D1287820

RENAISSANCE CONCEPTS OF METHOD

THOSE RULES OF OLD DISCOVER'D, NOT DEVIS'D,
ARE NATURE STILL, BUT NATURE METHODIZ'D. Pope

Renaissance Concepts of Method

By NEAL W. GILBERT

Columbia University Press, New York 1960

The Stanwood Cockey Lodge Foundation has generously provided funds
to assist in the publication of this volume.

About the Author

Neal Ward Gilbert received his
Ph. D. degree from Columbia in
1956. He is currently Assistant
Professor of Philosophy at the
University of Buffalo.

Published in Great Britain, India, and Pakistan
by the Oxford University Press
London, Bombay, and Karachi

Library of Congress Catalog Card Number: 60-6638

Manufactured in the Netherlands

To Paul Oskar Kristeller

PREFACE

The following study in the history of ideas owes
its inception to the author's work in philosophy at Columbia
University, during which he became convinced that Renaissance
discussions of method had not been sufficiently explored in their
full breadth. How could such an extensive and prolonged examination of the ways in which men acquire and communicate
knowledge fail to be significant for European intellectual
history? To be sure, medieval Schoolmen were masters of
disciplined debate and were by no means totally inept at edu-
cating themselves and others. But it may well have been true,
as Renaissance Humanists liked to maintain, that new forms of
inquiry and argument had to be found before new results could
be obtained. Sixteenth-century scholars sought these forms in the
writings of the ancients, while the philosophers of the seventeenth century claimed to have forged them for themselves. But
those who read this study will see, I hope, that not many of the
ideas on method for which the later period took credit escaped
the notice of these sixteenth-century students of classical thought,
even though they presented their conclusions in more modest
fashion.

I have tried to make the translations in the text as literal as
possible, although on occasion I have been forced to paraphrase
slightly in order to make sense out of the original. Part of the
difficulty in translating Renaissance Latin is due to the punctuation of the printed text, which is usually chaotic and sometimes
absolutely perverse: I have altered the punctuation whenever the
sense seemed to require it.

I should mention that when the research for this study was

being done, there had not yet appeared two works that would have expedited my work considerably. I refer to two excellent recent studies: Wilbur S. Howell's *Logic and Rhetoric in England, 1500-1700,* and Walter J. Ong's *Ramus, Method, and the Decay of Dialogue.*

Many libraries have been helpful in the preparation of this book. The Special Collections Staff of Butler Library at Columbia University has been of great assistance in facilitating use of Columbia's fine collection of Renaissance books. Other libraries in which I have worked include the New York Public Library, the library of the New York Academy of Medicine, the library of the Union Theological Seminary, Sterling Memorial Library at Yale University, and the Library of Congress. Microfilms of rare works have been obtained from various libraries, including the Bibliothèque Nationale, the British Museum, the Widener Library of Harvard University, and the University of Illinois.

For advice and help, my chief debt of gratitude is to Paul Oskar Kristeller. There is no need for me to say how much Renaissance scholars owe to his tireless efforts, but I should like to record one more personal debt owed to him. Helpful suggestions have also been received from Ernest A. Moody, John H. Randall, Jr., James Gutmann, and Martin Ostwald. My wife has been a great help at all stages of the work.

NEAL W. GILBERT

University of Buffalo
January, 1960

CONTENTS

Influence of the New Interest in Mathematics upon the Aristotelian Theory of Scientific Demonstration, 86; Humanistic Method in Faculties Other than the Arts, 92; The Rise of Legal Methodology, 93; Discussions of Methodology in the Medical Schools, 98; Leoniceno: Humanist Exegesis of Galen, 102; Manardi Continues the Humanist Exegesis of Galen, 104; Triverius of the Medical Faculty of Louvain, 105; Humanism and the Method of Theology, 107; Melanchthon's *Loci communes,* 108; Zanchius and Strigelius: More Protestant Methodology, 110

PART TWO

INTRODUCTION

Not so long ago people used to think of the modern period in philosophy as beginning with the publication of Descartes' *Discours de la Méthode* in 1637. Descartes, with his rejection of dogmatic enunciation and of reliance on authority, was considered to have inaugurated the new era by his insistence on the use of a critical method of inquiry. Yet the subject of method was not new when Descartes wrote his treatise. On the contrary, questions about the order and method to be employed in the arts and sciences had been discussed actively in Europe during the previous hundred years or more. By the end of the sixteenth century, when Galileo was beginning his researches into physical phenomena, the subject of method was indeed almost hackneyed. It had been the object of heated, if not always lucid, controversy; teachers of logic and of medicine had joined in praising and extolling the virtues of method, while differing considerably over its contents and application.

It has been suggested, with considerable plausibility, by modern students of intellectual history, that these sixteenth-century debates over method foreshadowed the great expansion of scientific research in the next century. In particular, it has been argued that Galileo was very much in debt to one trend of thought for his methodology—the Aristotelian. In his *Das Erkenntnisproblem,* Ernst Cassirer noted that significant changes were taking place in men's thinking within the Aristotelian tradition, and he singled out the development by Jacopo Zabarella of Padua of two "methods"—the compositive and the resolutive— as especially important because of the later use of these methods by Galileo.

Recently this thesis has been taken up by John H. Randall, Jr., in his study on the rise of scientific method in the school of Padua. Randall traces the continuous evolution of this concept from certain germinal ideas in Aristotle and Galen. This development took place chiefly at Padua, which was the leading scientific center of Europe during the sixteenth century. One would certainly expect advanced ideas on scientific method to be developed there, if anywhere.

The present study grew out of an interest in this thesis and out of a suspicion—which research soon confirmed—that the discussion of method in the Renaissance was considerably more widespread and perhaps more involved than one would be led to expect from the brilliant but brief suggestions of Cassirer and Randall. For talk of method was by no means the monopoly of teachers of logic or medicine, although it flourished among them. It was also current among Humanistically inclined writers of all sorts, some of whom attacked the medical tradition explicitly. In order to understand the historical context in which the teachers of Padua developed their doctrines, then, it is necessary to know something of their rivals in the field.

The more one reads in the writings of the sixteenth century, the more one begins to feel the need of determining precisely what meaning was given the term "method." For how are we to judge of the relationship between this academic talk and the practice of men of science unless we first make sure just what the talk was about? Such was the motivation behind this study; it gives it, perhaps, a somewhat philological tone. Yet it is difficult to escape the concern for words and their precise use that characterized the writers of the Renaissance. For it was during the late Renaissance that medieval philosophical and scientific terminology was beginning to give way to the modern, and Latin words were beginning to take on new meanings or to be superseded by Greek terms. Renaissance writers were fully conscious of this transformation of language: they were infatuated, indeed almost obsessed, with the etymology and history of the words they used. Since modern philosophical terminology takes its points of departure from these words transplanted into the various European vernaculars during the sixteenth and seventeenth centuries, we moderns have ideas which we associate with them (or "our own ways of using them," if you prefer). But we cannot understand this period of transition at all if we do not guard constantly against the danger of reading back into its language the philosophical significance which these words came to have later.

This is especially true of such a seemingly innocuous word as "method": it is hard to think of it as having a meaning much different from that which it has today, and so it is difficult to realize that the talk of method in the Renaissance may not have concerned *scientific* method in our modern sense at all. In this study we have tried to present sufficient material from the sixteenth century to enable the reader to form his own impression of this Renaissance controversy over method.

II

Perhaps we should pause for a moment to spell out, by way of contrast, some of the details of the modern scientific method that began to prevail during the seventeenth century, and to which we attribute our present vast accumulation of knowledge about the world in which we live. It would be best to remark at once that scientific method dictates not so much the detailed procedures of the researcher as the general grand strategy of his campaign. The strategy dictated is that of a sober and dispassionate determination to get at the facts by actual empirical research, instead of giving full play to poetic fancy or unbridled speculation. It is this aspect that is suggested when scientific method is eulogized as over against what is usually considered its predecessor, "primitive thinking" or "superstition."

The determination to get at the facts and find explanations for them that do not resort to the supernatural or the superstitious—this forms the central, generally accepted meaning of "scientific method." Beyond this lies a variety of doctrinal details which, it must be confessed, result not so much from divergence of opinion concerning the actual practice of investigators as from the acceptance of different disciplines as "sciences." Students of the developments in scientific research during the seventeenth or eighteenth centuries generally concede that the following characteristics were increasingly in evidence: (1) selection of a certain class of phenomena to investigate; (2) collection of the factual data relevant to this class of phenomena by some means available to any competent observer; (3) formulation of some hypothesis which, when combined with particular initial data, yields theoretical results capable of being verified or falsified; (4) testing of these results by experimental means; and (5) further testing of the hypothesis by determination of other theoretical results and of the degree to which it jibes with other relevant hypotheses.

Now no one at all conversant with earlier science, especially Greek science, would deny that it exhibited some or occasionally all of these features, at least in rudimentary form. But where Greek scientists started from direct contact with the subject matter, or from crude and unanalyzed data supplied by other cultures, Renaissance scientists found themselves in a world already theorized to death, so to speak—already interpreted or misinterpreted by centuries of intellectual effort. The seventeenth century had to fight its way back to a fresh view of nature by stripping itself of centuries of this kind of interpretation not uncontaminated by sheer superstition. The books of the past, which contained these interpretations, had come under grave suspicion: hence the repudiation of bookish learning that we find so marked from about the turn of the seventeenth century. Such a repudiation would be folly today, and, indeed, it was partly hypocritical at the time, for not even the haughty Descartes discarded the books of Euclid, Pappus, or Diophantus. But the percentage of serious error incorporated in the books that Renaissance students had at their disposal was sufficient to justify their complete discarding of such books—especially since the more valuable ideas were retained anyway.

Another source of dubious beliefs lay in the dabbling in

magical and hermetical practice of which the Renaissance was so fond. The extravagances of the nature philosophers, the Rosicrucians, and the Light-Metaphysicians also cluttered up the intellectual landscape. Small wonder that the seventeenth century felt the need, in Locke's phrase, of clearing away the underbrush.

These facts explain why modern science, in its earlier stages, and indeed down to the present, has been so predominantly *critical*—so careful, that is, to weed out, at every stage of its transactions, the valid from the invalid. At each step in the process outlined roughly above, the scientific investigator is willing to reject certain possibilities as unacceptable. He might forego the investigation of angels, for example, while being willing to undertake the investigation of something as trifling as the behavior of iron filings under magnetism. He might reject "factual" data that are accessible only to an observer whose sanity is not beyond question. He might reject a hypothesis so grandly formulated that no conclusions follow from it which could conceivably be subjected to empirical test, even when it is combined with other theories. He must surely stand prepared to accept the refutation of his own hypothesis when the facts do not bear it out. Finally, he must be willing to reject the hypothesis even if seemingly confirmed, if it cannot be squared with other scientific theories—unless he is willing, like Einstein, to attempt a still more major revision of these theories as well.

Throughout the modern enterprise of science, then, it is this critical aspect which predominates and which stamps its procedures as carried on by the scientific method. The characteristics which we think of as essentially modern and peculiarly scientific —such as the exact measurement of physical properties and the formulation of hypotheses in equations which permit the mathematical manipulation of these quantitative results—are important in part because they contribute to the discrimination with which we reject or accept theories. The development of mathematical theory would not have made the difference it did to physics and astronomy had not some men been willing to use mathematics to develop theoretical results so precise that only a near-perfect fit with the facts would justify retention of the theory.

Similarly, the development of instruments of observation made possible a greater discrimination of expected from unexpected results and helped to bring about a degree of observational refinement adequate to the demands of more refined mathematical theory. In sum, the development of mathematics and of instrumentation helped to narrow the region of neutrality between permissible and nonpermissible statements, and thus increased the critical demands of scientific method. A statement now had to pass more severe tests in order to qualify as valid.

This critical procedure carried with it, in the minds of its great early exponents, the obligation to stand by those theories or propositions which passed muster as well as to reject those which did not. Each provided a test of the scientist's loyalty to the method which had distinguished the false from the true, and enabled him to reject the former and accept only the latter.

Common sense, of course, also distinguishes the false from the true and stands by its dictates with the fervor of dogmatic conviction. But common sense does not weigh the evidence for alternatives with the care that scientific method requires. Often the dogmatic conviction of common sense is born of a lack of the ability to envisage alternatives that characterizes the true scientist. Aristotle was a master of this device; the alternatives he rejected have sometimes proved more suggestive than the doctrines he settled upon.

All of these aspects of the modern attitude toward scientific research figure in varying degrees in the scientific method employed in the different and sometimes quite disparate disciplines that we call sciences. Developments in anatomy in the Renaissance resulted not from any mathematical approach but simply from the resolution of Vesalius to dissect the human body himself and to observe it accurately—a revival of the spirit of Galen's method, not essentially a variation of it. In contrast, the mathematical analyses of motion by Galileo displayed the hypothesizing and mathematical characteristics in a high degree and constituted an epoch-making stage in the development of scientific method. The vigor with which Galileo was forced to campaign against the notion that mathematical analyses could not be exactly applied to such things as the paths of projectiles or the fall of heavy bodies testifies to the stubbornness with which these ideas were resisted by his contemporaries.

However, these developments are material for the historian of science, who alone is qualified to judge of the contributions made to the techniques and concepts of a science by Galileo or any other scientist. The analysis of ideas about *method* expressed by scientists falls, on the other hand, to the historian of philosophy—especially when a broad philosophical significance is attributed to them by the investigator or by others. The historian of philosophy should be more aware of the intellectual climate of the day and more sensitive to the significance of the language used by the investigator when he tries to explicate the procedure he himself follows, or would like to follow. Only after his actual procedures have been analyzed and evaluated by the historian of science, and his views on method have been analyzed by the historian of philosophy, can the two be juxtaposed and evaluated as a whole. It may then quite possibly turn out that they do not form a whole; that the ideas expressed by an investigator were quite commonplace and trite and did not correspond to his actual procedure at all. Or it might turn out that while his ideas on method were revolutionary, his actual achievements using that method were minimal, or were made by some other method. Or, finally, his techniques and his ideas about them might square perfectly, and represent contributions both to the substantive science and to methodology. But this could result only from an extraordinary combination of the absorption required for achievement in a scientific pursuit and the detachment required to analyze the methods used in the pursuit. Not to all scientists are these gifts given. Many of the greatest have left no clue as to the techniques they so successfully employed and no reflections whatsoever as to the philosophical significance, if any, of those techniques.

On the other hand, some signal contributions to the methodology of science have been made by men who have not contributed
one iota of factual information or of theoretical construction to
the sciences whose methods they studied. Nor is there any
intrinsic necessity why they should have made such first-level
contributions in order to make valuable estimates of the way in
which scientists have proceeded.

The conclusion to be drawn from these observations is that we
cannot afford to neglect ideas about method simply because their
exponents were not in the remotest connected with what we
would call scientific investigation. Ideas about method may very
well form part of the general climate of opinion and may help
to make that climate favorable to the growth of actual science.
It is this possibility which we shall be exploring in our study of
these Renaissance "methodologies."

III

If we find that a Renaissance writer seems to be groping for
a modern conception of scientific method, we shall expect him to
emphasize the critical nature of his method, that is, the degree to
which his method separates truth from falsehood and certainty
from uncertainty. We shall expect some doctrine of experimentation, the deliberate and purposeful manipulation of the natural
phenomenon under investigation. We shall expect him to discuss
with some care the role that mathematics plays in the development of science by his method.

In these particular expectations we shall be disappointed, in
most of our inquiries. Few of these writers seem to have thought
of their method as a definite program by means of which we may
start from intellectual scratch and slowly and painfully build up
a body of trustworthy knowledge—that programmatic aspect of
method which Descartes was to stress so powerfully. Hence
although one can find writers who speak of method as separating
truth from falsehood, this separation is not the crucial sieve that
it became in the next century, sifting all experience and retaining

only the indubitable. Missing from these expositions is the deliberate scrapping of all that has previously called itself knowledge, in order to start only from what is certain and sure. Furthermore, one feels a lack of that sense of intellectual exploration, of the conquest of new facts and the discovery of new theories, that is so impressive in the later period.

On the other hand, perhaps we are unfair in our expectations. If it should turn out that these Renaissance methodologists were engaged in a much more modest enterprise, we would not be so severe in our expectations, and hence not so disappointed in the results of our search. If we lay aside our preoccupation with scientific method, as we must if we are to arrive at a just estimate of this philosophical debate of the past, we find that a very considerable part of it was addressed not to the sciences but to the arts. This ancient Greek category has almost completely disappeared from our conceptual arsenal; we think of pure or basic science, of applied science, and of common sense as categories of knowledge. But the Renaissance still moved in an intellectual framework in which the arts or *technai* comprised a very important group of disciplines which occupied an intermediate place between routine mastery of a skill and demonstrated knowledge and which had to be accounted for in any scheme of knowledge-getting. Like so many other conceptual schemes, this one of the arts and sciences outlived its usefulness: one could argue that the low esteem in which the arts were held, as compared with the sciences, constituted a major block in the free development of knowledge. For example, the Greek disdain for computation, retained even into the Renaissance, may have had something to do with the fact that the formal manipulations of algebra received such tardy recognition from writers on mathematics, who preferred to analyze the traditionally respectable field of geometry. With the merger of the practical and the theoretical which has proved so fruitful in modern times, the category of the useful arts has been replaced by that of the "applied" sciences. In his *Reconstruction in Philosophy*, John Dewey explored some of the implications for modern ways of thought of this discarding of the category of the practical arts, somewhat menial and degrading as their cultivation was thought to be, as compared with that of the theoretical sciences. However, neither Dewey nor subsequent students have realized that a concurrent reform was taking place in the way in which men regarded these purposeful pursuits. These reforms were involved in the discussion of method, which took account of the methods of the arts as well as those of the sciences. To this genre of methodological thought, our questions are somewhat foreign, even as the category of the useful arts has become somewhat foreign to our ears. One would hardly look for a doctrine of experimentation in a treatise on grammar or rhetoric, yet these Renaissance students were naturally as much, if not more, concerned with these arts as they were with the science of astronomy, and with the methods successfully employed in their cultivation.

Because the arts as a separate and distinct category have more or less sunk out of sight, we are inclined to discount in advance the significance of a controversy over their methods. Yet I would contend that this aspect of the methodological discussions of the Renaissance is essential to an understanding of the thought of the period, and even, perhaps, to that of our own, for I believe that the reforms in education, in law, in the writing of history, and in theology which Renaissance students subsumed under this portmanteau label of "method" had great cultural significance. As a theoretical reflection upon these reforms, the "artistic" methodology fully deserves our interested scrutiny.

IV

Since the late Renaissance was above all a period of voracious scholarship, the discussion of method took the form of rival interpretations of passages dealing with method in the works of antiquity. These references were collected and explicated with great zeal, for aside from the chief issues of the day, which were theological, method was the subject that most interested these scholar-philosophers. It is as though Renaissance thinkers, impressed by the results of Greek thought, hoped to recover the methods which had yielded those results. They sought them not so much by an analysis of actual inquiry in philosophy and science (although beginnings of such examination can be found) as by the scholarly explication of references to method in the writings of the ancients.

This methodological discussion has been almost entirely lost from historical view, although it is currently being rediscovered in piecemeal fashion. Modern scholars have not been attracted to the verbose commentaries and polemical works in which the discussion was for the most part contained. It is much easier to assume that all nonmodern figures from the period are "medieval" and hence not worth reading. In a transitional period such as the Renaissance, historians like to look for figures who can be called either "modern" or "reactionary" (in this case, "medieval") and tend to neglect those who genuinely belong to the transition period. This fate has overtaken the writers who dealt with method in the sixteenth century, for they were certainly not medieval, nor were they clearly modern. The historians of philosophy have focused their attention on men like Paracelsus, Bruno, and Telesio because they seem to stand out from a drab background of dull academic nonentities usually lumped together as "rigid Aristotelians," who are mentioned in the history books only for the sake of contrast.

Strangely enough, if we read the writings of some of these "rigid" Aristotelians, we find in them some of the very characteristics which are supposed to distinguish their forward-looking contemporaries. For example, it is frequently maintained that one of the unusual features of those "modern" men who somehow got born a century before they should have been is their lack of respect and reverence for authority. As a matter of fact, there were few sixteenth-century authors who did not protest at one time or another their complete independence of authority. Most of these protests were then followed by a complete reliance on traditional philosophy and a conspicuous lack of original ideas. However, this lack of originality characterizes many of the revolutionaries as well. The most notorious anti-Aristotelian of the sixteenth century, Peter Ramus, turns out to be a very timid thinker when embarked on philosophical enterprises of his own, relying almost entirely on Aristotle and the Ciceronian tradition for his ideas.

The most significant changes in men's ideas were taking place not independently of the authorities but within their consideration, in changing interpretations of Aristotle and Plato. Scholars were deriving new ideas from old sources by seeing them in a different light. Such considerations suggest that it is not altogether fair to judge sixteenth-century philosophers solely by their possession or lack of originality. We should judge them also by their scholarship and grasp of the thought of antiquity, which was prodigious. The major historical archievement of the late Renaissance, it could almost be argued, was to hand on a more complete and accurate knowledge of the whole range of classical thought, from Plato and Aristotle to the Stoics, Sceptics, and Epicureans, and their interpreters from late antiquity. This meant that the seventeenth century had a much richer and more stimulating philosophical tradition to draw upon—or to reject.

Since many philosophers of antiquity discussed the methods of philosophizing or of achieving sound knowledge in the arts and sciences, there was a wide range of questions to be considered under the general heading of method. Generally speaking, these questions dealt with how the arts and sciences were first found, how they were "disposed" or presented, and how they were demonstrated. At the risk of oversimplification, we may divide the entire discussion of method into two large categories, that dealing with *artistic* method and that dealing with *scientific* method.

The first category of methodological thought, the artistic, was concerned with the teaching of the arts and with communication in general. The source of this tradition was Socrates, who was interested in the subject of the arts and their teachability primarily because of the question—raised by the Sophists—as to whether virtue could also be taught like an art, and because of the related question as to whether knowledge could be transmitted by one who claimed to be able to speak persuasively on every subject. The stringent requirements that Socrates set up for the possession and teaching of the arts exercised an influence far beyond his most important pupil, Plato, although the Platonic dialogues were the most important source for the methodological doctrine of Socrates, one which the Renaissance drew upon to a surprising degree.

The other category of methodological thought, the scientific, was the contribution of Aristotle, who developed explicit criteria of demonstrative procedure that went beyond what Socrates had demanded of an art and that represented, in a sense, a carrying out of the mathematical program of the older Plato. These two categories represent the poles of methodological thought and form a convenient scheme for orienting ourselves in the methodology of the Renaissance.

It should be pointed out that we shall be dealing, especially in the second part of this work, only with those writers of the Renaissance who used the term *methodus* in its Renaissance senses, not with those who were interested in what some present-day philosophers might consider subject matter for the methodologist. This means that we shall be forced to neglect many prominent thinkers who may have made the most original contributions to the period, and indeed gave it its distinctive tone. I do not intend to claim that the writers whom I present, often obscure and unfamiliar to the student of philosophy, are more worthy of attention than men like Patrizzi, Pomponazzi, and their like. I do maintain that these were the leading figures in the debate over method.

One might suppose that the best place to begin an inquiry of the kind we are about to undertake would be to plunge into an analysis of the writings of the Renaissance. But if we should try this approach, an embarrassing fact would soon make itself evident. Many of the ancient philosophical writers discussed in the Renaissance were better known then than they are now, even to our historians of philosophy. Galen, for instance, who was, next to Aristotle, the most influential writer on scientific method, is only a name in histories of philosophy. Hence if we are even to begin to understand the methodology of the Renaissance, we must first devote some time to exploring at least briefly some of the authorities then discussed. Another reason for starting with the methodology of the Greeks is that our judgments concerning the views of the ancients have a way of influencing our judgments of later writers who resurrect or uphold ancient views. Many a study of later thought that seems on the surface to represent an objective evaluation turns out to be an exercise in anti-Platonism or anti-Aristotelianism in disguise. We shall try to avoid this harmless deception by first examining the sources of Renaissance methodology and bringing our prejudices—if we have any—into the open.

PART ONE

Chapter 1. THE ANCIENT AND MEDIEVAL SOURCES OF RENAISSANCE METHODOLOGY

THE PLATONIC DIALOGUES: GREEK METHODOLOGY AT ITS SOURCE

The thought of Socrates as portrayed in the Platonic dialogues is fundamental to the understanding of the genesis of Greek thought on method and furnishes an essential key to the subsequent developments. For our purposes, we may focus our attention on the *Phaedrus*, and especially upon that section (from 265D to 277C) in which Socrates outlines what he would consider to be a true *art* or *techné* of rhetoric, as opposed to the teaching of the Sophists or the superficial manuals of rhetoric which contained these teachings. After describing the two processes of διαίρεσις and συναγωγή which the "dialecticians" (as Socrates calls those who make use of the methods) have originated, Socrates draws a comparison between the manner (τρόπος) of the healing art and that of the rhetorical art, which he says are the same, involving the analyzing of a nature or φύσις. Just as the physician needs to know the nature of the body, so the rhetorician needs to know the nature of the soul, which cannot be known without that method (μέθοδος) which Hippocrates advocated.[1] The description which follows, together with all of the many other

---

[1] The nature of the exact "method of Hippocrates" which Socrates advocates in this passage is the subject of the famous "Hippocratic question," which turns in part upon the interpretation of the crucial phrase "the nature of the whole." For a persuasive recent interpretation, see P. Kucharski, "La 'méthode d'Hippocrate' dans le Phèdre," *Revue des études grecques*, LII (1939), 301-57. But see also Wilhelm Nestle, "Hippocratica," *Hermes*, LXXIII (1938), 1-38, especially p. 17; and W. H. S. Jones, "'Hippocrates' and the Corpus Hippocraticum," *Proceedings of the British Academy*, XXXI (1945), 103-25. Most of the writers on this question, except Emil Littré, seem to have overlooked the evidence to be found in Galen's comparison of the doctrines of Hippocrates and Plato, which, although perhaps not too reliable, ought not to be disregarded entirely.

passages in the Platonic dialogues on the subject of method, was tremendously influential in Greek philosophizing.

Hippocrates is evidently brought into the discussion by Socrates because his art of medicine is preeminently a useful art, and one in which the man of understanding obviously has the advantage over one who has acquired his skill by mere practice and routine. His knowledge of the art of medicine was acquired by a *method*, as opposed to its acquisition by chance or routine. This passage contains the germ of the idea which later was to prove so pervasive, namely, that there is a method in the acquiring of a useful art which can be applied to all of the useful arts because it sets up criteria to govern the activities of the investigator who wishes to establish an art. Someone, on the other hand, who pretends to have mastered the art of medicine or that of rhetoric *without this method,* Socrates says, would be like a blind man (270D). Thus, in a valid art, the "artist" will first set up the problem of his art, which is to explicate the means of achieving its goal. His first step then is to show the nature (*physis*) of that which the art deals with, and whether it is simple or multiform. Secondly, he will describe the action and reaction of the various parts thus discovered. Thirdly, he will classify these parts and specify the causes of their actions and reactions. The illustration of this procedure which Socrates gives is the art of rhetoric, but the discussion can easily be applied to any useful art or *techné.*

We are here witnessing Greek methodology at its very formation. For whatever may have been the influence of the methods of medicine or of mathematics and of Eleatic dialectic upon Plato, it is clear that he and his master were the first to reflect consciously upon the methods of knowing exemplified in those arts and to attempt to articulate them. The ideas suggested by Socrates were taken up by Plato and his pupils, especially Aristotle, and by the Stoics, and continue to be identifiable at the very final stage of Greek thought, when school labels become almost meaningless, and Peripatetics, no less than Platonists, drew upon the dialogues and upon Academic school doctrine for inspiration in matters of method.

Actually, as Platonists in antiquity already realized, the "dialectical method" of Plato is not a single method but a varying compound of methods: school doctrine soon singled out (by a process which sounds suspiciously like that recommended in the *Phaedrus*) four which came to be known as the analytical, the definitive, the divisive, and the apodeictic methods. The characteristics and relative merits of these methods thus "method-ically" extracted from the dialogues of Plato occupied scholars for centuries and were still being discussed in the Renaissance. Accidents of textual transmission account for the fact that one of these four methods—the divisive—occupied the attention of the early Middle Ages almost exclusively, and then in a form far more abstract than that medical one to which Socrates drew a parallel in the *Phaedrus*. But the other dialectical methods were never completely lost sight of.

The *Phaedrus* passage explains much that is obscure in sub-sequent philosophizing: the close relation of *techné* and *methodos*, which sometimes seem to merge, yet always remain distinct con-cepts. The basic pattern of division—that of determining the end of an art, then analyzing the different parts and functions with a view to evaluating their relative merits and functions in respect to that end—prevails, in recognizable fashion, through many changes of detail and language. It may be said that Greek methodology never quite outgrew its initial orientation as a defense against deceptive Sophistry, and remained basically dialectical to the end. One school—that of the Stoa—did attempt to break away from this dialectical orientation. In only one Greek writer whose works have been preserved do we find a thoroughgoing "logical empiricism" that clearly separated the intellectual or logical from the sensory or experiential and rec-ognized that method could prevail in both. This writer was Galen, and it is surely no accident that Galen's writings came into their greatest esteem during a period in European history when empirical observation and experiment were again being recognized as essential ingredients in scientific inquiry, a period that also saw the revival of interest in Aristotle's biological writings. Galen himself remarked[2] that the student of Plato's divisive method would do well to consult Aristotle's *Parts of Animals* before becoming overconfident as to the ease with which results may be expected from application of that method.

Study of the *Phaedrus* will well repay the effort for one who wishes to understand Greek thought upon the subject of method. He will be able, among other things, to recognize the peculiar interplay which develops later in Greek thought between *method* in the singular (which refers to Art, and especially to the peculiarly Greek art of dialectic) and *methods* in the plural (which are the dialectical devices so beloved of Socrates). The methods can be applied to the "material" or subject matter of any art, and when so prosecuted result in a particular art, or method. This latter identification is not made explicitly by Plato, nor by Aristotle, who retained the dialectical sense of method in the singular and virtually discarded the methods in the plural. Aristotle was a consummate master of the "artistic" methods described by Plato, but he gave only one version of them himself, namely, the *Topics*. He regarded the syllogism as a method not of art but of science. Only in dialectic do *method* and *methods* merge and become confused. In the other arts the method is the result of the *methods* of dialectic. It goes without saying that the methods or techniques of shoemaking, e.g., as used in our modern sense (say, of how to sew leather or fasten heels), had no interest whatsoever for Socrates, or for Greek philosophers in general.

Of course other Platonic dialogues also deal with method—the dichotomizing of the *Sophist* or the mathematical discussion of the *Republic*—but no Renaissance Platonist was so thorough as to bring all of the dialogues into consideration. Besides, dialogues are notoriously difficult material to assimilate: Renaissance methodologists preferred short and easily quoted sayings which could be elaborated into full-fledged doctrine by the liberal use of constructive imagination. In contrast to Aristotle's works,

---

[2] Galen, *De methodo medendi*, in *Medicorum Graecorum Opera quae exstant*, ed. Carl Gottlob Kühn (26 vols., Leipzig, 1821-30), X, 26. Hereafter referred to as Kühn.

which abound in dicta easily cited without regard to context, Plato's dialogues must be understood as a whole and then paraphrased in order to be made use of in discussion. Sixteenth-century writers found little in the way of maxims and aphorisms on the subject of method in Plato: they could only cite his praise of method in the *Philebus* as the "gift of *some* Prometheus" and even this citation was usually altered to read more definitely, "*Prometheus'* gift to man." Thus although most students sensed the historical importance of the dialectic practiced by Socrates, they tended to believe that what was valid in Plato had been methodically distilled by Aristotle.

ARISTOTLE: THE MASTERY OF METHOD

Unfortunately, Aristotle did not write a treatise on what we would call scientific method. The closest he came to it was the *Posterior Analytics*, which is an analysis of the conditions under which we may be said to know something with scientific certainty. Since the most secure knowledge of Aristotle's time consisted of geometry and arithmetic and the allied disciplines of optics, harmonics, and astronomy, his analysis of science was intended to apply to these sciences, with the emphasis not so much on finding theorems as on their demonstration.

Aristotle's own scientific writings are not themselves examples of such demonstrated sciences (with the possible exception of the *Prior Analytics*): they are rational examinations of well-defined subject matters in a wide range of fields of knowledge. He does follow certain standard procedures in almost all of his inquiries, such as first collecting the views of his predecessors on a subject and evaluating them before undertaking his own analysis. But the complaint frequently heard from students of Aristotelian philosophy during the late Renaissance—that Aristotle had not dealt with method—was certainly justified. He does frequently discuss his manner of proceeding, usually at the start of his works, and he does throw out many valuable hints as to what we would call his own "scientific method," but these hints are scattered throughout his writings and represent flashes of insight rather than parts of a single explicit "methodology." It is not possible—or at any rate not easy—to make these scattered observations into a coherent and fixed pattern of method, because Aristotle's methods vary with the subject matter. In natural history he advocated and practiced a decidedly empirical procedure, but in other subjects, such as metaphysics, he was more concerned with the analysis of concepts. Once, in the *De anima*, he inquires whether it is possible that there could be just one method that will yield scientific results in all inquiries concerning substance, and comes to a reluctantly negative conclusion.[3]

This situation raised difficulties for Renaissance Aristotelians. So far as scientific demonstration goes, the answers to all problems could be found in the *Posterior Analytics*. But when pressed for a doctrine of how the sciences could be found by one who did not have the advantage of starting with the text of Aristotle, they were forced to attempt to coordinate and harmonize scattered references from Aristotle into a single methodology of science. A few were honest enough to admit that it could not be done and tried instead to develop a doctrine of their own, but most insisted that Aristotle must have dealt with the subject of method and tried to reconstruct his thought.

Another embarrassment awaited Aristotle's defenders. For it is a regrettable fact that Aristotle, although full of philosophical insight, is nevertheless often obscure in his presentation. The obscurity of Aristotle, even in his native language, had been a standing grievance with the Humanists, who were sensitive, perhaps unduly so, to the nuances of style. Hence they could add to Aristotle's neglect to furnish a treatise on method the charge that he followed no clear method in his writing, which is a still more damaging accusation. This led to a defensive examination of Aristotle's procedures by Aristotelians, some of whom began to wonder whether the *Posterior Analytics* had all the answers after all, and whether Aristotle had not recommended one method sometimes and followed another (or others) himself. The naive

---

[3] 402a14.

assumption that whatever Aristotle preached concerning method he actually practiced began to come under suspicion with Renaissance Aristotelians. Had he indeed presented the *Nicomachean Ethics* by the "resolutive order," as centuries of commentators had assured them? Was the *Physics* set forth by the "compositive method," which the commentators specifically required of a purely contemplative science? [4] Questions like these could not be so glibly answered by merely citing a dictum from anywhere in the Aristotelian corpus, but had to be solved by extensive and accurate scholarly inquiry.

To be sure, this search was not conceived in such a bookish manner. For the Renaissance, the confrontation of Aristotle's dicta on method with his manner of proceeding in the treatises was an empirical test, equivalent to confirmation by the most objective means available. This "empirical" test proved a great stimulus to the thinking of Renaissance Aristotelians. At the least it resulted in the collation of passages on method from all of Aristotle's works and the comparison of the methods thus found with Aristotle's own procedures in various inquires. At the most it resulted in a fairly critical evaluation repudiating the assumption so readily made that a man's practice automatically corresponds to his preaching.

To the extent that Aristotle's method is dialectical, the *Topics* may be regarded as his methodology. The "method" of the *Topics* (Aristotle uses the word in quite a Socratic way for the contents of the work) is still, like Plato's, aimed at the true and logically correct, which—man being the rational animal that he is—is more persuasive and hence more effective than that which is false or misleading. It is a way of discussing a subject and arguing about it that will lead us to the truth, in so far as the truth is ascertainable by that means. Since for Aristotle there is no impassable gulf between logic and rhetoric, the latter being indeed only a looser form of argument applied to persuasion, it

---

[4] For the difficulties encountered even by a modern scholar in answering such questions as the latter, see Paul Tannery, "Sur un point de la méthode d'Aristote," AGP, VI (1893), 468-74.

is not correct to say that the *Topics* is "merely" rhetorical. It was intended to guide one in philosophical inquiry as well as in debate. Aristotle frequently characterizes arguments in his other works as "only dialectical," but by this he does not mean that they are invalid or superficial, but simply that they do not carry the conviction that scientific or apodeictic argument does.

Hence so far as rational pro-and-con discussion of any given subject can produce knowledge, Aristotle did provide rules, those to be found in the *Topics*. The medieval practice of disputation was profoundly influenced by the *Topics*,[5] and represents an approach to the truth not too foreign to that of Aristotle or his fellow Greeks. The Schoolmen of the Middle Ages shared Aristotle's faith that in matters not susceptible of strict proof, the truth can be arrived at through disciplined debate.

When the practice of disputation began to lose favor in the Renaissance, largely through the adverse criticisms of the Humanists, one might have expected this classical delineation of the method of disputation to have fallen into disrepute also, but such was not the case. The Humanists challenged not the validity of the procedure outlined in the *Topics* but the use to which it had been put: the zeal for forensic victory and for glory, so they held, had replaced the search for truth. They themselves were by no means above making use of the *Topics* for their own purposes, as we shall see. The *Topics* formed one of the essential ingredients of Renaissance methodology.

The ultimate goal of Socrates' methods had been always the same, namely, the discovery and comprehension of moral truth; but since this moral insight was equivalent to knowledge, his methods could be considered ways of reaching other kinds of truth as well. When Aristotle developed his syllogistic method, from an analysis of the Greek practice of debating,[6] he then applied it to other domains than the moral, especially to the

[5] See Martin Grabmann, *Die Geschichte der Scholastischen Methode* (Freiburg im Breisgau, 1909), II, 219-21.

[6] See Ernest Kapp, *Greek Foundations of Traditional Logic* (New York, 1952), and Friedrich Solmsen, *Die Entstehung der Aristotelischen Logik und Rhetorik* (Berlin, 1929).

sciences well advanced at his time. But his discussion of these sciences is still largely nonempirical, that is, concerned not so much with rules intended to govern the investigator in his inquiry into a subject, along the lines of John Stuart Mill's canons, as with the formal structure of those sciences. If we call this exceedingly complex discussion Aristotle's scientific method, as Renaissance Aristotelians usually did, we then face the even more complex problem of the relation of this method to mathematical and scientific practice. We shall see that the complexity of this problem forced Renaissance Aristotelians to a divorce of mathematics from Aristotle's theory of science that estranged it from the nascent mathematical analysis of nature probably still further than Aristotle would have countenanced had he lived to see the development.

So much for more particular Aristotelian methods. If we take the broadest possible view of his procedure, of his methods of philosophizing, there is much that the Renaissance, and we ourselves, can learn from Aristotle's example and from his comments on his procedure.[7] But we shall look in vain for such broad consideration during the Renaissance.

STOIC DOCTRINES OF ART

The Socratic doctrine of *techné* was also transmitted, in hardly recognizable and rather doctrinaire fashion, by the Stoics, who took the elements of Socrates' analysis and made them into a fixed pattern which emphasized both the origin of the materials of an art out of "grasping sense impressions" and the usefulness of the art in life. Zeno asserted that an art was a "set of percepts exercised together toward some end useful in life."[8] As originally conceived, this was an epistemological doctrine, for *katalepsis*,

---

[7] Aristotle's philosophical method has been studied by Rudolph Eucken in a still useful monograph, *Die Methode der Aristotelischen Forschung in ihrem Zusammenhang mit den philosophischen Grundprincipien des Aristoteles dargestellt* (Berlin, 1872), which gives relevant excerpts from the text of Aristotle. A recent work, J. M. Le Blond, *Logique et méthode chez Aristote: Étude sur la recherche des principes dans la physique Aristotélicienne* (Paris, 1937), is more specialized.

[8] The favorite Renaissance source for this Stoic doctrine was Lucian's dialogue on the *Parasite*: "An art, as I heard some wise man say, is a system of grasping

literally "a grasping," was a Stoic technical term for a sense impression conveying the truth so powerfully as to defy shaking by reasoning. When translated into Latin by Cicero[9] and other writers, the doctrine at first retained its epistemological flavor. Medieval versions of the doctrine jumbled the key word *perceptio* into *praeceptio*, with the result that an art became a "system of precepts" or rules—a fruitful error, for the resultant idea, that of a set of rules, was a very useful one. This notion of an art as a set of rules may have influenced medieval logic;[10] it could have been found in grammatical works easily accessible to students of the arts in early medieval universities.

Because of the close synonymy between *techné* and *methodos* in antiquity, this Stoic doctrine of art tended to infiltrate the methodology of other schools, in spite of its radically different philosophical orientation. The substitution of *praeceptio* for *perceptio* neutralized the materialistic epistemology of the original doctrine and made it acceptable to all schools of thought. We shall see later how this Stoic doctrine helped to introduce into Aristotle's thought a concept of method that was not his own.

---

sense impressions exercised together toward some end useful in life." The Greek is given by Hans von Arnim, *Stoicorum veterum fragmenta* (4 vols., Leipzig, 1903-24), I, 21, 6. The definition is definitely attributed to Zeno by Olympiodorus in another fragment given by Arnim, I, 21, 3. This Stoic definition of an art is found in many other places, including Galen's works (Arnim, II, 30, 25).

[9] Cicero's version occurs in a grammatical work that was destined to have wide influence on subsequent grammatical teaching, that of Diomedes, a fourth-century grammarian. Diomedes's work begins with a general discussion of art: "Ars est rei cuiusque scientia usu vel traditione vel ratione percepta tendens ad usum aliquem vitae necessarium." There follows the quotation from Cicero: "Tullius hoc modo eam definit, 'ars est perceptionum exercitatarum constructio ad unum exitum utilem vitae pertinentium.'" *Grammatici Latini*, ed. Heinrich Keil (7 vols., Leipzig, 1857), I, 421. Cicero's fragment is given in Arnim, SVF, I, 21, 19. Another definition of art, attributed to Cicero throughout the Middle Ages, is to be found in the *Auctor ad Herennium*, I, 2: "Ars est praeceptio quae dat certam viam rationemque dicendi.".

[10] The following version may be found in a manuscript on logic attributed to the late twelfth century: "Utile est autem propter hos cognoscere primo, quid sit ars. Solet autem notificari ars: ars est collectio preceptorum ad unum finem tendentium. Hoc est dicere: ars est praeceptio sive regula collecta." Quoted by Martin Grabmann, "Bearbeitungen und Auslegungen der Aristotelischen Logik aus der Zeit von Peter Abaelard bis Petrus Hispanus," *Abhandlungen*, PAW, No. 5 (1937), p. 17. See also our quotation from Lambert of Auxerre's treatise on dialectic, p. 57 below.

Even though the original Greek version of this doctrine was well known in the Renaissance, the derived idea of a set of rules directed toward some end useful in life continued to be influential. Upon this notion of an art many Renaissance Humanists based their revolt against medieval Terminist logic, which, in their view, did not furnish a clear-cut set of rules to guide one in the pursuit of some useful end. The complaint was often made by Humanists that the Terminist logicians spent their time disputing over the very rules which they were supposed to furnish to other disciplines. The Humanists of course did not realize that the same Stoic doctrine had been used in medieval dialectic: they were notoriously apt to overlook medieval antecedents for their innovations.

THE SCIENTIFIC METHODOLOGY OF GALEN

The writer on scientific method whose authority most nearly rivaled that of Aristotle throughout the Middle Ages and on into the modern period was Galen, *logicus* as well as *medicus*. Few scholars shared the apprehensions of Pico della Mirandola and Nizzoli [11] that Galen, while trustworthy in medicine, must be dealt with cautiously in logic. These two derogatory voices compare with the almost unanimous [12] acceptance of Galen as a

[11] Pico rejected Galen's astrological doctrine with regard to critical days in illness and warned his contemporaries to "deal cautiously with the man when it comes to nonmedical matters." Giovanni Pico della Mirandola, *Disputationes adversus astrologiam divinatricem,* ed. Eugenio Garin (Florence, 1946), I, 338.

Mario Nizzoli endorsed Pico's warning, adding that although Galen frequently praises Aristotelian demonstration as a most precious thing, he nevertheless confesses that none of the books of the dialecticians are of any use in learning this science. Marius Nizolius, *De veris principiis et vera ratione philosophandi contra pseudophilosophos libri IV,* ed. Quirinus Breen (2 vols., Rome, 1956), II, 181-82.

[12] I select just one witness of the many who might be called upon: Bartholomew Keckermann, who was widely read in logic: "Eius namque tempore, i.e. Antonini, Galenus vixit, Medicorum parens et princeps post Hippocratem merito dictus, qui libros aliquot Logicos scripsit, ex quibus duo hodie reliqui, prior *de sophismatibus quae in verbis contingunt,* alter *de optimo genere docendi contra Phavorinum Ephecticum,* quem Des. Erasmus primus in Latinum vertit.... In reliquis scriptis medicis plurima infinitis locis praecepta Logica immiscet: ex quibus cuivis facile apparet, quanta fuerit viri huius in Logica Peripateticorum (quam solam in honore habet) excellentia." Bartholomaeus Keckermannus, *Praecognitorum logicorum tractatus III* ... (Hanover, 1606), p. 20. The parenthetical remark may not be too well founded, but the general sentiment is clear.

foremost theoretician of logic and science. He was regarded as
the most reliable commentator on Aristotle, one whose achievements in medical science entitled him to very respectful consideration in matters of science.

Galen's epistemology was fundamentally Aristotelian, although
he retained considerable respect for the methodology of Hippocrates and Plato. In matters of demonstration, he largely accepted
the views of the "older" writers (Aristotle and Theophrastus).
Galen was convinced early in life of the reliability of the linear
method of mathematical proof, as he tells us in a passage which
was well known to his sixteenth-century admirers.[13] Throughout
his life he held to a strict ideal of scientific proof and campaigned
against the lax methods of his fellow physicians, who were inclined to accept received views without seeking a sound basis for
them in experience or logic. He insisted that the characteristic
of the doctor who seeks to achieve a firm grasp of the principles
of his craft must be, not respect for the opinions of Plato or
Aristotle or anyone else, but only regard for the truth.

So far as analysis of scientific method goes, Galen was content
to remain within the Aristotelian framework, supplemented by
some doctrines from Plato and the Stoa, with certain emphases
which seemed to be called for by the state of medical instruction
in his day. Demonstration, in order to be scientific, must begin,
not with Stoic etymologies, but with *ennoiai koinai* or *emphytoi*,[14]

---

[13] Melanchthon knew the passage: "Galenus fatetur se pene in amentiam Pyr-
rhoniorum delapsum esse, nisi Geometria vidisset tantam vim esse demonstrationum."
Melanchthoniana Paedagogica, ed. Carl Hartfelder (Leipzig, 1892), p. 183. Robert
Recorde mentions the passage: "And that caused Galene to saie of hymself, that he
could never perceive what a demonstration was, no not so muche, as whether there
were any or none, till he had by Geometric gotten abilitie to understande it, although
he heard the beste teachers that were in his tyme." Robert Recorde, *The Pathwaie
to Knowledge* . . . (London, 1574), preface to the second book. Christopher Clavius,
the Jesuit mathematician, also mentions the passage in the prolegomena to his
edition of Euclid, "Euclidis atque Geometriae commendatio," *Euclidis Elementorum
libri XV* . . . (Rome, 1574), unpaged.

[14] The presence of these Stoic terms in Galen's little introduction to logic led
Carl von Prantl to deny its authenticity, but this was subsequently vindicated by
Kalbfleisch, who edited the work. Although he opposed the Stoics, especially
Chrysippus, in many points, Galen was certainly strongly influenced by them. It is
interesting to note that he wrote a work with the title, "That Geometrical Analysis
Is Better than That of the Stoics."

and these principles of science must exhibit *enargeia*, or clarity.[15] This appeal to common notions so clear as to be universally accepted was very congenial to sixteenth-century minds, who found in the doctrine a means of escape from "Pyrrhonian scepticism"— always a very distressing prospect. This scepticism they feared does not seem to have been so much a real threat—although we read of students who fell into sceptical doubts concerning the validity of what was being taught them (as well they might). It was more a philosophical position delineated in the Greek and Latin sources. The best-known writer of the period who supported the necessity for *ennoiai koinai* as an indisputable basis for morals and law as well as for science was Melanchthon, whose respect for Galen is well known;[16] yet he was by no means alone in championing this Galenian position.

Galen's general conception of logic included more than rules for syllogizing: logic for him concerns the weighing of scientific evidence as well.[17] Galen devoted a special treatise to the subject of demonstration in which he developed his own methodology of science, based on the work of the "ancients," including Plato, Aristotle, Theophrastus, and the Stoics.[18] This work was lost sometime after the sixth century, a loss that was bemoaned many

[15] Ἐνάργεια was originally an Epicurean technical term. Kurt Sprengel considered Galen's usage to be Epicurean, in his "Briefe über Galens philosophisches System," in *Beiträge zur Geschichte der Medizin*, I[1] (Halle, 1794), 117-95, on p. 136. However, F. H. Sandbach has suggested that it was adopted by the Stoics as an obvious synonym for *prolepsis*: "Ennoia and Prolepsis in the Stoic Theory of Knowledge," *Classical Quarterly*, XXIV (1930), 44-51, at p. 50. Yet it would seem that the attribution of the term to Theophrastus in precisely the sense used by Galen (in Sextus Empiricus, VII, 217 = fr. XXVII, Wimmer) ought to be strong evidence that the term was introduced into the Aristotelian theory of science by Theophrastus, and subsequently taken up by Galen. Proclus, in his commentary on Euclid, uses the adjective ἐναργής as synonymous with "not needing proof" and regards his meaning as "more precise" than that of the Stoics. Ptolemy also used this criterion in his Περὶ κριτερίου καὶ ἡγεμονικοῦ, ed. Ismael Bullialdus (Paris, 1663), mentioned by Franz Boll in his article on Ptolemy, cited on p. 23 below.

[16] Heinrich Maier, "Melanchthon als Philosoph," AGP, N.F., IV (1898), 73-132 and 212-45, esp. p. 88.

[17] Carl von Prantl considered this concern for evidence in the sciences a lowering of logic from its status as a pure science. Yet he also notes that Galen was one of the very first champions of the *mos geometricus* in philosophy, as an antidote to scepticism, surely a significant step. Carl von Prantl, *Geschichte der Logik im Abendlande* (4 vols., Leipzig, 1855-70), I, 561-62.

[18] For a brilliant reconstruction of Galen's treatise *Concerning Demonstration*

times during the Renaissance. Deprived of this explicit discussion, scholars were forced to rely instead upon the many references in Galen's other works to this lost treatise and to
demonstration. Yet Galen's influence on Renaissance methodology remained as fragmentary as the sources upon which scholars were forced to depend. Not a single scholar undertook the
total reconstruction of Galen's thought on the subject of method,
which, if truth be told, would be a strenuous assignment even for
a modern scholar. Since Galen had a great deal of respect for
the geometrical method—'linear demonstration,' as it was called
at the time—one might think that some one of the many medical
mathematicians of the Renaissance would have been interested in
reconstructing his thought on demonstration in general science.
But this was not the case; it is not until the seventeenth century
that Galen's answer to Pyrrhonian scepticism—the resort to linear
proof—was taken up again, by Descartes.

   Since Galen's major work on scientific method was lost, Renaissance students derived their knowledge of his doctrine from
his other works, in which he frequently alludes to his methodology. The picture which emerges is a complex and confused
one, even if we take all the relevant passages into account—which
none of our Renaissance scholars did. We may make a beginning
by examining the famous *Ars parva* passage. Here, at the start
of his most influential work, Galen describes three forms of
teaching; it is clear that he considers that he has used all three
of these forms in his own medical texts. The first of these ways
of teaching, that "arising from the notion of the end according
to analysis," [19] is exemplified by his work 'On the Establishing of
the Medical Art, to Patrophilus'.[20]

---

from references in Galen and other writers, see Iwan Müller, "Ueber Galens Werk
vom wissenschaftlichen Beweis," *Abhandlungen, philosophisch-philologische Classe,*
BAW, XX (1897), 405-78. Galen's importance as a theoretician of science during
his own time and during the Middle Ages and Renaissance is just beginning to be
generally recognized. See Ludwig Edelstein, "Recent Trends in the Interpretation
of Ancient Science," JHI, XIII (1952), 573-604. Much information is contained
in Richard Walzer's *Galen on Jews and Christians* (Oxford, 1949).
   [19] Kühn, I, 305. τρεῖς εἰσὶν αἱ πᾶσαι διδασκαλίαι τάξεως ἐχόμεναι πρώτη μὲν,
ἡ ἐκ τῆς τοῦ τέλους ἐννοίας κατ' ἀνάλυσιν γιγνομένη.
   [20] Kühn, V, 224-304.

Although this work is largely medical in content, it contains some observations on method. Galen wrote it at the behest of a friend, Patrophilus, who was anxious to learn medicine "by method and proof" (p. 224). Accordingly, he intends to show that medicine is established by the same method as all the other arts (p. 227). First, one needs to know what genus of arts the healing art belongs to, whether to the theoretical, the practical, the productive, or the possessive (p. 228). Galen decides that medicine belongs to the productive arts, and he compares it to the building of houses or architecture (Galen's father was an architect). Just as by *analysis* and *dialysis* (a term which Galen uses almost as a synonym for analysis) we understand the finished house, so by anatomy we understand the body of man, which is the subject matter of the healing art (p. 231). Yet medical technicians differ from housebuilders in having to understand not only the parts of their subject matter but also the operation (ἐνέργεια) of each of its parts (p. 232). Furthermore, we also need to know the use of all the parts found by anatomy as well (p. 236). This method of examining the number and operation of the parts has the same power (δύναμις), no matter what the subject matter (p. 237).

At the end of the sixth chapter, Galen has a very interesting passage in which he explains the combination of factors necessary to a "person seeking anything," in order that, "whether he knows the truth or not, he may not despair of discovering it." Such a person must possess seven characteristics: (1) he must have a keen natural endowment, so that he can follow logical study readily; (2) he must have education and training from childhood in the elementary disciplines—in particular, he ought to be exercised in arithmetic and geometry, "just as Plato advises"; (3) he should listen to the lectures of those who seem to be the best men in his day; (4) he must love to work, so that he will devote himself to nothing but his studies day and night; (5) he must have a passionate desire for truth and be zealous in its pursuit throughout his life, despising all else eagerly sought by the many; (6) he must learn thoroughly the method by which truth is distinguished from falsehood, for it will not suffice just to desire the truth only for the finding of what we seek, but it will be necessary also to provide oneself with the means (δύναμιν) of discovery; and finally (7) he must practice this method, so as not only to know it, but to be able to use it as well. "For if rhetoricians, who pursue an inferior art, do not seem to think it enough to know their method, but apply themselves to its practice all their lives, so much the more should those who are seeking great things practice their method." All seven of these factors are needed: the absence of any one of them will incapacitate the seeker after knowledge.[21] One can detect in this prescription an echo of Galen's own biography. It is precisely this fact that makes Galen's methodology impressive, for it was by a program such as this that Galen achieved his own quite substantial contributions to medicine.

Galen often lashes out at those who are so stupid as to fail to learn and to practice demonstrative method (ἀποδεικτικὴ μέθοδος). There is no use in even talking to such people (p. 250). Those pseudo-philosophers who are entirely ignorant of demonstration are to be shunned, unless one is prepared by being versed in logical theory (γεγυμνασμένος ἐν θεωρίᾳ λογικῇ) (p. 254). In the tenth chapter he observes that the analogy of the healing technician is not so much with the builder as with the repairer of houses (p. 257).

Referring to works in which he presents other parts of medicine, Galen says (p. 267) that there is not room in one book to comprehend all medicine, "nor was this our intention, but [we intended] only to state the methods (μεθόδους), and to point out, concerning the establishment of an art, from what and from how many principles it is developed, and by what ways (κατὰ τίνας ὁδοὺς) it is developed. Thus it was not proposed to go through the exposition of all the parts of medicine, but only to point out that, just as all the other arts are developed from the conception of the end (ἀπὸ τῆς κατὰ τὸ τέλος ἐννοίας), so also does the establishing

21 Kühn, V, 244-45.

of this art take place" (p. 302). He concludes by again calling
attention to the analogy with the other productive arts.

The second way of teaching mentioned by Galen in the *Ars
parva* passage is the "synthesis of those things found according
to analysis." [22] Although he does not state in this passage what
works of his are written in this synthetic manner, it may be
assumed that Galen's magnum opus, his *Method of Healing*,
proceeded by this mode of teaching. This textbook, the longest
and most imposing work of Galen we possess, came to be known
in the Middle Ages as the *Liber megategni*, the "full art," in
distinction to the *Liber microtegni*,[23] the "short art"—which was
the name given to the *Ars parva*.

In the *Method of Healing*, Galen set out to present his art by
a full and complete method: it was his answer to the claims of
rival teachers that they could teach the art of medicine to prospective learners in a few months. In the course of his exposition,
Galen constantly inveighs against Thessalus, the most successful of his rivals, who, according to Galen, simply stated his
medical doctrines dogmatically without rational support of any
kind.

And simply to declare that all the diseases in life are two [he says to Thes-
salus], without proffering a method (μέθοδον), a demonstration (ἀπόδειξιν),
a persuasive belief, or an explanation—not anything at all, except a def-
amation of the ancients—this is the work of a tyrant, not a teacher. Let
us grant, to silence [your objections], that you will find these by a logical
method but then you have to provide a criterion for the truth of your words.
For logical methods have the power to find what is sought, but for confirming what has been well found, all men have two criteria: reasoning
(λόγος) and experience (πεῖρα).[24]

---

[22]   δευτέρα δὲ, ἡ ἐκ συνθέσεως τῶν κατὰ τὴν ἀνάλυσιν εὑρεθέντων. Kühn, I,
305.
[23]   The origin of these names, which are garbled versions of Greek words, presents
an interesting problem. They are not Galen's titles; for he called the major work
θεραπευτικῆς μεθόδου βίβλια Δ and the short one τέχνη ἰατρική. Might these
names reflect Stoic methodology? They must have been current in late antiquity,
since the Arabs were responsible for garbling them.
[24]   Kühn, X, 28.

Reasoning and experience are the two criteria which Galen always invoked to combat the one-sided rationalism or empiricism of two of the schools of medical thought of the time.[25]

Although Galen, in his characteristic way, has methodological asides scattered throughout the whole of this work, he speaks most concretely in the fifth chapter of the "methods which I established in the work *On Demonstration.*" He intends to follow these methods in his present work:

For in those books it has been shown that the beginnings (archai) of all demonstration are the appearances which are clear both to sense perception and to the intelligence; and in the case of all things inquired into, one must take [careful] consideration of the names.... And in this you see all of them untrained, so to speak, not only the physicians of our day, but most of the philosophers as well. For few of them know how to distinguish the differences in words from those in subject matter. But the *method* for this was explained in our logical theory, and now is a fitting time for that, if ever. What then is this *method*? To begin with the differences in things, not those in names, and to show, for example, four things close to one another, and then in turn to make certain by demonstration that the content of the problem set forth is neither more nor less than these. And then, according to each separate name established for things, to pursue the subsequent discussion without changing the meaning of one word in any way, but accurately preserving it as you yourself have fixed at the beginning of the subject.[26]

This was a thrust against those who failed to notice the ambiguity of their terms.

Much more methodological advice is contained in this major work of Galen, but this should suffice to give some idea of the suggestiveness of his remarks, buried as they are underneath an immense mass of verbiage. Latin translations of the *Methodus medendi* were known in the Middle Ages,[27] but the work circulated in the Renaissance chiefly in the translation of Thomas Linacre (c.1460-1524), the famous English physician and Greek scholar; his version was first published in 1519 and was reprinted

[25] See Müller, "Ueber Galens Werk," BAW, XX, 436.
[26] Kühn, X, 39-44.
[27] See Hermann Diels, "Die Handschriften der antiken Ärzte. I Teil. Hippokrates und Galenos," *Abhandlungen*, PAW, No. 3 (1905), pp. 91-92.

many times.[28] These Renaissance translations of Galen undoubtedly helped to provide an additional stimulus to medical methodologists, since they furnished a variety of different concepts of method, inherited from all ancient schools but the Epicurean. We shall see what detailed attention Peter Ramus gave to a lesser work, written by Galen to show that Hippocrates and Plato agreed substantially in many doctrines. Unlike the *Methodus medendi*, this work did not exist in a medieval Latin translation,[29] and hence the new translations made in the folio volumes of Galen's works printed during the sixteenth century constituted a new influence.[30]

In this work Galen emphasizes the usefulness of the method, which he says is common to Hippocrates and Plato, of distinguishing the like from the unlike.

In order to arrive at the accurate diagnosis of the like and unlike, it is necessary that the beginning of the finding of these be made from the natural criteria, which are sense perception and intelligence. And as I have often said on many occasions, you may call this *mentality* or *mind* or *logic* or whatever you will, if you keep the notion that Hippocrates intends. For just as we agree with him that perception is the criterion of the perceivables, so [we agree] that there is another power for the intelligibles, which one can name as he likes—to keep what is incidental from assuming a greater importance for us than the work itself. For we use names, and all our discourse with one another, for the sake of showing the beliefs concerning the soul [one subject of Galen's treatise] which we acquired from examining the nature of things. It is ridiculous to abandon this [intent] in favor of a contention about words. And how does Hippocrates say the nature of things is found? By beginning from the greatest and easiest: the greatest for us, the easiest for our intelligence. For nature has given us both of these: the criteria themselves and our

---

[28] *Galeni methodus medendi, vel de morbis curandis, T. Linacro ... interprete, libri quatuordecim* (Paris, 1519). The work was edited by Budé and praised by Erasmus.

The Latin translation given by Kühn in Volume X of his edition of Galen's works seems to coincide closely with Linacre's translation. Linacre used *methodus* in rendering the Greek, e.g.: "sic demum tentare in proprias ea differentias diducere, secundum eam quam sapientiae professores tradiderunt methodum ..." (p. 27).

[29] Diels, "Die Handschriften der antiken Ärzte," PAW, No. 3 (1905), p. 74.

[30] For instance, Johann Sturm, during his early printing venture, brought out an edition of Galen in 1531 which may have been the one used by his pupil Ramus as a basis for his attack upon the medical methodology.

untutored confidence in them. The criteria themselves are both the instruments of the perceptions and the powers using the instruments. . . .

But if the products of the arts seem useful to the life of man, it surely was the men who trusted the natural criteria who made the standard for them. We are to this extent more fortunate than they, that we learn in a short time what was found useful by our forefathers only after much time and trouble and thought. If then, for the rest of our life, we do not exercise the arts as a sideline, but instead always consider the diagnosis of the like and the unlike, nothing prevents us from being better than our forefathers. How then shall we train and exercise ourselves? By beginning from things easy to know, just as Hippocrates said. For these are what have a great usefulness for the whole of life, and are distinct from one another.[31]

The stress on *askesis* and usefulness is obviously Stoic.

The last of the three teaching ways mentioned by Galen in the *Ars parva* is a kind to which he gives a number of designations: the breaking up of a definition (his own term), or the "unwinding" or "analysis" or "division" or "as some others say, the unfolding, or still others, explicating."[32] This manner of teaching, although inferior to the first or analytic in point of prestige and method, is nevertheless more useful for the synopsis of the whole (art), and for helping the student to remember its parts. The *Ars parva*, according to its author, is written in this manner, starting with the definition of medicine and analyzing it.

This passage illustrates (1) the looseness of Galen's terminology, (2) the diversity of philosophical influences to which he was subjected, and (3) the difficulties in arriving at any clear notion of what Galen meant. It is small wonder that the whole passage became a perennial stumbling block for medical lecturers and gave rise to a host of variant interpretations. Pending a thorough study of Galen's philosophy of science, one should not speak too confidently of his theories, but it seems clear that

---

[31] [*Claudii*] *Galeni De Placitis Hippocratis et Platonis,* ed. Müller (Leipzig, 1874), p. 733. (There is no ancient evidence for the name "Claudius," which seems to have been bestowed on Galen by tradition, on the basis of some resemblance to the astronomer Ptolemy.)

[32] τρίτη δὲ, ἡ ἐξ ὅρου διαλύσεως, ἢν νῦν ἐνιστάμεθα. καλεῖν δ' ἔξεστι τὴν τοιαύτην διδασκαλίαν, οὐ μόνον ὅρου διαλύσιν, ἢ ἀνάλυσιν, ἢ διαίρεσιν, ἢ, ὡς ἕτεροι τινες, ἐξάπλωσιν, ἢ ἐξήγησιν, ὡς ἄλλοι. Kühn, I, 305.

Galen adopted several methodological traditions—and never quite made his own view consistent.

In an astronomical authority from the same period, the outlines of a methodological eclecticism similar to Galen's could have been found by sixteenth-century students of science. Claudius Ptolemy also rejected the overrefinements of Stoic dialectic, and yet also made some use of Stoic concepts within a generally Aristotelian framework.[33] Although Ptolemy is mentioned by Renaissance writers on method only seldom, he was certainly familiar to those who were at all informed in astronomy, and his name does appear now and then as an authority on method also.

Galen and Ptolemy were typical of their period in drawing upon a variety of traditions for their doctrines of scientific method while still remaining fundamentally loyal to the Aristotelian theory of scientific demonstration. The other major philosophical schools of antiquity, since they offered little in the way of explicit methodology, found few adherents in the Renaissance controversies. At most they contributed a few concepts or doctrines to the generally accepted Aristotelian theory of proof. Stoic notions in particular exercised a good deal of influence, but this influence was indirect, being transmitted by means of stray quotations in writers of other schools, or by their incorporation into the doctrines of eclectic writers. As for Stoic dialectic, it was commonly called a "bramble patch" in the Renaissance, and its thorns were compared with those of medieval Terminist logic—a comparison that was more justified historically than the Humanists who drew the comparison knew. There was no one to suggest, as did Johann Sturm with respect to the similar brambles of medieval theology, that "even these thorns might have their roses." Few Renaissance scholars were in a position to realize the extent to which Stoic doctrine had crept into the writings of Galen, who was assumed to be a good and faithful Aristotelian.

Although Epicurus did not develop a very complex epistemology,

---

[33] Franz Boll, "Studien über Claudius Ptolemäus: Ein Beitrag zur Geschichte der Griechischen Philosophie und Astrologie," *Jahrbücher für classische Philologie,* Supplement-Band XXI (1894), 49-244.

he did have views on the manner of acquiring sound knowledge. These, however, were not explored thoroughly until the seventeenth century, when the scholarly Gassendi adopted an Epicurean epistemology. The sceptical later Academy was *ex professo* not a good source for doctrines on method.[34]

METHOD IN THE GREEK COMMENTATORS

Next to the works of Plato, Aristotle, and Galen, by far the richest source for Renaissance methodologists was the corpus of Greek commentaries on Aristotle. In these works Renaissance philosophers could find a great deal on the subject of method, particularly in those written by the scholar-scientists of Alexandria, who frequently combined an interest in the exact sciences with a scholarly and philological approach to the exegesis of philosophical texts. Most of these commentators were, like Galen, students of many or all of the philosophical schools of their time—or at least were familiar with the doctrines of other sects. Consequently they brought to their reading of Aristotle much of the terminology and lore of other schools. It is to their period that we owe the codification, so to speak, of the methodologies of antiquity. The Platonic doctrine had already been reduced to a list of four dialectical methods, division, definition, demonstration, and analysis: since many commentators were Platonists, it was necessary for them to correlate these dialectical methods of Plato with the logical doctrines of Aristotle found in the treatises under consideration.

In general, originality is not to be looked for in a commentator: his task, as he conceived it, was the linguistic and philosophic explication of a text. So far as doctrines of method go, the discussions of the commentators were intended only to explicate references to the subject in Plato or Aristotle. Only a few of the commentators suggest that these are methods that can be put to use in independent philosophizing. One such was Ammonius

---

[34] See Melanchthon's dismissal of all but Aristotelian philosophy, CR, XIII, 656-57. In the early sixteenth century it was still unorthodox to champion any of the minor Greek philosophies that found adherents later on.

Hermiae, who remarked that the above-mentioned four dialectical methods of Plato can be used by philosophers "to find out about any subject." [35]

A perennial question in such treatments was one concerning the relative merits of the various methods thus distinguished—whether, for example, definition was "subservient" to demonstration or conversely. Just as Plato, after distinguishing the different faculties of the soul, was interested in determining which faculty or part should dominate, so these commentators argued over which variety of dialectical method should dominate. They extended the same kind of analysis to the sciences as a whole, and argued as to which science should be the master science.

The external form of commentaries was set for the medieval period and for the Renaissance as well by these Greek writers, especially the form of the preamble or introduction that preceded the commentator's exposition of his text. Although the contents of these preambles varied somewhat from author to author, they usually took up the purpose of the work, its authenticity, its usefulness, its inscription or title, and its place in relation to the whole of philosophy. This standard (and rather useful) form of introduction[36] was transmitted to the early Middle Ages by Boethius, who himself followed neo-Platonic models. Within

---

[35] Ammonius was discussing Porphyry's *Isagoge*. Porphyry had said that the five predicables of Aristotle are useful for division and for demonstration, which gave Ammonius the opportunity of discussing the methods of Plato and Aristotle. "For dialectic according to Aristotle follows five judgments, as he has set forth in the *Topics*, and dialectic according to Plato is fourfold, according to Division, Definition, Demonstration, and Analysis.... The sense of the passage is, then, to be taken as if Porphyry had said that this work contributes not only to the treatises of the philosophers, but as if, without there being any treatises, it contributes to the very methods of the philosophers (εἰς αὐτὰς τὰς τῶν φιλοσόφων μεθόδους)." *Ammonius in Porphyrii Isagogen sive V voces*, CAG, IV³, 34-5. Ammonius would have made such a point only, it seems to me, if it had been counter to prevailing conceptions.

[36] See Prantl's *Geschichte der Logik*, I, 649-50; also Martin Grabmann, "Methoden und Hilfsmittel des Aristotelesstudiums im Mittelalter," *Sitzungsberichte*, BAW, Jahrgang 1939, Heft 5, esp. pp. 18-19. For a very thorough and scholarly account of the medieval version of these Greek preambles, see Edwin A. Quain, "The Medieval Accessus ad Auctores," *Traditio*, III (1945), 215-64. Father Quain regards the Greek commentators on Aristotle as the most likely source for the common medieval practice of prefixing an *accessus* to the examination of a work. He found

the confines of these preambles, much Greek and medieval methodology developed, for almost any of these standard topics, and
especially the last, could give rise to general considerations of
the methodology of the arts and sciences. This sequence of topics
for discussion continued to be consciously employed by editors
of Aristotle and commentators on his works up to the sixteenth
century. For instance, an Italian named Francesco Vimercato
(c.1500-1570), who taught philosophy in Paris, noted the practice
with approval in the preface to his commentary on the third book
of the *De anima*.[37] In handing down this standard sequence, the
commentators also passed on some standard problems, the most
famous of which was Averroes' discussion of the "way of
doctrine" at the start of his commentary on the *Physics*.[38] Another was the problem of the order of the books of the *Organon*.
The dispute that raged for centuries over this problem was no
mere bookbinder's quarrel, as it must appear to one not familiar
with the preambles of the commentaries: it concerned the relative
functions of the various parts of Aristotelian logic. Such a dispute
served to illustrate in concrete fashion the abstract issue of the

---

traces of the practice in medieval grammar, rhetoric, dialectic, and canon and civil
law. See also Richard W. Hunt, "The Introductions to the 'Artes' in the Twelfth
Century," *Studia mediaevalia in honorem admodum Reverendi Patri Raymundi
Josephi Martin* (Bruges, n.d.), pp. 85-112.

[37] "Consuevere Aristotelis interpretes quotquot hactenus vidimus, Graeci, Latini,
et Arabes, omnium eorum librorum, quos interpretandos susceperunt, quam σκοπόν
Graeci, subiectum Latini alio nomine nuncupant, utilitatem et divisionem, inter
multa alia initio praemittere, ea ratione (nec immerito) arbitrati id, quod in libris
eiusmodi traditum esset, ardentius expetitum, pleniusque et facilius ab omnibus
intellectum iri. Intentio enim authore Simplicio, recte perspecta, intellectum nostrum
dirigit, ut non vagemur, et temere atque frustra in diversa trahamur, sed ad ipsam
omnia referamus. Utilitas promptiores nos ad huiusmodi doctrinam persequendam
efficit, ea namque natura sumus ut nihil quod alicui usui non sit, raro aut nunquam
aggrediamur. Divisio totum librum ob oculos ponit atque uniuscuiusque partis ad
universam intentionem usum, et opportunitatem praestat, eam imitata speculationem,
quae a medicis de incisione scientia appellatur." Franciscus Vicomercatus, *Commentarii in tertium librum Aristotelis De Anima . . .* (Venice, 1574), p. 3. Vimercato, then professor of Greek philosophy at the Collège Royal, was one of the judges
adverse to Ramus in the famous debate with Goveanus. See Charles Waddington,
Ramus, sa vie, ses écrits, et ses opinions (Paris, 1855), p. 43. On Vimercato as an
"Averroist," see Ernest Renan, *Averroès et l'Averroïsme* (Paris, 1866), p. 425. See
also Henri Busson, *Le rationalisme dans la littérature française de la Renaissance*
(Paris, 1957), pp. 191-212.

[38] See pp. 165-70 below.

"order of doctrine." Similarly the heading which dealt with the inscription of the work gave rise to differences of opinion among scholars. The title of the *Analytics* (*Prior* and *Posterior*) was a constant source of bewilderment to the commentators. What was being "analyzed" in these works? And (since analysis always requires a corresponding synthesis for the sake of symmetry) what "synthesis" corresponded to this "analysis"? Unfortunately Aristotle did not write a *Synthetics*, although commentators for centuries taxed their ingenuity to discover a possible meaning for such an enterprise.

THE MEDIEVAL COMMENTARIES ON ARISTOTLE

Although those Humanist methodologists whom we have called the methodologists of the arts considered themselves under no debt of gratitude whatsoever to their medieval predecessors, the "scientific" methodologists could look upon their activity as a continuous development from the earliest reception of Greco-Arab science to their own days, for the Aristotelian texts upon which they based their analyses, and the works of Galen which supplemented them, had been commented upon and studied since the twelfth and thirteenth centuries. Of the vast number of medieval commentaries on Aristotle, few have been thoroughly studied by modern scholars. If we reflect that in order to understand these Latin commentaries at all adequately we need to know something of the Arab writers whom they knew and discussed, and, further, something of the Greek commentators upon whom both Arab [39] and Latin writers drew, and then think of the lack of scholarship that shrouds both the Arabs and the Greek commentators—we are appalled that anyone can confidently pretend to evaluate the medieval material at the present time. The danger of attributing originality to a writer for expressing a view which he and his contemporaries knew full well to be

[39] On the indebtedness of the Arab commentators to their Greek predecessors, see Ernest Renan, *Averroès et l'Averroïsme*, pp. 88-94, and Richard Walzer, "Arabic Transmission of Greek Thought to Medieval Europe," *Bulletin of the John Rylands Library, Manchester*, XXIX (1945), 160-83, esp. pp. 174-75.

derived from an Arab or Greek source lurks in wait for the unwary scholar. Or, most embarrassing of all, a thought that seems strikingly modern when expressed by a thirteenth-century Aristotelian turns out to be contained in the works of Aristotle himself!

The methodology one finds in these Latin commentaries on Aristotle represents basically Platonic and Aristotelian doctrines of dialectical or scientific method variously compounded with Stoic or neo-Platonic elements. During the earlier medieval period the neo-Platonic elements, which fitted in with Islamic and Christian theology, were given greater emphasis in philosophy in general, and this emphasis may be seen even in methodological doctrines. The basic metaphor of method, that of a way leading somewhere, could easily be adapted to moral and religious purposes, especially when conceived as a vertical ascent. Hence doctrines of emanation and other cosmological notions readily found their way into the most sober Aristotelian methodology, while in the Platonic dialogues they already had been given such metaphorical significance.

In general, the fact that the Greek commentators, although commenting upon texts of Aristotle, still felt the obligation to do justice to Platonic views meant that they attempted to reconcile or to merge the schematized fourfold "dialectical method of Plato" with Aristotle's theories of demonstration or of argumentation. Frequently this merger was little more than a listing of methods drawn from both philosophers. The pagan Ammonius, the Christian Philoponus, and the Byzantine Bishop Eustratius, all had lists of methods varying somewhat in language but little in content; and lists of this sort were familiar to the Arab Averroes and to his Latin heirs in the commenting tradition.

The medieval Latin commentators did not realize what a mélange their methodology was. The attempt to understand the thought of ancient writers directly and only from the Greek sources was a product of the Renaissance. It was not until Humanist criticism began to require the identification of doctrines at their source that it could be realized to what an extent these doctrines of method were simply pastiches from Platonic, Aristotelian, neo-Platonic, and Stoic sources.

Often, of course, the exact Aristotelian source of a doctrine is given, and there is then no problem of determining its parentage. Thomas Aquinas, for example, identified the beginning of the *Physics* as the source of his "mode of resolution," according to which we proceed from the "composite to the simple," and from the "whole to the part."[40] But at other times Aristotelian notions appear blended, in this Scholastic methodology, with neo-Platonic doctrines that could not have been identified as Aristotelian, such as the idea that "causes are simpler than effects" (a relic of the *Liber de causis*), in the method known as the "resolutory process."[41]

Thus the study of medieval commentaries on Aristotle[42] must be reckoned a very delicate pursuit. Fortunately, for us the problem is not central, since we shall find that with only a few exceptions, the great medieval doctors were seldom discussed in

[40] "Est autem duplex via procedendi ad cognitionem veritatis. Una quidem per modum resolutionis, secundum quam procedimus a compositis ad simplicia, et a toto ad partem, sicut dicitur in primo *Physicorum,* quod confusa sunt prius nobis nota. Et in hac via perficitur cognitio veritatis, quando pervenitur ad singulas partes distincte cognoscendas.... Alia est via compositionis, per quam procedimus a simplicibus ad composita, qua perficitur cognitio veritatis cum pervenitur ad totum. Sic igitur hoc ipsum quod homo non potest in rebus perfecte totum et partem cognoscere, ostendit difficultatem considerandae veritatis per utramque viam." Thomas Aquinas, *In II Metaphysicorum,* Lect. 1, n. 278.

[41] "Quod quidem si, sicut est prius in cognitione, ita etiam sit prius in esse, non est processus resolutorius, sed magis compositivus; procedere enim a causis in effectus, est processus compositivus, nam causae sunt simpliciores effectibus. Si autem id quod est prius in cognitione est posterius in esse, est processus resolutorius; utpote cum de effectibus manifestis iudicamus, resolvendo in causas simplices." *Summa theologica,* Ia IIae, qu. 14, a. 5. These and many other references in Aquinas to resolution and composition are collected by S. Edmund Dolan, "Resolution and Composition in Speculative and Practical Discourse," *Laval Théologique et Philosophique,* VI (1950), 9-62. See also Louis-M. Régis, "Analyse et synthèse dans l'oeuvre de saint Thomas," *Studia mediaevalia in honorem admodum Reverendi Patri Raymundi Josephi Martin,* pp. 303-30. Régis notes Latin writers previous to Aquinas who employ similar dichotomies, including Chalcidius, Boethius, Scotus Erigena, and Albertus Magnus.

[42] A. C. Crombie's book, *Robert Grosseteste and the Origins of Experimental Science, 1100-1700* (Oxford, 1953), contains a wealth of information about medieval methodology of science. Of particular interest is his section on the "foundations of Grosseteste's theory of science," pp. 52-60. The section on Galileo in this book, pp. 303-10, contains references to the most recent secondary literature on the subject of Galileo's methodology.

the sixteenth century. It is true that the methodology of the commentators—Greek, Arab, and Latin—formed the background for the traditionalists of the late Renaissance. But under the pressure of Humanist criticism, they began to sift through this assortment of doctrines and to pick out those which were genuinely Aristotle's. One of the first stages in this process was the elimination from consideration of those commentaries which were not written in Greek. The second stage came with the realization that even the Greek commentators were not entirely reliable, for they often labeled the non-Aristotelian source of their doctrines quite clearly themselves. The next stage, and the final one for the history of Aristotelianism, was the elimination of all but two considerations: Aristotle and the Truth. With Descartes, even Aristotle was dismissed, and the modern era indeed began.

This explains why Renaissance Aristotelians, with the exception of the Spanish neo-Scholastics and those Italian Scholastics who were influenced by them, showed relatively little interest in the commentaries of Aquinas, Albert, or any of the many other Scholastics in whom doctrines of method could be found. The one medieval commentator who continued to enjoy great prestige in methodological matters was Averroes, "the" commentator—but even he was not above the suspicion of having lifted his doctrines bodily from Philoponus, Themistius, or Alexander of Aphrodisias, and he remained in favor only in Italy.

The application of Platonic or Aristotelian "methods" to education was a subject that received little attention in any of the commentaries. True, doctrines concerning the "order of cognition" could easily be applied to the learning of geometry, for example, but for the most part methodological issues were conceived in the abstract and pedagogical considerations were definitely of minor importance.[43] The conduct of schooling was not

---

[43] An exception is the Byzantine writer Eustratius (died c.1120), who says that the four dialectical methods are ones by which all teaching (πᾶσα διδασκαλία) and scientific learning (μάθησις ἐπιστημονική) are carried on. But Eustratius drew on all of the sects for his doctrines, and this note may very well be Stoic: he also speaks of "conceptual" methods (μέθοδοι ἐννοηματικαί) which also suggest Stoic influence. *Eustratii in Analyticorum Posteriorum librum secundum Commentarium,* CAG, XXI¹, 4-5.

a theoretical concern of the Aristotelian tradition; aside from a few remarks in the *Politics* and *Ethics,* Aristotle did not deal with pedagogy in any detail. This explains why it was that the Humanists, with their programs of education, could enter the philosophical arena without seeming at first to do more than supplement Aristotle. In a later chapter, we shall see that this apparently innocent reform of educational methods finally developed into a general intellectual revolution that threatened to alter medieval habits of philosophizing as well as education.

GEOMETRICAL METHOD IN THE GREEK COMMENTATORS

A constant if somewhat elusive ingredient in the methodology of the commentators is the pair of methods drawn from geometry, namely, those of "analysis" and "synthesis." Geometrical analysis, the first of these methods, is mentioned by Aristotle in terms specific enough to suggest that both the terminology and the concept were current among the geometers of his time.[44] The question whether this geometrical analysis was the invention of Plato—a theory entertained even in late antiquity—has been the subject of scholarly controversy concerning Plato's relation to actual investigation in mathematics. Since it is generally conceded by most authorities on the history of mathematics that the geometers of Plato's time were in command of quite subtle methods of inquiry and proof, it seems more likely that Plato's twofold way of dialectic was based on current geometrical procedure than that the latter sprang into being at his instigation,[45] but this is

[44] *Nicomachean Ethics,* 1112b20—a passage which was one of the chief sources for the later Scholastic doctrine that the "practical sciences" must proceed by the resolutive order. Another reference to geometrical analysis is found in the *Sophistical Elenchies,* 175a28-30. Cf. Sir Thomas Heath, *Mathematics in Aristotle* (Oxford, 1949), pp. 270-72.

[45] Which is not to say that Plato and the Academy may not have been very active in promoting the study of mathematics. For secondary literature on the subject of geometrical analysis and synthesis, which usually deals incidentally with the question of Plato's relation to mathematical research, see the references in Thomas Heath's edition of *Euclid's Elements* (Cambridge, 1926), I, 139. To this should be added more recent studies: Friedrich Solmsen, "Platos Einfluss auf die Bildung der mathematischen Methode," *Quellen und Studien zur Geschichte der Mathematik, Astronomie, und Physik, Abteilung B: Studien* (Berlin, 1931), I, 93-107; Kurt von Fritz, "Platon, Theätet, und die antike Mathematik," *Philologus,* LXXXVII (1932), 40-62,

admittedly a complex problem. At any rate, by Euclid's time (a generation or so after Aristotle's death), geometrical usage was certainly fixed; we find short characterizations of both geometrical analysis and synthesis in the thirteenth book of the *Elements*.[46]

By the second and third centuries of our era, this geometrical language had begun to permeate philosophical writings, indicating that these geometrical methods were known, by name at least, to scholars of various philosophical schools. Alexander of Aphrodisias, the first Greek commentator on Aristotle whose works are preserved to us in any extent, mentions the geometrical meaning in his commentary on the *Prior Analytics*, in that part of the preamble in which he discusses the "inscription of the work."[47] Geometrical analysis is only one of nine different senses of ἀνάλυσις current in philosophical thought, and we can see from this list how the various meanings could interact and become blurred in subsequent philosophy.

Somewhat earlier, Clement of Alexandria (c.150 A.D.), in the book of his *Stromateis* devoted to logic, had also described a kind

---

and 136-78; Francis M. Cornford, "Mathematics and Dialectic in the Republic VI-VII," *Mind*, XLI (1932); 37-52, 173-90; Richard Robinson, "Analysis in Greek Geometry," *Mind*, XLV (1936), 464-73; and Paul Tannery, "Du sens des mots analyse et synthèse chez les Grecs et de leur algèbre géométrique," *Mémoires scientifiques* (16 vols., Toulouse, 1912-43), III, 162-69.

[46] Although the authenticity of this section has been challenged. See *The Thirteen Books of Euclid's Elements*, ed. Thomas Heath (3 vols., Cambridge, 1926), III, 442.

[47] "And he [Aristotle] called them *Analytics* because the resolution of every compound into those things out of which the synthesis [is made] is called *analysis*. For analysis is the converse of synthesis. Synthesis is the road from the principles to those things that derive from the principles, and analysis is the return from the end to the principles. For geometers are said to *analyze* when, beginning from the conclusion they go up to the principles and the problem, following the order of those things which were assumed for the demonstration of the conclusion. But he also uses analysis who reduces composite bodies into simple bodies, and he analyzes who divides the word into the parts of the word; also he who divides the parts of the word into the syllables; and he who divides these into their components. And they are severally said to analyse who reduce compound syllogisms into simple ones, and simple ones into the premisses out of which they get their being. And further, resolving imperfect syllogisms into perfect ones is called analyzing. And they call analysis the reducing of the given syllogism into the proper schemata. And it is especially in this meaning of analysis that these are entitled *Analytics,* for he describes for us a method at the end of the first book with which we shall be able to do this." *Alexandri in Aristotelis Analyticorum Priorum librum I Commentarium*, CAG, II¹, 7. (My translation.)

of analysis which could be the geometric, but Clement does not give the converse process the name *synthesis*, nor does he speak of this analysis specifically as geometrical.[48] A contemporary of Galen, Albinus,[49] who heard the lectures of the same Platonist teacher (Gaius) under whom Galen studied, listed a kind of analysis which could have been geometrical among a list of purportedly Platonic procedures; and he listed its converse as the "synthetic manner." One would suppose that Galen, the enthusiastic champion of the geometrical or "linear" demonstration, would have adopted this doctrine of analysis and synthesis, and made it central in his epistemology. This does not seem to be the case. Although Galen speaks of synthesis and analysis, he never, so far as I have been able to determine, takes cognizance of the two correlative geometrical methods, but always gives to the terms meanings they had received in the philosophical tradition.[50] In short, we find an absorption of the geometrical

---

[48] "Demonstration differs from *analysis,* in which each of the things to be proved is proved through some things that are [already] proved, and these in turn are proved by others, until we run back to the things which are certain in themselves or are clear to sense-perception and understanding [εἰς τὰ πρὸς αἴσθησιν τε καὶ νόησιν ἐναργῆ —the Theophrastian doctrine again: cf. Galen's version given above, p. 20]: this is called *analysis.*" Clemens Alexandrinus, *Opera omnia,* ed. Reinhold Klotz (Leipzig, 1832), pp. 300-1.

[49] Albinus divides dialectic into five subspecies instead of the usual Platonic four, in his Epitome of Platonic philosophy, which is in reality a mixture of doctrines from various schools. One of the five parts of dialectic is *analysis,* which is of three kinds. Both the second and the third kinds are suggestively close to the geometrical: "The second species of analysis is as follows: that which is sought must be assumed; and one must consider what is prior to that; and demonstrate, going from the posterior to the prior; until we come to the first and conceded [notion]; beginning from this, we return to the thing sought by the synthetic manner (συνθετικῷ τρόπῳ) .... Analysis by hypothesis (ἐξ ὑποθέσεως) is as follows: the inquirer assumes what he is seeking; then, he considers what follows from his assumption; and after that, if it be necessary to give a reason (λόγον) for his hypothesis, making another hypothesis, he seeks if the prior assumption, in turn, is consequent upon the other hypothesis; and so he does until he arrives at an unassumed principle (ἀρχή)." Albinus, *Épitomé,* ed. Pierre Louis (Rennes, 1945), pp. 25-27. A Latin translation of this work was published in 1469, the work of Petrus Balbus; but the most influential Renaissance translation was made by Marsilio Ficino: it may be found in his *Opera* (2 vols., Basel, 1576), II, col. 1948.

[50] In the work on the doctrines of Hippocrates and Plato, Galen calls *synthesis* that process which Socrates describes in the *Phaedrus* as the other part of dialectic beside the divisive. *De placitis Hippocratis et Platonis,* p. 767. He also mentions a number of forms of division (p. 826) "which some philosophers ... call also *analysis.*" But the two methods are not correlative for him, nor are they geometrical.

terminology into both Aristotelian and Platonic philosophizing
(if we may speak of this epitomizing and commenting as "philosophizing") during the second and the early part of the third
century of our era.[51]

The most detailed and interesting account of the geometrical
methods (here called ὁδοί not μέθοδοι) was given later by Pappus
of Alexandria, who flourished about 300 A.D. His description
has the ring of authority about it, for its author was a competent
geometer and was writing for "those who wish to acquire a
facility in the resolving of problems" in geometry.[52] Pappus
remarks that a number of writers have dealt with the "analytical
topos," as he calls his subject: Euclid, the author of the *Elements*;
Apollonius Pergaeus; and Aristaeus the Elder. Probably his own
account is a compilation from these earlier ones. However,
Pappus exercised no influence upon medieval methodology, for
his work was not widely diffused until the Latin translation made
by Federigo Commandino (1509-75) was published in 1589 at
Venice.

The medieval Scholastics, deprived of this most detailed
description, had only the earlier philosophical accounts to study—
which, as one can see, are quite vague and secondhand. Many of
the Greek commentators on Aristotle, Themistius especially, refer
to Euclid's *Elements* when discussing Aristotle's theories of
demonstration but, not being skilled mathematicians, do not develop the subject of geometrical method. In short, the analysis
and synthesis of geometry, while never quite lost from sight in the
commentaries, do not emerge into the full light of day until the

---

[51] Prantl, in his *Geschichte der Logik*, I, 655, found a "scholastic" distinction
between analytic and synthetic procedures in Philoponus' commentary on the *Prior
Analytics*, in a quotation from the Venice, 1536, edition of Philoponus, which I
have not been able to verify. The passage he cites refers definitely to geometrical
analysis and synthesis. But it is certainly not the first mention of them in the Greek
commentators on Aristotle.

[52] *Pappi Alexandrini Collectionis quae supersunt,* ed. Friedrich Hultsch (3 vols.,
Berlin, 1877), II, 634-37. The possibility of some infiltration of Stoic logic into
this geometrical methodology has never been suggested, much less explored, but it
is a tempting one. Pappus' language is very similar to that of Clement of Alexandria,
who followed Chrysippus in much of his doctrine, or of Albinus; both these writers
were receptive to Stoic ideas.

late sixteenth century, when they quickly became the common property of philosophers as well as scientists. Previous to this time they tend to be blurred and lend themselves to identification with all sorts of other kinds of "analysis" or "synthesis"—as, for instance, those listed by Alexander.

RENAISSANCE ATTITUDES TOWARD AUTHORITY

Such were the authorities in philosophy to whom, if we believe the histories of philosophy, medieval and Renaissance philosophers paid unconditional homage. The authority of Aristotle in philosophy, Galen in medicine, and Ptolemy in astronomy, we are told, reigned supreme and with a "dead hand" over men's minds. (The authority of Euclid in geometry, being still quite weighty, is usually conveniently omitted from this list by the historian.) A few bold and independent thinkers heralded the dawn of the new age by proclaiming that the authority of Aristotle was not absolute. The rest remained sunken in medieval slumber, knowing nothing but the *verbum Magistri* and swearing upon it. A dismal picture, if true: but we must examine it and see how much truth it does contain.

First of all, what do our sources tell us? Do we hear of anyone who wished to be known as a blind follower of Aristotle during the sixteenth century? The answer, in spite of the histories, is that we do not. To a man, Renaissance writers proclaim their unyielding devotion to the Truth, and to the Truth alone. Aristotle must be given serious attention, yes, but blind adulation, no. Aristotle was, in a common phrase of the times, *non Deus, sed vir,* capable of erring like the rest of us, and the privilege of challenging his authority had been claimed repeatedly since Petrarch. The boldness of these declarations of intellectual independence strikes us forcefully when we read them in the writings of a Bruno who died for them—but when we read more widely and find similar declarations made by those whom the histories call "dogmatic Aristotelians," we begin to realize that Bruno was only expressing a common attitude.

Yet there is a sense in which the histories are correct in regarding most Renaissance philosophers as slaves of the word, and that, curiously enough, to a greater degree than their medieval predecessors. For the Renaissance "philosopher" was a man who read his authorities in the original language and who permitted no deviations of doctrine that were not sanctioned by the original language of the author. The philosopher who did not read Greek felt himself under a considerable handicap, and sometimes apologized for his lack of linguistic ability. In other words, even the philosophers, at this late period in the Renaissance, had become Humanists, that is, students of the ancient languages and of the classics written in them. It is impossible to separate philosophers of the period into two neat categories, the one ("traditional") upholding the authority of Aristotle, and the other ("Humanist") attacking it. By this time many professors of philosophy had learned the Greek language and had read widely in the Greek sources of their subject. The phrase "Humanist Aristotelian," while it may offend readers of history books, accurately describes many Renaissance philosophers. Furthermore, anti-Aristotelianism was not limited to Humanists but could be professed by serious students of Plato or other writers as well.

There is another consideration that must be taken into account. In the effort to understand Aristotle in the Greek, Renaissance philosophers, dogmatic Aristotelians as well as Humanists, scorned the medieval commentaries, which were so clearly based on Latin translations, and turned instead[53] to the Greek commentators and to other Greek writers, especially Plato, for illumination and help in understanding difficult points in the text of the Master of those who know. Thus we have what, by some modern interpretations, would be the curious paradox of two strongly "Aristotelian" opponents of Peter Ramus—Schegk and Carpentarius—quoting extensively and seriously from Plato's dialogues. Yet they were typical of their day.

Scholars of every conviction were becoming more aware of the

---

[53] With the exception of the Italian Averroists, who still read the commentaries of Averroes (in Latin, of course).

interplay and rivalry between ancient schools of thought and were beginning to gain more of a feeling for the actual historical development of the doctrines of Aristotle, particularly for his indebtedness to Plato. There was no longer the antagonism between followers of Plato and followers of Aristotle that the earlier Renaissance had inherited from the Byzantine scholars. The views of Plato and Aristotle were now considered by many to supplement and corroborate one another. "Let us love both," was Melanchthon's conclusion,[54] and most students agreed.

Thus the attitude professed by the great majority of Renaissance writers toward the authorities, and particularly Aristotle, was one of respectful attention but not blind devotion. When we compare these professions with the performance of those who made them, however, it soon becomes clear that the authorities did indeed exercise an almost hypnotic fascination upon men's minds. When one could acquire a great reputation as a "philosopher" simply by dint of linguistic ability and diligent reading, why venture to think for oneself and run the risk of being scorned for not recognizing the superior merit of the ancients? *Auctoritas,* then, was indeed in the ascendant in the Renaissance,

---

[54] For a typical expression of a Renaissance "Aristotelian," see Melanchthon's declamation on Plato given in the year 1538: "Cum igitur [Plato] eam, quam toties praedicat, methodum non saepe adhibeat, et evagetur aliquando liberius in disputando, quaedam etiam figuris involvat, ac volens occultet, denique cum raro pronunciet quid sit sentiendum, assentior adolescentibus potius proponendum esse Aristotelem, qui artes quas tradit explicat integras, et methodum simpliciorem, ceu filum, ad regendum lectorem adhibet, et quid sit sentiendum, plerunque pronunciat. Haec in docentibus ut requirantur multae graves causae sunt. Ut enim satis dentibus draconis a Cadmo, seges exorta est armatorum, qui inter se ipsi dimicarunt, ita si quis serat ambiguas opiniones, exoriuntur inde variae ac perniciosae dissensiones. Paulo ante hanc aetatem Bessarion et Trapezuntius hostiliter inter se dissenserunt, cum hic Aristotelem, ille Platonem anteferret. Id certamen diremit Theodorus Gaza, inquiens suum cuique locum tribuendum esse: ita lectionem Platonis multum profuturam esse, si quis in Aristotele recte institutus, postea Platonem legat. Nam cum afferet lector Aristotelicam methodum, facile quasi intra certas metas includet eas res, quae apud Platonem late dissipatae sunt. Et hanc fuisse Aristoteli causam arbitror, cur methodum adeo exiliter consectaretur, ut ea quae a Platone acceperat, collecta et quadam oeconomia atque ordine distributa, posteris integre traderet. Etsi quaedam limare etiam ac corrigere voluit, rerum tamen in summa non magna est dissimilitudo.... Amemus igitur utrunque, et cum in Aristotele mediocriter versati fuerimus, alterum etiam propter politicas materias et propter eloquentiam legamus. Habet suos quosdam locos, propter quos eruditos delectare potest." CR, XL. cols. 423-24.

so far as philosophy proper is concerned, perhaps even more so than it was during the high Middle Ages, when it was balanced or even overbalanced by a *ratio* which showed great constructive vigor and which could assert that *auctoritas* after all had a *cereum nasum*. For now in the printed word was to be found all human knowledge and even, so it was beginning to be held, the key to what little additional knowledge the human race might aspire to—the *method* of the ancients.

Chapter 2. THE HISTORY OF METHOD AS A PHILOSOPHICAL TERM

The history of the concept of method is quite unintelligible without some knowledge of the history of its terminology, and hence we offer—with apologies to those who, with Galen, consider the choice of words to be a matter of complete indifference—a chapter sketching briefly the use of μέθοδος and *methodus* as technical terms in philosophical writing. The derivatives of these words in vernacular languages are so common and ordinary that it is not easy for a modern reader to realize that *method* has had a varied career as a philosophical term. But unless we become sensitive to its nuances, the rather interesting history of the development of that concept of method to which we pay lip service today must remain a closed book. For it is very difficult to avoid the almost irresistible temptation to smuggle into early discussions of *methodus* our modern conceptions of scientific method; and yet, unless we can do this, we destroy the fabric of intellectual history altogether. Let us turn then to the word as it first occurs in a European language.

Μέθοδος IN PLATO AND ARISTOTLE

The Greek word from which our *method* comes is μέθοδος, which is a compound of μετά and ὁδός meaning "following after." The word is missing from pre-Socratic philosophy,[1] where the

---

[1] See Ottfrid Becker, "Das Bild des Weges und verwandte Vorstellungen im frühgriechischen Denken," *Hermes, Einzelschriften*, Heft 4 (1937). Becker's study originated in an interest in *aporia* in Plato's dialogues; he was led, in the course of examining the root *poros*, to investigate *odos* as well. "Die Aporie (ἀ - πορία) beruht auf dem Bild des 'Weges.' Neben sie stellt sich daher der von Platon geschaffene Begriff der 'Methode' (μέθ - οδος) und aus dem Gebiet des Mythischen etwa der Aufstieg zum Licht im Höhlengleichnis und anderes. Des Wegbild erweist sich als wichtiges Motiv einer platonischen Bildersprache." *Ibid.*, p. 2.

language in general is commonplace or poetic rather than technical, although "way" does appear. Parmenides, for example,
spoke of the ὁδός which the Goddess pointed out to him, and the
metaphor of the way or path was common in early Greek thought.
As a technical term, μέθοδος is first found in the dialogues of
Plato.[2] The *Phaedrus* passage which we discussed in the previous
chapter (265D-277C) contained in embryo all of the connotations
which the word was later to acquire in Greek. Only the man who
has the μέθοδος can be said to have a sound knowledge of an art,
and it is this μέθοδος which enables him to teach the art to others.
A person who has mastered the methods of διαίρεσις and συναγωγή
was called by Socrates a "dialectician." These are the basic "dialectical methods."

Discussion of these methods is everywhere in the Platonic dialogues, so that it is difficult to overlook the fact that Plato used
the word in a technical sense.[3] Plato's ideas on method may have
been suggested in part by Hippocrates or the Eleatics, but the
terminology originates with him.

Not so obvious is the fact that Aristotle also uses μέθοδος in a
technical sense. If we examine all the passages in which Aristotle
uses μέθοδος with Plato's usage in mind, we see that the Stagirite
was still very much under the influence of his master's doctrine.
The μέθοδος of the *Topics* (100[a]18) is Aristotle's answer to Plato's
demand for a systematic treatment of the art of arguing and
debating. In other works when Aristotle speaks of proceeding
κατὰ μέθοδον, he usually means the method of διαίρεσις or the analysis of a phenomenon into its parts and the examination of their
interrelated functions—which we might call the "Hippocratic"
method. It is a rational way or reasoned procedure for arriving
at sound conclusions through discussion. Thus Aristotle's usage
is still not too far away from that of Socrates, which was enunci-
ated in answer to the Sophists' claim that they could transmit, by

[2] Rudolph Eucken, *Geschichte der philosophischen Terminologie* (Leipzig, 1879),
p. 17.
[3] For the various uses of the term μέθοδος in the earlier dialogues, see Richard
Robinson's fine study, *Plato's Earlier Dialectic*, 2d ed. (Oxford, 1953), pp. 62-69,
and on the phrase "dialectical method," the subsequent pages, 69-92.

means of the art of speaking, all the other arts, including the art of governing men. Since the art of speaking played such a major role in Greek civic and private life, it is only natural that the primary sense of the τέχνη or μέθοδος of dialectic which Socrates developed should continue to prevail in subsequent usage. Philosophy's feud with rhetoric thus gave μέθοδος a distinctively argumentative flavor which it long retained in the ancient schools, with the possible exception of the Stoic. The early Stoics, being fundamentally opposed to too much talking and discussion, would be expected to adopt a more down-to-earth and practical concept of method.

Aristotle wrote a work, now lost, with the title τὰ μεθοδικά, but the notices of it that we find in Dionysius of Halicarnassus and Diogenes Laertius do not lead us to expect anything but another treatment of debating methods.[4]

One thing is clear in Aristotle: μέθοδος never refers simply to any way of investigating or pursuing an inquiry but only to a certain *definite* way, a "reasoned way." In his *Index Aristotelicus*, Bonitz distinguishes two primary meanings which Aristotle gives to the word: (1) *via ac ratio inquirendi* and (2) *ipsa disputatio ac disquisitio*. In the first meaning μέθοδος is supposed to be more abstract: any number of different inquiries may be pursued by one "method." The second meaning is less abstract: it refers to a single inquiry prosecuted by a "method." (Bonitz notes a possible third meaning, which *non multum differt ab hoc usu, quod* μέθοδος *perinde ac* πραγματεία *usurpantur ad significandum aliquam disciplinam ac doctrinam.*) Yet as instances of the first meaning, Bonitz lists such phrases as ὁ τρόπος τοῦ μεθόδου from the *Parts of Animals* (646ᵃ2), which would be a pleonasm quite foreign to Aristotle's careful manner of speech. The word τρόπος, indeed, may mean simply the "manner of pursuing an inquiry," but in Aristotle μέθοδος certainly retains more of its Platonic

---

[4] It has been suggested by the most recent writer on the subject of the lost works of Aristotle, M. Paul Moraux, *Les listes anciennes des ouvrages d'Aristote* (Louvain, 1951), p. 66, that the title refers to the *Topics*, a view which was also held by Rose and Zeller. But cf. Dionysius of Halicarnassus, "πρὸς ''Αμμαιον," *Opuscula,* ed. Hermann Usener (Leipzig, 1899), I, 266.

connotation and refers to dialectical method of one sort or another.

The peculiar usage of μέθοδος in Aristotle has always baffled translators of his works who face the problem of capturing its elusive sense with a suitable Latin or English word. We may take a modern illustration from an Aristotelian text which is itself a long exercise in the analytic method: the *Politics*. Sir Ernest Barker, in the introduction to his admirable translation of the *Politics* (Oxford, 1946), considers μέθοδος, in that work, to be equivalent to "section," and maintains that there are six of these "methods" or "sections" presented in the work (pp. xxxvii-xxxix). Yet he himself sometimes translates the word in such a way as to indicate that he is sensitive to its Platonic orientation, as for instance, in translating it (in 1252ᵃ18) by "according to our normal method of analysis." Barker's limitation of μέθοδος to a particular "section" of the *Politics* illustrates the lengths to which a translator may go in coping with the problem of rendering μέθοδος. It represents an attempt to make the term even more concrete than in the third meaning suggested by Bonitz. Such attempts are plausible only to the extent that the particular passage which is supposed to be denoted by each "section" or μέθοδος actually comprises a complete application of one of the Platonic methods—in other words, when the sense of method as dialectical inquiry governed by certain rules still predominates. In the language of Plato, a person who has really mastered an art is able to teach it to others because his knowledge is *method*-ical. Hence the Latin word *doctrina*, frequently used in medieval and Renaissance translations of Aristotle, has a certain amount of justification. Yet *doctrine*, in English as well as in Latin, tends to convey the impression of a finished product, the residue of the dialectical inquiry, which the word certainly lacks in Greek. Although Aristotle, very infrequently, does use μέθοδος and τέχνη as synonymous,[5] he nowhere defends this synonymy with an explicit doctrine linking method and art. This synonymy seems to be a general heritage of Greek philosophy from Socrates.

----

[5] As in the *Sophistical Elenchies*, 171ᵇ11.

Μέθοδος AND Τέχνη IN STOIC USAGE

The close relationship between *method* and *art* persisted in Greek philosophy, even down to the last of the Greek commentators on Aristotle. The Stoics, as we have seen, gave to τέχνη its most succinct definition, although it must be confessed that the Stoic formula loses its appearance of precision when examined too closely (the diversity of Latin translations, even among classical authors, testifies to this). This standard definition of an art gained a wide acceptance in antiquity, no doubt because of the attention which the Stoics gave to the theory of the liberal arts. It appeared at the beginning of many grammars and "arts" of rhetoric.

There was another Stoic definition of τέχνη whose existence is something of a puzzle, for it seems superfluous in view of the fact that the Stoics had the very definite and acceptable definition of an art as a "system of percepts" already. It is given by a scholiast on the Greek grammar of Dionysius of Thrace, who says that it is Zeno's: τέχνη ἐστὶν ἕξις ὁδοποιητική ,[6] to which the scholiast adds, "that is, making something by means of a way and method."

The question might well be asked, why did Zeno offer these two "definitions" of τέχνη, if such they are? The solution we suggest is that while the official definition of an art was that of a "system of percepts," this alternative description was an etymological derivation of the word used since Socrates' time for τέχνη—namely, μέθοδος. What we know of Stoic habits of discussing concepts leads us to suspect that Zeno took the etymology of μετὰ - ὁδός seriously and derived from it the notion that art creates or shapes a "way with" reason, or "by means of reason."

The subsequent course of methodological thought within later Greek Stoicism is a subject to which insufficient scholarship has been devoted. The recent interest in Stoic formal logic may

---

[6] Arnim, SVF, I, 20, 30. Later Stoics carried on the doctrine, as for instance, Cleanthes, who said (Arnim, SVF, 1, 110, 8) that an art is a habit of producing all things by a "way." Here Cleanthes used the less specific and less Socratic ὁδός rather than μέθοδος.

eventually lead to an investigation of the general theory of science of the later figures in that school, some of whom were well known as scientists as well as philosophers. In particular, the possible influence of Stoic logic upon formulations of geometrical method needs exploring. Galen's relation to this later Stoic methodology is another gap in scholarship.

One finds assertions in secondary literature that Polybius was indebted to Stoic philosophy, and the evidence usually presented is his use of some term considered Stoic. Such influence has been found[7] in the phrase "methodical experience" (ἐμπειρία μεθοδική), opposed by him to routine or "chance" experience. If this were true, Polybius would indeed have been responsible for an important innovation in Greek thought. Yet in this case, as in the case of other purportedly philosophical terms in his writings, Polybius' usage is rather general and hardly sufficient evidence for his assimilation of philosophical doctrine.[8]

Μέθοδος IN GREEK GEOMETRY AND MEDICINE

The fact that method was conceived to bear a close relation to art explains the absence of such a phrase as "scientific method" from early Greek philosophy. When Aristotle set up his criteria for a strictly demonstrated science in the *Posterior Analytics,* he spoke of "scientific syllogisms," but not of "scientific method," for method suggested an art which could be taught but was not demonstrated rigorously in the fashion outlined by the creator of the theory of demonstration. Greek mathematicians indeed were accustomed to speak of their μέθοδοι, and in later thought one can trace the interaction of these two vocabularies of Platonic dialectical methods and the methods of geometry, for example in the work of a mathematically inclined Platonist such as Proclus.

---

[7] By Rudolph Eucken, who gives the passage in his *Geschichte der philosophischen Terminologie,* p. 32. It occurs in I, 84, 6 and in IX, 14, 1 of Polybius.

[8] References to "methodical knowledge," as in X, 47, 12, are likewise much too general to trace to any one philosophical sect. On this whole subject, see Kurt von Fritz, *The Theory of the Mixed Constitution in Antiquity* (New York, 1954), pp. 54-59.

However, it would be difficult, I think, to make out a case for the influence of this very specialized terminology upon the language of philosophy in general.

On the other hand, there may well have been some assimilation of doctrines and terminology of the methodist school of medicine in writers such as Galen, even though he was not very sympathetic to the teaching of Thessalus, its leader. But this remains to be seen: unfortunately, the sources from which we gain our information about this school of Greek medicine are not as explicit as we could wish.[9]

THE METHODOLOGICAL LANGUAGE OF GALEN

However it may be with the intervening centuries, by the second century of our era usage had crystallized so that Galen (c.129-199) could speak of "scientific methods" without being aware of any discordance in doctrine. It may be that the Stoic school with its materialistic orientation had developed a conception of empirical method to combine with dialectical method in establishing scientific truths, and that Galen's usage reflects this development. Yet just as Galen's general philosophic position is difficult to determine precisely (he attended all the major schools of philosophy at his time), so his terminology is hard to trace, and may indeed be partly original with him. As a medical man and a careful student of both Hippocrates and Plato, Galen was struck by the parallel drawn by Socrates in the *Phaedrus* between the method of the art of medicine and that of dialectic. He devoted part of his work *On the Doctrines of Hippocrates and Plato* to a discussion of method.

Galen speaks of "logical methods," "demonstrative method," and "scientific methods," but he also speaks of method in the singular, as though all the other methods he discusses were part of a single method. In one passage he mentions the method of dividing a genus of things into its different parts as "the method

---

[9] See the article "Methodiker" on the methodist sect by Ludwig Edelstein in Pauly-Wissowa, RE, Supplement-Band VI, 358-73.

which the philosophers have handed down to us." [10] Galen's
language is not very exact, nor was he the sort of man to make
his terminology consistent: he himself was fond of saying that
words make no difference so long as we grasp the idea. But
what idea of method are we to grasp from among all these words?
Peter Ramus was not far wrong in singling out, as we shall see,
four senses of "method" from Galen's verbose and rambling
asides on the subject. This inexactitude of expression makes it
extremely difficult to trace the influence of Galen on medieval
or Renaissance thought. Medical commentators throughout the
centuries found his methods very hard to expound: one need only
glance at any two commentaries on the *Ars parva*, for example,
to see what diverse doctrines could be drawn from one passage
by different commentators. The fact that Galen merged Aristotle's theory of science (to which he gave the non-Aristotelian
designation "demonstrative method") and Plato's dialectical
method(s) with the extremely elusive method of Hippocrates
made his methodology a nightmare for exegetes, especially those
who were not familiar with the Platonic dialogues.

Μέθοδος IN THE GREEK COMMENTATORS ON ARISTOTLE

Since Aristotle presented no single body of thought on the subject of method, yet used the word μέθοδος frequently in his
writings, his commentators were faced with the difficult task of
explicating these occurrences without explicit instructions from
their author. It is substantial evidence for the correctness of our
views of the Platonic origin of Aristotle's μέθοδος that these
Greek commentators almost always introduced a résumé of
Plato's dialectical methods on such occasions: this practice, very
common with the philosopher-scholars of Athens and Alexandria,
would seem somewhat arbitrary were it not for the historical

---

[10] Galen, *De methodo medendi*, Kühn, X, 27: οὕτως ἤδη πειρᾶσθαι τέμνειν εἰς
τὰς οἰκείας διαφορὰς αὐτά, καθ᾽ ἣν ἐδίδαξαν ἡμᾶς οἱ φιλόσοφοι μέθοδον. The context does not enable us to tell whether this is "the" method taught by the philosophers, or one of the many methods.

connection between the "method" coined by Socrates in the
Platonic dialogues and the usage of Aristotle.

In these commentators we can trace a gradual assimilation of
Stoic doctrine, which begins innocently enough with Alexander
of Aphrodisias, who flourished in the early part of the third century A.D. His definition of method is cited by a later commentator, Simplicius, in an explanation of the opening passage of
the *Physics*, that *bête noire of* Aristotelian interpretation. In this
passage Aristotle speaks of "all methods of which there are
principles or causes or elements," and this gives Simplicius the
opportunity to introduce Alexander's definition of method:
μέθοδος ἐστὶν ... πᾶσα ἕξις θεωρητικὴ τῶν ὑφ' ἑαυτὴν μετὰ λόγου. [11] This
"definition" is not Aristotle's, for he gives no such account of
μέθοδος: in fact, he gives no account of it at all. It was thereupon
easy for later commentators to introduce Zeno's definition of
τέχνη to explicate Aristotle's μέθοδος, as we shall see. The definition of method that Alexander gives is quite similar to Aristotle's
definition of τέχνη in the sixth book of the *Nicomachean Ethics*,
as a "certain habit of producing according to true reason"
(1140[a]20). Hence it is not surprising that a later commentator,
Johannes Philoponus (sixth century A.D.), in discussing the same
passage of the *Physics*, introduced not Aristotle's definition of

---

[11] Simplicius' commentary on the *Physics,* CAG, IX, 4. Cf. the Renaissance
translation by Gentianus Hervetus: "Num ergo ipse est attendendus Aristoteles, qui
accurate dixit cognitionem quae est ex scientia evenire in omnibus rebus, neque in
omnibus cognitionibus, sed in omnibus quae certa via et ratione traduntur disciplinis,
quae Methodos appellant. Si enim Methodus est, ut ait Alexander, 'omnis contem-
plativus habitus eorum quae sibi subiecta sunt,' cum 'ratione', hoc est, cum causa
(idem est autem potest cognosci), non fuerit videlicet Methodus cognitio principii,
sed ea quae est ex scientia, quae fit ex principiis et causis eius quod potest cognosci."
*Simplicii Commentarii in octo Aristotelis Physicae auscultationis libros cum ipso
Aristotelis contextu, a Gentiano Herveto Aurelio, nova ac fideli interpretatione donati*
(Venice, 1551). Simplicius may have been referring to the statement introduced as
a premise in a syllogism given by Alexander of Aphrodisias in his commentary on
the *Prior Analytics:* πᾶσα ἕξις μετά τινος λόγου τῶν ὑπ' αὐτὴν οὖσα θεωρητικὴ
μέθοδός ἐστιν (CAG, II[1], 275), in which the order of subject and predicate is inverted
so that ἕξις can serve as a middle term in a syllogism proving that politics is a
method. However, it seems more likely that Simplicius had in mind some other
passage in Alexander, possibly lost to us, in which method is discussed thoroughly,
not just introduced in this incidental fashion.

τέχνη but Zeno's : μέθοδος δ'ἐστὶν ἕξις ὁδοποιητικὴ μετὰ λόγου,[12] substituting μέθοδος for τέχνη. According to Melanchthon, it was this sense of method that the "dialecticians" of the Renaissance adopted for the "most correct order of explication . . . for thus the Greeks define it."[13] Obviously such a doctrine was indeed more or less the joint work of the Greeks, since the germ of the idea could be found in the Platonic dialogues; definitions of art similar to this one could be found in Aristotle's *Nicomachean Ethics*; while the explicit identification of μέθοδος and τέχνη was made originally by the Stoics and then incorporated into commentaries on Aristotle by the commentators.

METHODUS AS A PHILOSOPHICAL TERM IN LATIN

Meanwhile a different fate awaited the term in Latin. The Latinized form of μέθοδος, *methodus*, never caught on in classical Latin as did other compounds of ὁδός such as *periodus, synodus,* or *exodus.* The occurrences of *methodus* usually given in Latin dictionaries are from a medical or mathematical context; they are clearly tranported bodily into Latin from some particular Greek passage in which a specific "method" is mentioned.[14] In neither the geometrical nor the medical usage does *methodus* have the

---

[12] Philoponus' commentary on the *Physics,* CAG, XVI, 6. Exactly the same definition of "method" may be found in Eustratius' commentary on the *Ethics,* CAG, XX, 7, but Eustratius undoubtedly copied the sentence from Philoponus.

[13] "Ut autem alias nomen μέθοδος significat rectam et compendiariam viam, ita Dialectici ad ordinem explicationis rectissimum transtulerunt hoc nomen: ac significat hoc loco μέθοδος rectam viam seu ordinem investigationis et explicationis, sive simplicium quaestionum, sive propositionum. Et sic Graeci definiunt: μέθοδος ἐστὶν ἕξις ὁδοποιητικὴ μετὰ λόγου, id est: Methodus est habitus, videlicet scientia seu ars, viam faciens certa ratione, id est, quae quasi per loca invia et obsita sentibus, per rerum confusionem, viam invenit et aperit, ac res ad propositum pertinentes, eruit ac ordine promit." *Erotemata dialectices,* CR, XIII, 573.

[14] One reference usually given is that of Vitruvius, who lived under Augustus. Vitruvius was explaining the arts an architect has to know, and he says that "difficult questions of symmetries are found by geometrical ratios and methods": "difficilesque symmetriarum quaestiones geometricis rationibus et methodis inveniuntur." *De architectura,* Liber I, 10. The medical reference is found in the poem by Ausonius (who died about 395 A.D.) in which the poet is listing things that occur in threes. The three sects of medicine are listed here: "triplex quoque forma medendi, cui logos aut methodos cuique experientia nomen." Ausonius, *Opera,* ed. Peiper (Leipzig, 1886), p. 203. Ausonius still has the Greek form of spelling.

broad and abstract meaning that Renaissance students (and we, following them) give to the term.

The chief reason for the failure of *methodus* to be carried over into classical Latin as a technical term was that Cicero, who was responsible for so much of Latin philosophical terminology, studiously avoided the word and never quoted it in Greek, although he quoted almost all the technical Greek terms he considered significant. Evidently Cicero did not consider the concept worth baptizing with a new Latin word, which would have had to be some compound of *via* or a word like *semita*, later used to translate μέθοδος by some writers.

There is a puzzle in connection with Cicero's terminology. Centuries of scholarly opinion have agreed that he used the phrase *via et ratio* for the Greek μέθοδος and the synonymy has gone unquestioned. Yet how can we be sure of this, since Cicero does not give the equivalence himself explicitly? It is certainly true that Cicero did not use the Latinized form *methodus*: this much is certain. But what is there to prevent us from saying that he used *ars* or *ratio* alone for μέθοδος? And that the phrase *via et ratio*, which he uses so often, is a rendering of the disjointed Stoic etymology of μετὰ - ὁδός, with *via* translating ὁδός and *ratio* replacing the phrase μετὰ λόγου?

At any rate, the result of Cicero's omission was that the specific Greek concepts of method were lost in the vagueness of circumlocution in Latin philosophy, only to be regained when writers using Latin once more had access to Greek works. Most ancient Latin writers on philosophy (there were not many of them) followed Cicero in avoiding the Latinized form *methodus*. Quintilian (c.38-c.100 A.D.), although he had ample occasion to speak of the "method" of his art of rhetoric, used Cicero's *via et ratio*, or perhaps the phrase *breve compendium*.[15] Apuleius (born c.123 A.D.) did not use *methodus* at all in his presentation of

---

[15] Renaissance writers insisted that Quintilian used *breve compendium* for the Greek μέθοδος, but they do not give any evidence. There is only one occurrence of the phrase in the *Institutiones oratoricae,* and it could just as well be a translation for σύνοψις or some other term in the Greek.

Platonic doctrine, in spite of the prominence given to the concept in Plato's dialogues.[16]

The honor of using *methodus* for the first time as a Latin philosophical term belongs to Boethius (c.480-524 A.D.), who used it in his translation of the *Topics* of Aristotle: *Propositum quidem negotii est methodum invenire per quam poterimus syllogizare de omni proposito problemate ex probabilibus, et ipsi disputationem sustinentes, nihil dicemus repugnans.*[17] Boethius does not employ the word himself when writing commentaries on Aristotle or Cicero, but only uses it to translate the Greek word when it occurs in Aristotle—thus setting a precedent which the Latin Middle Ages followed for the most part. Medieval translations of Aristotle, especially those made directly from the Greek, tended to follow the lead of this translation in the *Logica nova* and to use the Latinized word for its Greek original, but not all translators did this consistently.[18] Early medieval

---

[16] *Methodus* does not appear in either the Greek or Latin form in the *Index Apuleianus* (Middletown, Conn., 1934).

[17] Migne, PL, LXIV, 909. If indeed this translation is that of Boethius. Its authenticity was called in question by Bernhard Geyer, "Die alten lateinischen Uebersetzungen der Aristotelischen Analytik, Topik, und Elenchik," *Philosophisches Jahrbuch*, XXX (1917), 25-43, who came to the tentative conclusion that the common medieval translation of the *Topics* was to be identified with that of Jacobus of Venice, made in 1128. Lacombe, in the *Aristoteles Latinus* (Rome, 1939), pp. 45-47, discussed the authorship of the *Topics* translation and came to the conclusion that it cannot be identified with that of Jacobus of Venice: he noted that an Oxford manuscript expressly attributes the translation to Boethius. It might be suggested that the use of *methodus* in the Latin constitutes a tiny bit of evidence for the medieval origin of the translation.

[18] Since most of Aristotle's methodological remarks occur at the very start of his treatises, it is possible to compare a good many manuscript translations of Aristotle simply by consulting manuscript catalogues or a work such as Lacombe's *Aristoteles Latinus.* The *Physics*, for instance, begins in one translation from a twelfth-century manuscript given by Lacombe (p. 125) with the words: "Quoniam agnoscere et scire circa methodos omnes accidit quarum sunt principia vel causae vel elementa...." Again, on page 136 of Lacombe's work, we have a comparison between one translation of the *De anima*, probably made in the twelfth century, with a translation by William of Moerbeke (1215-86), the famous Flemish Dominican who made so much of Greek philosophy available to his contemporaries. Where the earlier translation twice has *scientia* for μέθοδος in the passage given, William of Moerbeke has *methodus*. Similarly, in translating the *De partibus animalium*, an unknown translator in a Paduan manuscript has (p. 179): "Circa omnem speculacionem et artem..." where William has: "Circa omnem theoriam et *methodum* ...." Robert Grosseteste, in translating a similar passage at the start

translations of Plato also use *methodus*,[19] but they are hardly as significant for the development of general philosophical terminology as the translations made of Aristotle's works.

At about the same time that the body of Aristotle's writings was being made known in Latin translation to the West, the Latin translations of the Arabs, especially of Averroes (1126-98), were reaching students of philosophy. These translations of Averroes' commentaries, made almost during his lifetime, were rapidly diffused through Europe, and were beginning to be known in universities by the third decade of the thirteenth century. Whatever Averroes' own terminology may have been,[20] all we need to know is that these Latin translations do not contain the term *methodus*. Somewhere along the line—in Syrian intermediary translations or in Averroes' own Arabic—the distinction between ὁδός and μέθοδος became blurred and the latter concept was lost. The result was that crucial passages such as that at the start of the *Physics*[21] lost their original sharpness and were swept into the general rubric of *via doctrinae*—that phrase which could lend itself to metaphysical and Platonizing interpretations. Philosophical terminology was plunged back into a pre-Socratic state in which "method" lost its abstract character and became identified once more with its metaphorical root, the image of the road. This does not mean that Latin students of Averroes took no cognizance of the new term: even when Averroes had raised a question in pre-Socratic terms, they some-

---

of the *Ethics* (p. 69), has: "Omnis ars et omnis *doctrina . . .*" another favorite medieval rendering.

[19] See the translation of the *Phaedo* made about 1161 (Socrates is speaking): "'unusquisque quidem michi videtur,' ait ille 'concedere, O Socrate, ex hac *methodo*, eciam vix docibilis, quoniam toti et omni similius est anima semper similiter se habenti quam ei quod minime.'" *Phaedo, interprete Henrico Aristippo*, ed. Lorenzo Minio-Paluello in *Plato Latinus* (London, 1950), II, 36. Cf. also p. 59 of the same edition.

[20] It is important to remember that the Latin translations of Averroes may not have done justice to the original: see Aldo Mieli, *La science Arabe et son rôle dans l'évolution scientifique mondiale* (Leiden, 1938), pp. 248-50.

[21] Lacombe gives the Latin translation used with Averroes' commentary on the *Physics* most conveniently (p. 214): "Quoniam dispositio scientie et certitudinis in omnibus *viis* habentibus principia et causas et elementa non adquiritur nisi ex cognitione istorum . . . ." Compare this with the other two medieval translations given above.

times discussed it, in Aristotle's own language, as one of "method."[22]

The Latin West, working both with Averroes in Latin translation and with Latin translations of Aristotle made directly from the Greek, faced the problem of correlating and coordinating doctrines from the Arabs with the Latin Aristotle. Subsequent philosophizing shows by its diversity that this correlation was not necessarily unambiguous. When Latin Averroism,[23] after its first

[22] In a passage near the start of the *De anima*, 402[a], Aristotle asks whether there is one method (μέθοδος) for all things of which we wish to know the substance. If there is such a method, Aristotle remarks, we certainly would want to know it. In Averroes' commentary, this becomes a question as to what the 'way' might be: "utrum demonstratio, ut dicebat Ypocras, aut divisio, ut Plato dixit, aut alia via, ut via compositionis, quam Aristoteles dedit in *Posterioribus*." Texts 4 and 5 in *Averrois Cordubensis Commentarium in Aristotelis De Anima libros*, ed. F.S. Crawford (Cambridge, Mass., 1953), pp. 6-9.

John of Jandun (died c.1328) was a master of arts at Paris who was regarded as an Averroist. He raised this question not in Averroes' terms but in Aristotle's: "Fortassis alicui quaedam sit investigandi quodquid est Methodus omnium habentium quodquid est." His conclusion is the following: "Non est una communis investigandi quodquid est Methodus quo ad propria, est tamen via ac communis modus quo ad universalem rationem sumendi quodquid est, qui ad Logicam spectat." Jandun justifies the last attribution by reference to the Arab definition of logic, "quae tradit cognitionem instrumenti deveniendi de cognito ad ignoti notitiam." *Ioannis de Ianduno viri acutissimi super libros Aristotelis De Anima subtilissimae quaestiones* (Venice, 1552), f. 7[r]. The capitalization of "Methodus" is common in Renaissance editions.

Taddeo da Parma, who also lived in the first part of the fourteenth century and who taught at Bologna, discussed the same question in his commentary on the *De anima*. See Martin Grabmann, *Mittelalterliches Geistesleben* (Munich, 1936), II, 249.

By shifting the terms thus, both Averroes and his Latin students were able to conclude that there was such a "way"—even though Aristotle had expressly decided that there was no such "method"—without being disturbed by the divergence of conclusions.

[23] "Averroism" is admittedly a difficult concept and has been used in many different ways. The label "Averroist" originated as a term of opprobrium hurled at certain medieval thinkers by their opponents (e.g., by Thomas Aquinas, or by ecclesiastical authorities). Later the label was taken up by scholars such as Renan, Charbonnel, and Busson, who were interested in tracing the growth of free thought or rationalism and who considered the 'Averroists' of the Middle Ages and the Renaissance to be the intellectual forebears of Italian or French scepticism and libertinage.

Can a concept that originated in this way be expected to prove useful in distinguishing purely philosophical trends? I take it that modern students of intellectual history are not primarily concerned with examining the religious orthodoxy of these "Averroists": it is not our business to condemn heretics. The second usage is more relevant: speaking for myself, I would not want to discard it too casually, for I still believe that Renan was on the track of an important movement of thought.

The suggestion that these determined secularists, call them what you will, were part of a growing and significant tradition of rationalism deserves exploration, at least.

The whole question of Latin Averroism is very complex and has given rise to an extensive scholarly literature since Renan first gave the term "Averroism" prominence. I cannot here review the discussion, but refer the reader to an illuminating recent summary, with a convincing appeal for caution in the use of the term: Stuart MacClintock, "Heresy and Epithet: An Approach to the Problem of Latin Averroism," *Review of Metaphysics*, VIII (1954-55), 176-99, 342-56, 526-45. To the works cited by MacClintock should be added some more recent ones: Paul O. Kristeller, *The Classics and Renaissance Thought* (Cambridge, Mass., 1955), pp. 33 and 37-38; and Ferdinand Van Steenberghen, *Aristotle in the West: The Origins of Latin Aristotelianism* (Louvain, 1955), pp. 198-208.

The chief difficulty with the term "Averroism" is that in order for it to be significant, it seems as if there ought to have existed at least one man whom scholars will agree to call a bona fide Averroist, and it would be best if he were a self-professed one. Such men are not easy to find: Siger of Brabant and John of Jandun have not met the requirements to everyone's satisfaction. It should be stressed, however, that so far no scholar has investigated in any detail the fifteenth and sixteenth century Italian Aristotelians among whom the most likely candidates are to be found. I mean such men as Nifo, Zimara, Achillini, or Odo, who were stigmatized by the Jesuits of the Coimbra commentaries as Averroists.

So far as single philosophical problems go, it is not difficult to discriminate "Averroist" approaches or solutions—although here we must be careful, for Mac-Clintock reminds us that even adherence to a proposition verbally identical may not permit us to lump together two philosophers as Averroists in any meaningful sense. But it is something else again to label a man's entire thought as "Averroistic" and to call him without qualification an "Averroist." Nevertheless, the door should not be closed upon this possibility. If we were to find that philosopher A adopted Averroistic solutions to a certain number of crucial philosophical problems, might we not call him an Averroist (especially if he himself adopted the label)? At any rate, until the evidence from Renaissance Italy is in, we are certainly not yet in a position to evaluate the Averroist movement or to substitute a better label for "Averroism." I suspect that the term will still prove useful, but that the antithesis to "Averroist" will turn out to be, not "Alexandrist" (or follower of Alexander of Aphrodisias) as once maintained, but the category I have called "Humanist Aristotelian." In other words, I think we will find two main camps of Aristotelian thought: those who discussed problems in terms derived from the Averroist tradition and those who discussed them (or related ones) in terms of the original Greek text and its historical context. University teachers of philosophy in Italy favored the Averroist approach, while teachers in France, Germany, and the rest of Europe favored the Humanist approach almost exclusively. The easiest way to distinguish the two approaches is by means of the language they employed, as Randall has suggested (in *The Renaissance Philosophy of Man*, ed. Ernst Cassirer, Paul Kristeller, and John Herman Randall Jr., [Chicago, 1948], pp. 259-60). Anyone who has looked into Aristotelian writings of the Renaissance period will recognize Randall's insight as valid.

To sum up, I think we can talk meaningfully and usefully about Latin Averroism without necessarily committing ourselves to the existence of a class of men who subscribed without reservation to every statement that Averroes ever made, or even to a specified number of them. To anticipate myself somewhat, I am not at all sure that I would call Zabarella an Averroist, but I would certainly want to maintain that his historical role cannot be assessed without reference to Averroism.

outbreak at Paris, began to flourish at Bologna in the early fourteenth century and later at Padua, terminological problems such as this had to be faced in Italy as well. When we come to examine some representative thinkers of the Italian tradition, we shall see to what lengths they went to justify their own doctrines in Averroistic terms. This involved them in an attempt to correlate Aristotle's μέϑοδος with Averroes' *via doctrinae* (and hence with the famous distinction at the start of the *Physics*, which is so reminiscent of Plato, between the way *a priori* and the way *a posteriori*). The Averroistic background of Italian philosophizing in the Renaissance explains why the subjects of "method" and "order" were dealt with so closely together in that country, for *via doctrinae* and *ordo doctrinae* were Averroes' distinction (although to be sure they may have Greek sources). As a result of seemingly trivial linguistic differences of this sort, a wholly different philosophical orientation was sometimes produced in medieval students who saw Aristotle through Arab eyes.

The Humanists of the Renaissance were later to look with scorn upon the early "crude" translations of Aristotle, with their importation of nonclassical words into Latin—and many modern scholars have been led to believe that these medieval versions do not convey the thought of the Greeks as faithfully as did the Renaissance translations. Yet it is entirely possible that a better idea of the thought of the Greek originals could be gotten by means of the old word-for-word translations (especially if supplemented by a modicum of knowledge of Greek) than from the ornate and stylistically superior versions of the Humanists. William of Moerbeke was one of the translators who consistently used *methodus* in his Latin when it appeared in the Greek, and we shall later have occasion to contrast the succinctness and veracity of his rendering, however un-Ciceronian, with the clumsy circumlocution of Renaissance Humanists.

The presence of *methodus* in Latin versions of Aristotle and other Greek authors did not mean that it was adopted as a technical term by medieval philosophers. For example, Thomas Aquinas (1225-74), who used at least some of the translations of

William of Moerbeke, did not have a doctrine of *methodus*,[24] but kept to the more traditional and neutral words *via, modus, ratio,* and *processus*—terms which had been used in the commentaries or in previous Latin philosophy. Aquinas also used *ars* for *methodus*, even when he was commenting on a text that contained the Greek word in such conspicuous fashion as did the *Politics*. If we consult his commentary on this work, we find that Aquinas speaks always of *ars*, never of *methodus*, in passages in which the Greek (and William of Moerbeke's translation) contains the latter word. *Methodus* does occur in the section of the commentary which Peter of Auvergne completed[25]—which shows that it was a matter of personal preference whether a medieval writer adopted the term or not.

THE LATER GREEK CONCEPT OF METHOD ENTERS LATIN PHILOSOPHY

There are also traces in medieval philosophy of the adoption of a sense of *methodus* which, although it is attributed to "the Greeks," does not represent the classical dialectical method of Plato or Aristotle, but rather a later and somewhat different, though related, concept of method. John of Salisbury (c.1110-1180), in discussing what an art is, mentions that "the Greeks also call it *methodon*," since it prepares a compendious way and thus avoids the waste (*dispendium*) of nature with respect to those things which it is in man's power to produce.[26]

[24] At the only occurrence of *methodus* given in *A Lexicon of St. Thomas Aquinas,* ed. Roy Deferrari and Barry (Washington, 1948), Aquinas finds the word so strange that he gives several alternative readings: "secundum eandem methodum, id est, artem, id est, secundum eandem artificialem considerationem" (from the commentary on the *Physics,* 8 Physics, 15a).

[25] For the authenticity of Aquinas' commentary on the first two books and part of the third book, see Martin Grabmann, "Die Werke des Hl. Thomas von Aquin," BGP, XXII[1-2] (1931), 267-68. According to a manuscript in the Vatican Library, the remainder of the commentary is the work of Peter of Auvergne.

[26] "Est autem ars ratio que compendio sui naturaliter possibilium expedit facultatem. Neque enim impossibilium ratio prestat aut pollicetur effectum; sed eorum que fieri possunt, quasi quodam dispendioso nature circuitu compendiosum iter prebet, et parit (ut ita dixerim) difficilium facultatem. Unde et Greci eam *methodon* dicunt, quasi compendiariam rationem que nature vitet dispendium, et amfractuosum eius circuitum dirigat, ut quod fieri expedit, rectius et facilius fiat."

The word *compendium*, which John of Salisbury here opposes to the *dispendium* of nature, was a very useful alternate rendering of μέϑοδος in its later sense, as found in the Greek commentators on Aristotle. It incorporates two ideas: that of gathering together scattered things into one place and that of shortening or saving time—both of which legitimately belong to method considered as a reasoned way of doing things. In a later passage, John states that one who intends to investigate things proposed in physics, ethics, or logic cannot do so unless he proceeds by the "compendious procedure" (*ratio compendiaria*) that logic alone teaches.[27] Again, in discussing the utility of the science of probabilities, John observes: Ethics, physics, and logic, therefore, "conduct inquiries separately, and although each is armed with its own principles, still logic furnishes them all with its methods (*metodos*), that is, its compendious procedures (*compendii . . . rationes*), and hence is most useful not only for exercising the mind but also for rebuttal (*obviationes*) and for philosophical training of all sorts. For (1) a person who has a method easily argues on a given thesis (*propositum*); (2) he who, knowing the opinions of the many, speaks not from irrelevant but from relevant evidence, makes rebuttal properly (*commode obviat*), changing whatever does not seem well stated; and (3) he who considers the surrounding reasons more easily distinguishes the true from the false in single cases and is made more skillful at understanding and teaching, because he demands the thesis (*propositum*) of the person philosophizing and requires [him to perform] his duty." This much is clearly the doctrine of Aristotle's *Topics*, as is what follows: "Since however dialectic is investigative, it has the way to the principles of all methods; since indeed any art at all has its methods, which we can interpret figuratively as entering roads or approaches, and discovery follows inquiry;

Ioannis Saresberiensis episcopi Carnotensis Metalogicon, ed. Clement C. J. Webb (Oxford, 1929), p. 28.

[27] . . . . licet enim quis perspicacem habeat rationem, anime virtutem dico, in philosophie tamen negotiis ad multa subsistit offendicula, si non habeat rationem propositi faciendi; que quidem est methodus, id est ratio compendiaria, propositi pariens et expediens facultatem. Versantur autem in his et que dicte sunt pertinentes ad logicam discipline." *Ibid.*, p. 67.

nor does he gain any fruit of science to whom the study of inquiry is displeasing. But demonstrative science seeks methods which are necessary and which reveal that inherence of things which it is impossible to dissolve."[28] In part John of Salisbury is here simply paraphrasing, or perhaps quoting, a section of the *Topics* in which Aristotle says that "dialectic, being investigative, has the way to the principles of all methods."[29] The latter phrase was incorporated into the standard medieval definition of dialectic[30] as the "art of arts and science of sciences, having the way to the principles of all methods," which appeared at the very beginning of the most widely used medieval textbook in logic, the *Summulae logicales* of Peter of Spain, written in the middle of the thirteenth century. This rather striking formula was often repeated by medieval logicians, and it naturally raises the question as to what these methods are to whose principles dialectic has the way.

Evidently this question occurred also to medieval students trying to master the *Summulae logicales*, for one writer, Lambert of Auxerre (fl. 1250), devoted part of his commentary on this work to the subject of method.[31] Lambert first gives a definition of art—the Stoic one in its modified form, which he could have found in many places—and then paraphrases Peter of Spain's first sentence.[32] It is interesting to note that Lambert considers

---

[28] *Ibid.,* p. 85. This is a difficult passage: my translation should be compared with that of Daniel D. McGarry in his excellent English version, *The Metalogicon of John of Salisbury: A Twelfth-Century Defense of the Verbal and Logical Arts of the Trivium* (Berkeley and Los Angeles, 1955), pp. 103-4.

[29] *Topics,* I, ii (101^{b}2-3)

[30] "Dialectica est ars artium et scientia scientiarum ad omnium methodorum principia viam habens." *Petri Hispani Summulae logicales,* ed. I. M. Bocheński (Turin, 1947), p. 1.

[31] Long excerpts from this treatise, which dates from about the same time as Peter of Spain's, are given by Martin Grabmann, "Handschriftliche Forschungen und Funde zu den philosophischen Schriften des Petrus Hispanus, des späteren Papstes Johannes XXI. († 1277), "*Sitzungsberichte,* BAW, Jahrgang 1936, Heft 9. I shall quote from the pages of Grabmann's reproduction.

[32] Ars est collectio multorum preceptorum ad unum finem tendentium, id est collectio multorum documentorum et multarum regularum, quae ordinatur ad finem unum, scilicet, ad cognitionem illius, de quo in arte principaliter intenditur ... Logica est ars artium, scientia scientiarum, qua aperta omnes aperiuntur et qua clausa aliae clauduntur, sine qua nulla, cum qua quelibet." *Ibid.,* p. 46.

the single end "intended" in an art to be the *cognition* of the things principally treated in it, which is quite different from the kind of usefulness in life that the Stoics had required and that Renaissance Humanists, in their use of the Stoic formula, were again to require. Dialectic (which Lambert distinguishes from logic as dealing with dialectical rather than with demonstrative syllogisms) is said to be the "art of arts, having the way to the principles of all methods." Lambert then gives a simile in which he likens art to a road and method to a short cut that leads to the same terminus but in a shorter and easier fashion.[33]

The very first sentence of the *Topics*—that one in which Boethius had introduced the word *methodus* to readers of Latin philosophy—became the point of departure with medieval commentators for philological excursions into the history of the term. Albert the Great (c.1206-1280), in his commentary on the *Topics*, noted the equivalence of "method" and "art" and then gave a metaphorical explanation for the former term.[34] Later on, he says that art is the "correction of operation," science the "correction of speculation," and that method, which he considers the main concern of the *Topics*, is the "demonstration of the way in both."[35]

---

[33] "Dialectica est ars artium ad principia omnium methodorum viam habens: sola enim dialectica probat, disputat de principiis omnium artium. Sed est sciendum, quod methodus est ars brevis et facilis et semite proportionatur. Nam sicut semita ducit ad eundem terminum ad quem data via, sed brevius et expedientius, similiter ad cognitionem ejusdem ducunt ars et methodus, sed facilius methodus quam ars." *Ibid.*, p. 47.

[34] Having given the first sentence of the *Topics* in a translation fairly close to that of Boethius, Albert continues: "Est autem quod dicimus *methodum* metaphorice: dicitur enim *methodus* brevis via, quae via est compendii, et vulgariter vocatur summa. Per similitudinem ergo transfertur ad istam scientiam proprie et artem: quia cum speculabilia et operabilia multa offerantur, sua multitudine et longitudine, distantiae quidem ipsorum dispendium faciunt, nisi per formam scientiae et artis ad compendium redigantur: et ab hac similitudine nomen methodi ad artem et scientiam transfertur." Albertus Magnus, "Liber I Topicorum, Proemium," *Opera omnia* (Paris, 1890), II, 235-36.

[35] Albert also includes the Stoic definition of art in this passage: "Ars autem, ut dicit Aristoteles, factivum est cum ratione principium: et ideo est collectio multorum praeceptorum ad eundem finem tendentium, quae est operatio artis: et sic est ars rectificatio operationis, scientia vero speculationis, et methodus est demonstratio viae in utraque. Methodus ergo pro isto toto supposuit libro, quia ea quae in primo libro dicentur, quasi universalia principia praesciuntur ad syllogizandum de omni problemate." *Ibid.*, p. 237.

Later commentators, even in the Renaissance, continued to introduce into their explanations of the *Topics* the notion of method as a "brief way." The famous Aristotelian exegete, Agostino Nifo (1473-1546), noted Albert's discussion of the passage at the start of the *Topics* and added that method is, as it were, a "short cut that leads us most quickly to the knowledge of anything." [36]

Now there is something strange about these derivations which insist that method is a short art, or a short cut to knowledge. For whatever else may be said about Plato's dialectical method, it certainly was not intended to be a short cut. One need only recall that passage of the *Phaedrus* (272C) in which Socrates, after giving a description of what he would regard as a valid τέχνη of rhetoric, asks Phaedrus if there is any shorter way (ὁδός) to reach the same goal—and reluctantly answers himself in the negative. Again, the argumentative "method" presented by Aristotle in the *Topics* is hardly designed to shorten debates but simply to facilitate winning them, or to guarantee the validity of inquiry, depending upon the use to which his method is put. Nor is the *Topics* itself a "brief art," so that it is hard to see the relevance of the "Greek meaning" suggested by Albert and Nifo to the method presented by Aristotle in the work upon which they were commenting. It would seem rather that the notion of method as a short cut has been intruded into the thought of Aristotle from some alien source. The most likely explanation would seem to be that the temporal aspect of the later concept of method was derived somehow from the Stoic doctrine that through reason an art presented a quick way of bringing into order those things out of which an art is to be constituted. The similarity of the descriptions of art or method in these accounts, together with the use of somewhat unusual words such as *compendium* or *compendiaria*,

36 "Per methodum [Aristoteles] brevem artem intelligit: nam licet μέθοδος graece, latine sit *semita*, transumitur tamen ad compendiariam artem, quae brevissima est, et cito nos ad rei cognitionem ducens...." *Aristotelis Stagiritae Topicorum libri octo, cum Augustini Niphi Medices Suessani philosophi clarissimi commentariis...* (Venice, 1555), f. 3r.

suggests a common source of doctrine that has thus far escaped me.[37] The ideas are familiar and could be found in Cicero, or in any work incorporating Stoic doctrine, but the exact provenance of the terminology is not clear.

Thus we find that John of Salisbury, Lambert of Auxerre, and Albert the Great—in discussing *methodus* as they found it in Boethius' translation of the *Topics* or in the standard medieval definition of dialectic—tended to emphasize the point that method is a short cut to knowledge, or a short art or *compendium*. As yet, however, no very well-developed doctrine went with this rather vague formulation, which, as we have seen, is somewhat foreign to both Plato and Aristotle, and which yet purported to be a "Greek" notion. In fact, *methodus* did not become a common philosophical term until much later, in the Renaissance, when, as Melanchthon observed, it was adopted by "the dialecticians" for the most correct order of explication.

HUMANIST DISTASTE FOR METHODUS

Part of the explanation for the neglect of *methodus* in the intervening period seems to lie in the aversion of early Humanists to Latin words of nonclassical or even non-Ciceronian origin. This aversion was strongest in the Italians: we have seen even in the medieval period how Aquinas, although he must have been familiar with the word as used in Greek, and although he inherited much of the methodology of the commentators and discussed it himself, used other Latin words in place of *methodus*. The distaste for Greek words would naturally be strongest in those whose vernacular language most resembled Latin, and who felt the strangeness most. Moreover, with the rise of the Humanists in the fourteenth century, non-Ciceronian words were not tolerated by the more fastidious, and Humanist translators strove to avoid them at all costs. An illustration of this may be seen in the accompanying table, which gives certain key passages in

---

[37] Quintilian might seem to be a likely source (see p. 49), were it not for the fact that his work was not known in its entirety before the fifteenth century.

which Aristotle used the word μέθοδος and compares the translation made by William of Moerbeke (1215-86) with those of two Renaissance Humanists, Leonardo Bruni (1369-1444) and Denis Lambin (c.1516-1572), teacher of eloquence and Greek language at the Collège Royal in Paris.

In avoiding the non-Ciceronian word *methodus*, Bruni has used no less than six different circumlocutions in six passages where William of Moerbeke consistently used one word: *methodus*. Lambin also avoids it, and uses long Latin phrases, although somewhat more consistently than Bruni. Obviously if there were a specific Greek sense of the word, it would have been hard for a reader of the Renaissance translations to become aware of it.

Bruni boasted that he had captured the true meaning of Aristotle in uncorrupted and pure Latin, and in the preface to one of his translations of Aristotle he vaunted the superiority of his versions over that of the "unknown medieval translator" who used barbarous Latin expressions and failed to transmit the sense of the original.[38] These prefaces occasioned an exchange of polemics between Bruni and a Spanish bishop, who undertook the defense of the "old version" against Bruni's attack.[39] In the light of the subsequent development of philosophical language, and the enriching of neo-Latin and the vernacular tongues with words from the Greek, it must be admitted that Bishop Alonso got the best of his Italian opponent, who would have eliminated such useful words as "oligarchy," "democracy," and "method" from the language of philosophy. Furthermore, as the Bishop remarked,[40] what loss is there if we use a short and precise Greek word in Latin, when to replace it would mean the substitution of a long and clumsy circumlocution?

---

[38] See the prefaces to Bruni's translations of the *Nicomachean Ethics* and *Politics*, given in *Leonardo Bruni Aretino, Humanistisch-philosophische Schriften*, ed. Hans Baron (Leipzig, 1928), pp. 70-81; also the treatise defending his stand, "De interpretatione recta," pp. 81-96.

[39] See Alexander Birkenmajer, "Der Streit des Alonso von Cartagena mit Leonardo Bruni Aretino," BGP, XX⁵ (1922), 129-210.

[40] In a passage cited by Birkenmajer, p. 169.

Aristotle: Politics	*Wm. of Moerbeke (1215-86)*	*Leonardo Bruni (1369-1444)*	*Lambinus (1516-72)*
Book I, 1, 1252ᵃ18	...manifestum autem erit quod a nobis dicitur, intendentibus *secundum subiectum methodum*. (p. 2)	...Sed haec vera non sunt, quod manifestum erit *secundum hanc doctrinam* considerantibus. (f. 1ᵛ)	...atque id quod a nobis dicitur, iis planum fiet qui hoc spectabunt *ex ea institutione ac docendi ratione* quam nos antea secuti atque ingressi sumus. (p. 378)
Book II, 1, 1260ᵇ36	...propter hoc *hanc* videamur inserere *Methodum*. (p. 58)	...ideo *hunc laborem* a nobis esse susceptum. (f. 14ᵛ)	iccirco *hanc disputationem* suscepisse atque institutisse videamur. (p. 405)
Book III, 8, 1279ᵇ13	...qui *circa unumquodque Methodum* philosophatur et non solum adspicit ad agere conveniens est non despicere neque praetermittere, sed declarare circa unumquodque veritatem. (p. 180)	Philosophantis vero circa *singulorum disciplinam*, et non solam ad agendum respicientis, proprium est nihil negligere, neque praetermittere, sed demonstrare in singulis veritatem. (f. 37ᵛ)	...ei autem qui *in unaquaque institutione* philosophatur neque ad agendum solum curas et cogitationes suas confert, convenit acriter et non negligenter rem de qua agitur intueri. (p. 464)
Book IV, 2, 1289ᵃ26	Quoniam autem *in prima Methodo* politiarum divisimus tres quidem rectas politias, regnum, aristocraticam, politiam... (p. 377)	Cum vero *in praecedentibus* dictum sit a nobis, tres esse rerumpublicarum species, regnum, optimatum, et eam quae appellatur respublicam. (f. 52ᵛ)	Quoniam *in disputatione atque institutione superiore* de rei publicae administrandae formis tali partitione ac... (pp. 495-96)

Book IV, 8, 1293^{b}30	...ultimo autem de tyrannide rationabile est facere mentionem, quia omnium minime politia haec est, nobis autem est *methodus* de politia. propter quam quidem igitur caussam ordinatum est hoc modo, dictum est. (pp. 406-7)	Merito autem postremo loco tyrannidem reservavimus: propterea quod ista minime est resp. nostra vero *materia* est de republica tractare. Qua igitur de causa sic ordinavimus dictum est. (f. 59^r)	...ad extremum autem ut de tyrannide mentionem faciamus, ratio postulat propterea quod, quamvis haec minime omnium sit rei publicae administrandae forma, a nobis tamen suscepta sit civitatis administrandae *institutio*. Quamobrem igitur talem ordinem secuti simus, dictum est. (p. 510)
Book IV, 10, 1295^{a}2	de tyrannide autem erat reliquum nobis dicere, non quasi sit multa sermocinatio circa ipsam, sed ut accipiat quis *methodi partem*, quoniam et hanc ponimus politiarum quandam partem. (p. 414)	Restat nunc, ut de tyrannide dicemus, non quod multis verbis indigeat, sed ut habeat *in hoc tractatu locum suum*. Quandoquidem hanc quoque posuimus partem esse aliquam publicae gubernationis. (f. 61^r)	De tyrannide autem nobis reliquum erat dicere, non quod longus de ea sermo habendus sit, sed ut *suam hujus institutionis partem* consequatur, quoniam etiam hanc in reipublicae administrandae formis numeramus. (p. 514)

William of Moerbeke, *Aristotelis Politicorum libri octo cum vetusta translatione Guilelmi de Moerbeka*, ed. Franz Susemihl (Leipzig, 1872). *Methodus* is capitalized as in the sixteenth-century edition.

Leonardo Bruni, translation of *Politics* in *Aristotelis Stagiritae Politicorum sive de Republica libri octo, Leonardo Aretino interprete, cum D. Thomae Aquinatis explanatione* ... (Venice, 1568). Moerbeke's translation also appears in this volume.

Dionysius Lambinus, translation of *Politics* in *Aristotelis Politica et Oeconomica ex editione Sylburgii* (Oxford, 1805), II, 377-666. (First published at Paris in 1567.)

RENAISSANCE ETYMOLOGIES OF METHODUS

By the sixteenth century, scholars who worked in the Greek sources were thoroughly familiar with the various senses which the term *methodus* had in Greek and were beginning to reconcile themselves to its use in Latin. The French scholar Guillaume Budé (1467-1540), in his philological commentary on the *Pandects*,[41] gave a list of source passages in Greek from which the various meanings could be drawn. This list became the standard reference of later scholars investigating the etymology of *methodus*, especially after its incorporation into the Greek *Thesaurus* of Stephanus under μέθοδος.

Thus the Latin purist Mario Nizzoli (1498-1566), in banning the word *methodus*[42] as barbarous and not to be used in polite learned discussion, was trying in vain to stem the tide. Even during his lifetime Italian philosophical writers had adopted the term, perhaps from new translations of Galen, or even from the old medieval translations of that writer. At any rate, Girolamo

---

[41] This work, a product of that legal Humanism which we shall take up in our next chapter, contains a long list of derivations and explanations of words which might occur in considering the *Pandects*, among which is the following: " '*Methodus.*' A Graecis methodus dicitur, quod verbum Theodorus *viam rationemque docendi* transtulit. Quintilianus duas grammaticae partes facit, methodon et historiam: *methodon* appellans quam Cicero *viam, artem,* et *rationem* vocat. Sic enim inquit libro primo *Institutionis:* 'Et finitae quidem sunt partes duae, quas haec professio pollicetur, id est, ratio loquendi et enarratio auctorum: quarum illam methodicen, hanc historicen vocant.' Idem alibi methodon *breve dicendi compendium* vertit, quasi brevem viam qua quam celerrime ad peritiam evadimus. Cicero, *De finibus:* 'Artes etiam ipsas propter se assumendas putamus, tum quia sit in iis aliquid dignum assumptione, tum quod constent ex cognitionibus, et contineant quiddam in se ratione constitutum et via,' etc." After mentioning the medical sect of methodists, Budé observes that Galen opposed the 'method' of these physicians with his own method of healing: "Galenus libro nono eiusdem *Therapeuticae* primum se dicit medicinam via et ratione tractasse, quod ipse μεθόδῳ θεραπεύειν appellat. Quam tamen viam Hippocratem primum secuisse dicit: sed viam ab eo sectam a se veluti stratam esse. Unde librum *methodon therapeuticam* nominavit. Duas enim partes omnis artis et scientiae facit, methodon et ascesin id est, viam et exercitationem. Neque enim possumus, inquit, alicuius nobis artis scientiam comparare, nisi et commentationem in universum viam quandam pernoverimus, et artis meditationem per singulorum exempla exercuerimus." Gulielmus Budaeus, *Annotationes ... in quatuor et viginti Pandectarum libros ...* (Paris, 1535), pp. 37-38.

[42] In the appendix of his Ciceronian lexicon, Nizzoli listed *methodus* among the "barbarous and non-Ciceronian" words, and suggested instead the phrase "ratio et via." *Nizolius, sive Thesaurus Ciceronianus ...* (Basel, 1583).

Borro (1512-92), professor of philosophy at Pisa, even wrote a book on the "Peripatetic Method of Teaching and Learning." In his etymology of the term, he takes over the later Greek concept of the "short cut," while recognizing that *via* is the standard translation for it.[43]

Much the same etymology is given by Rudolph Snell (1546-1613), a Ramist and the father of the discoverer of Snell's law in physics. Snell stressed the metaphor of the road as central to the word's meaning in Greek.[44] In this passage we may see once again the importance attributed to the speed and ease with which method leads us to our goal, and also a hint of the Ramist doctrine that it is the disposition of the "matter" of an art that yields this speed and efficiency. In the words of an English Ramist, George Downham (died 1634), method applies not to the finding of arts nor to the arts themselves, but to their "common form, by which the precepts are disposed."[45]

But an observation of this sort presupposes the Ramist movement, which itself was only a part of the reform of the arts that Humanistically trained educators tried to bring about in the

---

[43] "Μέθοδος est vox graeca, quae latine *viam* significat, non tamen quamlibet, sed brevem illam quidem, qua una duce, ad peritiam quam celerrime ducimur, aut breve compendium, aut brevem artem et rationem addiscendi atque docendi; graecam hanc methodi vocem, multi iidemque primae classis latini authores ita transtulerunt, ut Budaeus in *Annotationibus in Pandectas,* Theodorus Gaza, in suis translationibus, Quintilianus in suis *Institutionibus,* et latinae eloquentiae princeps Cicero, compluribus in locis: horum exempla, dignissima quidem quae imitentur, secuti, nos pro graeca *methodo,* latinam *viam* usurpamus. ..." Hieronymus Borrius, *De peripatetica docendi atque addiscendi methodo* (Florence, 1584), pp. 12-13.

[44] "Videtur autem methodus metaphora quadam a viatoribus deducta. Μετά enim *cum,* et ὁδός *viam* significat: hinc methodus, quae Ciceroni *via et ratio* dicitur, Quintiliano *breve compendium.* Quemadmodum enim viatores quam possunt brevissima via ad metam tendunt: sic etiam methodus nos deducit via compendiaria ad cognitionem artium rerumque hoc ordine dispositarum, cum perpetua serie appareat veluti ante oculos suo loco quidque collocatum." Rudolphus Snellius, *De ratione discendi et exercendi logicam* ... (Herborn, 1599), p. 141. I should add that I have not been able to find any passage in Quintilian that would justify Snell's statement, or Budé's.

[45] "Methodus autem, quae hic docetur, non significat vel artem ipsam doctrinamve aut tractatum aliquem, vel rationem aliquam investigandi et inveniendi artes ... sed communem earum formam, sive compendiosam illam viam rationemque, qua praecepta artium inventa jam, suoque vel syllogismi judicio judicata, pro sua quaeque naturae claritate disponit. ..." George Downham, *Commentarii in P. Rami regii professoris dialecticam* ... (Frankfurt, 1605), p. 752.

Renaissance. From such declarations we can see how method became the party slogan it was for the Renaissance. An art is brought into method by being presented in short, easily memorized rules set forth in a clear manner so that the student may master the art in as short a time as possible. In order to qualify as methodical, the rules of an art require to be disposed in a certain order. Thus method is almost synonymous with art (as with the Greeks), but is distinguished from it by the fact that it facilitates or speeds up the mastery of the art. The emphasis on speed and efficiency sets apart the Renaissance notion of method—at least, the "artistic" branch of it—from the ancient concept. The Middle Ages helped to transmit the idea, but never gave it the importance that the Humanists of the Renaissance attached to it. The notion that method can provide a short cut to learning an art did not seem crucial to medieval students or educational reformers. Only when the milieu had become more time-conscious did method become the slogan of those who wished to speed up the processes of learning. Even then the doctrine was not made explicit, for the Humanists who advocated this reform were not philosophically very articulate. But they were tremendously influential, and their elevation of method to the leading criterion of educational success had to be met by those who felt that the disposition of the rules of art was a matter of rhetoric, not of science, and that thorough mastery of a subject was more important than speed in learning it.

Chapter 3. THE INFLUENCE OF HUMANISM
ON METHODOLOGY IN THE VARIOUS SUB-
JECTS OF THE UNIVERSITY CURRICULUM

During the Renaissance, Humanism took on the character of a movement for reform in education, not so much an abstract reform as a practical one, which soon began to threaten established modes and methods of teaching. Throughout the Middle Ages, indeed, there had been educational reformers such as John of Salisbury, Roger Bacon, or Vincent of Beauvais who deplored the current state of education and often suggested alternatives that resembled in some ways those which the Humanists were later to advocate. But these were single voices easily ignored by institutionalized education. The Humanists, however, constituted a much more serious opposition to established medieval practices, to which they had been unalterably opposed since the days of Petrarch. The two chief medieval forms of teaching, the *lecture*, or reading and exposition of a written text, and the *disputation*, were reflected in the written *commentaries* and *quaestiones*.[1] It was upon these forms of educational discourse that the Humanists[2] directed their attack: the technical jargon

---

[1] For a good discussion of Scholastic method, see Friedrich Ueberweg's *Grundriss der Geschichte der Philosophie*, Zweiter Teil, *Die patristische und scholastische Philosophie*, ed. Bernhard Geyer (Berlin, 1928), Chap. 17, "Scholastische Methoden und Literaturformen," pp. 152-57.

[2] I use the term "Humanism" in the widest sense current in the Renaissance, to denote the activity not only of the professional teachers of the *studia humanitatis*, with whom the term originated, but also the nonprofessional students of ancient languages and literatures. See Paul O. Kristeller, "Humanism and Scholasticism in the Italian Renaissance," *Byzantion*, XVII (1945), 346-74; and Augusto Campana, "The Origin of the Word 'Humanist,'" *Journal of the Warburg and Courtauld Institutes*, IX (1946), 60-73. In the broader sense, many professional teachers of philosophy during the sixteenth century may be called Humanists, while some were at one time or another in their careers also Humanists in the strict professional sense.

used in them, especially the syllogistic form of argumentation, displeased these lovers of style immensely.

How to teach and what teaching methods to use are perennial problems of teachers wherever there is institutional transmission of knowledge, but so long as there is a generally accepted *status quo* in education, there will be little in the way of theoretical pedagogy: it took the Sophists to provoke Plato's scheme of education. Thus theoretical consideration of methods of teaching only began to assume prominence in Europe when the Humanists, in their struggle against the "useless disputations" of the Schoolmen, offered their own educational programs.

TREATISES ON EDUCATIONAL METHOD

Beginning with lower schooling and the humble fields of grammar and rhetoric, the Humanists gradually revamped traditional curricula and methods. These changes, first made in Italian schools, were described and advocated in small and unpretentious pedagogical treatises such as Pier Paolo Vergerio's *De ingenuis moribus et liberalibus studiis* and Battista Guarino's *De ordine docendi ac studendi*, both fifteenth-century works, but printed often in the next century. Like all reform movements, Humanism is more attractive at its inception: more conscious of its ultimate objective—in this case, the finished scholar—and less concerned with the mechanisms by which that objective is to be achieved. Part of the inspiration for this reform came from the classics themselves, especially Quintilian.[3]

Where earlier works of Humanist pedagogy were concerned with the development of the "whole man," soon more technical and partial treatments of education began to appear, dealing not with a whole program of education but with the mode of

---

[3] "The impetus given to the enthusiasm and to the educational method of the humanists by the production of Guarino's rendering of 'Plutarch's' treatise *On Education* in 1411, and by the discovery of the complete Quintilian in 1416, and the *De Oratore, Brutus,* and *Orator* in 1422, was fully felt by Vittorino." John E. Sandys, *A History of Classical Scholarship* (3 vols., Cambridge, 1908), II, 53. The influence of the latter works, those of Cicero, was also felt by Renaissance methodologists, as we shall see.

presenting particular subjects. At first these treatises dealt chiefly
with the traditional subject matters of Humanists: the fields of
grammar, letter writing, poetry, speaking, and history. In works
such as these, the titles reflect the character of the presentation,
which is elementary. Words like *via, ratio, ordo, modus,* and,
finally, *methodus* appear in them not as standing for clear and
well-defined concepts, but simply as neutral names used both for
the content of a discipline and for any manner of investigating or
teaching it.[4]

Not only do the words *methodus, ordo,* and *ratio* appear as
nouns in the nominative case in the titles of textbooks, but they
also appear in the subtitles, stating that a grammar, for instance,
had been written "in a certain manner" or "by a certain method."
Here we begin to discern a reflection of Humanist dissatisfaction
with the method of presentation of the traditional disciplines, in
which there was no clear order or controlling scheme. The number of school subjects "brought into order" or "reduced to art"
during the late Renaissance is almost unbelievable.[5]

THE STOIC CONCEPT OF ART IN THE RENAISSANCE

As we have noted, *methodus* was held to be a "short form of
art" by Renaissance etymologists, and it is this meaning which is
reflected in its use in the titles of textbooks. Now the concept of
an art upon which almost all writers leaned for support was the
Stoic idea of an art as a "system of percepts exercised together
toward some end useful in life." This Stoic definition met scholars everywhere in the writings of classical antiquity, but especially
in a number of works that were favorites of the Humanists: the

---

[4] It should be remarked that earlier Italian methodological works, in all fields,
generally do not use the term *methodus*: only in the sixteenth century do we begin
to find it used. For a representative list of titles of pedagogical work from the
sixteenth century, see our Appendix.

[5] A representative but by no means exhaustive list of such texts from the sixteenth and early seventeenth centuries may be found in the Appendix. I have
selected mostly titles in which *methodus* appears in the nominative case: to include
works in which *methodus* appears in an oblique case would have been almost equivalent to compiling a complete list of pedagogical works from the period, so widespread was the fashion for using it.

writings of Cicero, Quintilian, Lucian, and the rhetorician Hermogenes.

An explicit doctrine adopting the Stoic definition of an art and also adopting the Stoic equivalence of method with art was never developed by Humanists or writers of textbooks. But the standard definition of an art was this one, which some writers knew enough to call Stoic. The fact that it can be attributed safely to the founder of Stoicism, Zeno, was overlooked, for the attribution is buried in Olympiodorus' commentary on Plato's *Gorgias*.[6] For that matter, the exact sponsorship of the Stoic idea is seldom correctly identified: the quotation of it by the "parasite" in Lucian's dialogue of that name, who heard it from "a certain wise man" (obviously a Stoic), was attributed to Lucian, as if he himself had originated the idea. The best one can find is a scholar who says that the definition exists *apud Lucianum*, as does Melanchthon.[7] Melanchthon was typical of the Humanists in thus seizing upon the phrase "some end useful in life" as a justification for his reform of education. The Stoic definition had been used by Rudolph Agricola (1443-85), the "Erasmus of the North," to show that dialectic is an art, and that the medieval version of dialectic—Terminist logic—was not.[8]

[6] Olympiodorus, *In Platonis Gorgiam Commentaria,* ed. William Norvin (Leipzig, 1936), p. 63. It is interesting to note that a whole list of definitions of art, many Stoic, should be introduced by a neo-Platonist of the sixth century into a commentary on Plato. See also Arnim, SVF, I, 21, 3.

[7] In his *Erotemata dialectica,* Melanchthon, after distinguishing science from art ("Aristotle often mixes them up," he remarks), gives the Stoic definition as found in Lucian and Quintilian: "Apud Quintilianum extat definitio stoica artis, ubi ars pro scientia sumitur. Eam definitionem Graecis verbis recitabo, ut apud Lucianum extat, quia verba Latina apud Quintilianum obscura sunt, et definitio ipsa propterea studiosis gratior esse debet, quia admonitionem de fine artium continet, quae in aliis definitionibus non recensetur. Ait enim artem doctrinam certam esse de talibus rebus, quarum aliqua sit in vita utilitas. Significat artes divinitus hominibus monstratas esse propter multas utilitates, quod in Arithmetica, Architectonica et multis aliis manifeste conspici potest. Et in discendo eligamus doctrinam vitae utilem, et saepe nobiscum cogitemus, ad quem finem ea quae discimus, referenda sint. Verba haec sunt: τέχνη ἐστι σύστημα ἐγκαταλήψεων ἐγγεγυμνασμένων πρός τι τέλος εὔχρηστον τῶν ἐν βίῳ, id est, ars est ordo propositionum, exercitatione cognitarum, ad finem utilem in vita. Vocat enim καταλήψεις propositiones certas et firmas, seu demonstrationes, quia κατάληπτα vocabant certo comprehensa, ut saepe Plutarchus loquitur." CR, XIII, 536.

[8] Agricola is discussing the "common opinion" that dialectic is an art, and he notes that it does satisfy two of the usual definitions of an art: "Dialecticen

Another influential educational reformer, Luis Vives (1492-1540), also adopted a version of the Stoic definition for use in his reform of the "corrupt arts."[9] At his hands it certainly received one of the most philosophical defenses the Humanists could muster.

HUMANIST METHOD IN TEACHING AS BRIEF AND SYSTEMATIC

In contrast to the oversubtle rules of Terminist logic, Humanist method could be applied with profit to any of the other arts, and when so applied would speed the student on his way to mastery of the arts. In the words of Girolamo Borro already quoted, method was the "brief way under whose guidance we are led as quickly as possible to knowledge" (p. 65). The insistence on speed is typical of the Humanists: the arts must be learned "as quickly as possible." In a phrase favorite with them, the Humanists had no intention of "growing old and gray in the study of logic," or in any of the other arts. The very earliest Renaissance Humanist, Petrarch (1304-74), had protested the spending of too much time in dialectic.[10] Thus Humanist presentations of

quidam ex artium genere voluerunt esse, quidam facultatem quandam vocavere. Verum utro dicatur modo, non est quod in praesentia valde nos solicitos habeat. Artem esse communis accepit opinio, et artem disserendi vulgo dicimus, hocque nomine editi de ea inscribuntur libri. Eritque nimirum indignum, artium eam excludere numero, quae reliquarum dux sit, et stabilitrix artium, et sine cuius praesidio tueri fines suos reliquae non satis commode possint. Quod si est ars (ut quidam definivere) *collectio multarum de una re comprehensionum, ad finem aliquem utilem vitae,* vel (ut alii) *recta ratio rerum faciendarum:* nemo ipsam dubitaverit artem vocare. Nam et multas comprehensiones colligit, quo pacto inveniendum sit argumentum, et quomodo iudicandum, ubi inveneris: et faciendorum istorum rectam tradit eatenus rationem, quatenus faciendi verbus potest istis aptari. Utilemque esse certum est, si falli, decipi, vera pro falsis, falsa pro veris accipi, inutile putamus." *Rodolphi Agricolae . . . De inventione dialectica, liber primus* (Paris, 1529), pp. 156-57.

[9] Cf. his *De causis corruptarum artium:* "Quae vero in regulas ac precepta non coguntur, minime sunt artes, sed generali nuncupatione *cognitiones* et *peritiae* quaedam, velut *rerum gestarum notitia, consideratio;* quare definiatur nobis ars: Collectio universalium praeceptorum parata ad cognoscendum, agendum, vel operandum, in certa aliqua finis latitudine . . ." Ludovicus Vivus, *Opera omnia* (8 vols., Valencia, 1782), VI, 252.

[10] See Petrarch's letter to Tomasso of Messina, translated by Hans Nachod in *The Renaissance Philosophy of Man,* ed. Ernst Cassirer, Paul Kristeller, and John

the arts were designed to facilitate the quick and efficient learning of the subject matter.

Nor was this methodical reform, if such it may be termed, limited to the enemy without, for within Humanism itself there seems to have been a reaction to the aimless and disorderly erudition which filled large folio volumes with poorly digested observations drawn at random from the author's reading. Complaints begin to be heard about the vice of *curiositas* and the danger of wasting time by darting from one subject to another. Possibly in connection with the severe discipline of editing *editiones principes* of classical authors, Humanist scholars felt the need of systematic and methodical study. Certainly systematic dictionaries, such as the *Thesaurus* of Stephanus and the Ciceronian lexicon of Nizzoli, date from this period, and must have required a methodicalness not conspicuous in the works of early Humanism.

To a certain extent also, the Humanist insistence on order and method seems to have been a reaction to the lack of organization which they felt in traditional teaching. "All teaching must come at the proper time and place," remarked the Humanist pedagogue, Claude Baduel (1491-1561), founder of the college at Nîmes, in a letter to Cardinal Sadoleto. "But today our masters distinguish neither time nor age nor methodical order. They mix everything up, confuse it all, teach everything at the same time. Greek, Latin, orators, poets, historians, dialecticians, philosophers, come at the same time, on the same day, at the same hour, to fill the minds of the students with confusion, overwhelmed beneath this indigestible mass of knowledge." [11] These were not idle complaints, for they came also from men engaged in setting up new schools and new curricula, such as Johann Sturm, who founded the school and university at Strasbourg. [12] The remedy

---

Herman Randall, Jr. (Chicago, 1948), pp. 134-39. See also Carl von Prantl, *Geschichte der Logik im Abendlande* (4 vols., Leipzig, 1855-70), IV, 153-55.

[11] Quoted in French by M. J. Gaufrès, *Claude Baduel et la réforme des études au XVIe siècle* (Paris, 1880), p. 47. Baduel had studied with Melanchthon.

[12] See Charles Schmidt, *La vie de Jean Sturm* (Strasbourg, 1855), pp. 230-31: "Pour que ce mouvement littéraire [i.e., the Humanist movement] produisit **tous**

for this lack of order in studies was felt by Melanchthon to lie in a greater awareness of the end or purpose of each art.[13]

The most methodical of Humanist educational reforms was the *Ratio studiorum* of the Jesuits, completed in 1586, although ratified in 1599. This rigid scheme for instruction in the humanities and sciences could just as well have been called a *Methodus ad eruditorum piorum fabricationem*, for it was in every respect the model of Humanist method: giving strict rules to be followed in instruction, setting time limits to study, and extremely conscious of the end to be achieved by the whole plan. It was at once the envy and the despair of Protestant educators. But just as the Jesuit system, while efficient, tended to stifle the free development of its students, so the methodical textbooks compiled in such quantity during the period of the late Renaissance, while no doubt efficient in their own way, tended to degenerate into empty formalism and pedantry. It soon became apparent that in producing a flood of such textbooks, the printing presses of Europe were facilitating a trend toward superficial education that would have to be offset by more thorough textual treatment of the various subjects dealt with in their pages. Melanchthon's little compendia, prepared to answer the need for methodical instruction in mathematics, Greek, rhetoric, dialectic, and so on, were immensely successful, but they set a dangerous precedent. When Peter Ramus put out an even more elementary and perfunctory set of textbooks on the liberal arts, some realization of the Pandora's box that had been opened began to dawn upon startled scholars. Soon Europe was deluged with small, convenient school manuals in which the life of traditional subjects was systematically and methodically eradicated and reduced to rules so simple that any child, literally, could learn them.

---

les resultats dont il contenait les germes, il fallut le régler, le ramener à des principes, l'organiser conformément à un plan rationnel. Il fallut en concentrer les éléments épars, réunir les forces qui se seraient épuisées dans l'isolement, en un mot, créer des écoles constituées d'après une méthode." See also L. Kückelhahn, *Johannes Sturm, Strassburg's erster Schulrector* (Leipzig, 1872), p. 51.

[13] See, for example, Melanchthon's preface to Cicero's *De officiis*, CR, XI, 257.

HUMANISTS AND THE REFORM OF LOGIC

One of the chief targets for writers of methodical textbooks was the subject of logic, which had been overrun, so the Humanists held, with Terminist subtleties and oversophisticated dialectic. The evil fascination that Terminist logic exercised upon the minds of the young and impressionable must be overcome by the use of textbooks in which the Properties of Terms—*supposition, ampliation, restriction*, and the like—were ruthlessly eliminated and the subject of logic reduced to its proper dimensions. Only then could the student be quickly instructed in what he needed to know of logic and sent on his way to higher learning, especially the humanities, where the wisdom of ancient Greece and Rome awaited him. The bare bones of Aristotelian logic, together with a few useful admonitions concerning method, were enough to equip him for life.

Ironically enough, the medieval basis or springboard for these Terminist commentaries, Peter of Spain's *Summulae logicales*, was itself a short and methodical textbook, designed to introduce the student to the subject of logic.[14] At least one Humanist, Johann Sturm, came to the defense of this medieval textbook, realizing that it was in fact pretty much what the Humanists were looking for in a textbook.[15] Most of the Humanist innovators, however, condemned Terminist logic in blanket fashion and did not stop to ask themselves whether the substitution of their Latin compendia for Peter of Spain's represented any progress so far as the beginner was concerned.

Not only were these Humanist logics "methodically" written, but they contained rules for the methodical treatment of other

---

[14] In his commentary on the work, Johannes Versor (died c.1485), a German Thomist, says that it is called *Summulae* because it is a short compendium: "Et quia iste liber brevis est, et compendiosus, ideo vocatur *summula* et definitur sic: *Summula* est quoddam breve compendium in brevi et generali comprehendens illa quae in libris logicalibus diffuse et in speciali tractantur." *Petri Hispani Summulae logicales, cum Versorii Parisiensis clarissima expositione* ... (Venice, 1580), f. 1ʳ.

[15] Facilius mihi probabitis Petrum Hispanum utiliorem esse gymnasiis, quam Aristotelem: nam et ordinem Aristotelis retinet, et supervacanea resecat: et obscura clarius, etc." *Ioannis Sturmii Prolegomena, hoc est, praefationes* ... (Zurich, n.d.) p. 131.

arts as well. These rules of method were usually to be found at
the end of the manuals of logic and represent, in the sixteenth
century, a new development in logic. A textbook fairly typical
of its class is one written by François Hotman (1524-90), a French
writer better known in political than in intellectual history, but
often quoted during the latter part of the century. In his logic,
Hotman first disposes of the predicables and categories of Aristotle, and then pauses to wonder whether he should next deal
with division or with definition. "This question cannot be satisfactorily answered until we have spoken of Method and the
procedure of teaching," he decides, and then gives his definition
of method: "Method is an art which demonstrates how every
discipline can be reduced to an art and fixed procedure." [16] This
of course is simply giving back to the concept its original Greek
name. Hotman was a lawyer, and his textbook is slanted toward
the legal reader. Hence it is not surprising that Cicero occupies
a prominent place among the authorities on method that Hotman
cites: the justification for citing him on a subject about which,
taken at the letter, he has nothing to say is that method for Hotman is an art—and of course Cicero had much to say about art.

Such sections on method in logic textbooks cannot be said to
have been exclusively the contribution of the Humanists, for into
them went also some of the current discussion which was carried
on by traditional logicians and Aristotelians, little suited though
it must have been to the requirements of elementary instruction.
These doctrines give the impression of being grudgingly included

[16] Hactenus primam Dialecticae artis partem videmur absoluisse. Deinceps ad
divisionem accedamus. Sed utri prior debetur locus, divisioni an definitioni? Huic
quaestioni responderi commode antequam de Methodo, et docendi ratione dis-
seruerimus, satis non potest. Nam ad huius artis cognitionem ea praemunitione est
opus. Quid est Methodus? Ars quae quemadmodum disciplina omnis redigi in
artem et certam rationem possit demonstrat. Hoc est, quemadmodum ex iis rebus
quarum ars nondum est, effici ars possit." "Institutionis dialecticae ex fontibus philosophorum libri IIII, exemplis plerisque e iure civili depromptis," *Francisci Hotmani
iurisconsulti operum tomus* (Geneva, 1599), p. 1173. Hotman then asks what an
art is, and gives in reply definitions from Cicero's *Orator,* from Aristotle, and from
Lucian. Of the three methods of compiling an art, "analysis," "synthesis," and
"diaeresis," he claims to have made use of the first in writing his own work. Hotman's logic was published in 1573 without indication of the place of printing, but
there may be an earlier edition.

as a concession to the need to present a rival doctrine to Humanist method. They sometimes appear side by side with material from Terminist logic, which was also being relegated to the rear of textbooks during this period.

Instruction in method was thus considered to be one way in which logic could be made useful to the student. Another was the emphasis on the doctrine of "finding," which, as Aristotle had maintained, was useful "for disputing, for overcoming opponents in debate, and for practice in philosophizing." What more could be asked? But the *Topics* had long since been translated into Latin: Cicero and Quintilian had adapted Aristotle's *topoi* to the *loci* of Latin school rhetoric. Rudolph Agricola weighed the merits of the doctrines as found in Aristotle with those in the Latin rhetoricians and decided for the latter as more concise and readily available.

This emphasis on *inventio* is considered one of the hallmarks of Humanist logic and has been called the "Ciceronian-rhetorizing" tendency, of which historians of logic[17] speak with so little sympathy. Yet the renewed interest in topical method which Rudolph Agricola spearheaded was a very influential movement in the late Renaissance and its repercussions in theology and law were not so unfortunate as one would be led to expect.

Emphasis on the finding part of logic[18] was not intended to exclude the syllogism altogether from consideration, for practically no Renaissance writer, Humanist or otherwise, challenged the

[17] Carl von Prantl viewed this development with some distaste as a hopeless weakening and superficialization of traditional Aristotelian logic, and his view is shared by many modern writers who know very much less about traditional logic than he did. Yet it must be pointed out that the *Topics* is, after all, a part of the *Organon* and not of the *Art of Rhetoric,* and that the precedent of centuries as well as Aristotle's explicit testimony justified its inclusion in the repertory of logical texts.

[18] The separation of logic or dialectic into two divisions dealing with finding and judging was, of course, not a Humanist innovation but an ancient one. Cf. Boethius, *De differentiis topicis*: "Omnis ratio disserendi quam Logicen Peripatetici veteres appellavere, in duas distribuitur partes: unam inveniendi, alteram iudicandi." Migne, PL, LXIV, 1173. Furthermore, Renaissance writers were thoroughly aware that this dichotomy was ancient: its sources were well known. See, for example, the work of Nicolaus Grouchius (1520-72) on the subject: in *Praeceptiones dialecticae ... Disputatio ... Quid de nomine dialectices et logices cum Aristotele sentiendum sit, quo singuli libri Organi Aristotelis pertineant* (Paris, 1553), f. 1r.

obvious validity of the Aristotelian syllogism on its own grounds, and even the Humanists were usually willing to concede it a minor role in the educational process. What they objected to, most vehemently, was the eristic use of it in disputation, which they considered completely futile. The aim of disputation, so the Humanists argued, was simply the "silencing of one's opponent," and the gaining of glory for the winner. Of what possible use could this practice be to the other arts?

In point of fact, the *Topics* had been part of logic or dialectic ever since the *Logica nova* became known in the twelfth century. (Even before then, Boethius' work *De differentiis topicis* had been part of the basic fund of dialectical knowledge.) Peter of Spain's *Summulae logicales* dealt with the *loci* at some length. Thus the conflict between the Humanist "dialecticians" and the Terminist logicians was not a question of introducing foreign material into the *Organon* and the teaching of logic, but of a different emphasis upon what had always been there. The Humanist dialecticians saw that the *Topics* was the only part of the *Organon* which could have any conceivable use in eloquence or speaking, and so they centered their attention upon it.

This conflict of purpose between traditional logic and Humanist dialectic occupied the latter part of the fifteenth century and the whole of the sixteenth. It helped to flood the learned world with so many books on logic that Bartholomew Keckermann, surveying the scene at the end of the sixteenth century, was able to remark that not since the beginning of the world had there been a century in which the interest in logic, the publication of logical texts, and the flourishing of logical studies could be compared to the peak reached at his time.[19]

METHOD IN TEXTBOOKS OF GRAMMAR AND RHETORIC

Although detailed doctrines on method were presented in logic textbooks, other arts could be presented methodically and could

---

[19] Bartholomaeus Keckermannus, *Praecognitorum logicorum tractatus III ...* (Hanover, 1606), pp. 109-10.

also reflect Stoic influence in their introductory remarks as to
what constitutes an art. There were ancient models for this
practice of beginning a textbook with a definition of art in
general and then proceeding to a definition of the particular art
being transmitted in the subsequent exposition. For example, the
grammar of Dionysius of Thrace, upon which many subsequent
Greek and Latin grammars were patterned, proceeded thus. And,
as we have seen, we owe the preservation of Zeno's etymological
derivation of *methodos* or "art," among others, to Greek
(Byzantine) commentaries upon this work.

Stoic doctrine could also be found in ancient textbooks on
rhetoric, and when rhetoric was made the object of special study
by Renaissance Humanists, it helped to diffuse still more the
definition of an art as a "system of precepts." Johann Sturm,
the Protestant schoolmaster of Strasbourg, especially cultivated
the rhetorician Hermogenes, who lived in the second century of
our era and who was strongly under Stoic influence. Sturm edited
and commented upon the *Partitiones* of Hermogenes,[20] as well as
the *De formis orationum* and *De ratione inveniendi oratoria*: he
was undoubtedly the greatest admirer of Hermogenes in modern
times. From Stoic doctrine found in the introductory sections of
the *Partitiones* and elsewhere, Sturm derived his emphasis on the
necessity for putting the precepts of art to daily use. Mastery of
an art requires nature, knowledge of the precepts, and exercise.
Sturm held that this exercise consisted in the reading and "resolution" of the speeches of Cicero and Demosthenes and in daily
use, in order that the student might express those things which
he reads and observes in the writings of the orators and imitate
them. Ramus, who was a pupil of Sturm at Paris, owes a great
deal of his own program to this doctrine of his teacher.[21] And
it was no doubt owing to Sturm's influence that Hermogenes was
also taught at Cambridge.

[20] Sturm's commentary on Hermogenes is entitled *Scholae in partitiones rhetoricas
Hermogenis* (Strasbourg, 1570).

[21] For an appreciative reference to Sturm by Ramus, see Schmidt, *La vie de Jean
Sturm*, p. 269. See also Walter J. Ong, *Ramus, Method, and the Decay of Dialogue*
(Cambridge, Mass., 1958), pp. 232-36.

METHODS OF READING AND WRITING HISTORIES

Another field of Humanist interest in which works of methodology were produced was that of historiography, or rather of the "reading and writing of histories"—for historiography as we conceive it had little in common with the stylistic and moral injunctions of the *artes historicae*, as these works were called. They were produced in considerable numbers during the sixteenth century, especially in Italy. A collection of these tracts (some from antiquity) appeared under the title 'A Store of Historical Art' in Basel in 1579,[22] attesting to the rising interest in the subject of history during the previous years when most of the works were written.

Jean Bodin's famous 'Method for the Easy Cognition of Histories,' first published at Paris in 1566, has been described as the reaction of a legally trained scholar against this unduly rhetorical treatment of history.[23] Unquestionably, Bodin was familiar with the talk of method in his day: he speaks[24] of the difficulty of

---

[22] Of the eighteen *artes historicae* contained in this collection, only one—Bodin's —contains *methodus* in the title. John L. Brown observes that the term is not used by the Italian writers of *artes* (see next note). Nevertheless the German editor of the collection says that they may all be called "methods of histories": ". . . coeperint viri eruditi, et qui plurimum studii atque temporibus historiis impertivissent, reliquis infinito labore modum ostendere: et ad ea quae longissimo tempore, summaque diligentia percepissent, quasi suorum ingeniorum lumina, cum magna laude, contra historiarum tenebras praeferre, in illis libris, quos Methodos historiarum non iniuria inscripserunt." Dedicatory epistle of Johann Wolf, dated August, 1576, in *Artis historicae penus* . . . (Basel, 1579).

[23] By John L. Brown in his excellent study, *The Methodus ad Facilem Historiarum Cognitionem of Jean Bodin: A Critical Study* (Washington, 1939), esp. Chap. 3, "The 'ars historica' before Bodin." Brown's monograph takes cognizance of the importance and wide extent of the methodological controversies of the Renaissance. Bodin was also influenced by the legal methodology of his time: see pp. 33-34 of Brown's study: "For if the book [the *Methodus*] was designed in part . . . as a reproof to the elegant emptiness of the Italian theorists of history, it was also written as a criticism of the inadequate methods of the law schools of his day."

[24] "Quae disputatio sit nimis ampla cuiquam ac diffusa videbitur, cogitare debebit, ea quae nullum exitum habent, cuiusmodi est historia rerum humanarum, non posse brevi methodo contineri. Quod si Galenus de sola methodo suae artis, quae certis regionibus concluditur, libros plus quam triginta, Diomedes vero de re grammatica sex millia librorum effudit, profecto non debet id quod de universa historia scripsimus, copiosum videri." *Methodus ad facilem historiarum cognitionem*, in *Oeuvres Philosophiques de Jean Bodin*, ed. Pierre Mesnard (Paris, 1951), p. 109.

comprehending history "within a brief method." In the second
chapter of the *Methodus*, Bodin speaks of "analysis,"

> that outstanding master of teaching the arts, which teaches us how to
> divide the universal into its parts, and to divide these parts again into
> parts, and then the coherence of parts and whole with one another. Syn-
> thesis need not be elaborated by us, since the members of almost all his-
> tories are so joined one to another and are fitted by scholars with great
> study into one body, as it were, although unskillfully separated by some.
> There is nevertheless such a coherence of parts and whole that if they are
> torn apart, they are in no way able to exist.[25]

History was an art, not a science; and it was a useful art to
the extent that one could profit from the lessons it taught. Yet
to assign a discipline to the arts was not to lower its prestige, in
antiquity or in the Renaissance, and Bodin's contributions to his
subject are an instance of the cultural implications inherent in the
simple observation that an art deals not with singulars but with
universals—for from this observation sprang a concept of comparative jurisprudence that was to have great significance. The
ties between the study of history and the historical or comparative
study of jurisprudence were close during this period. Since both
subjects were pursued chiefly by Humanistic writers, most of the
historical or legal methodology belongs in the "arts" category,
and shows only slight influence from the medical or "scientific"
school of methodological thought.

Because of the fad for using *methodus* in the titles of textbooks
in the arts (*artes*), many sixteenth-century books that seem
promising to a modern scholar interested in learning about Renaissance "method" are bound to disappoint. A method of studying grammar or an order of reading histories may not be an
essay in methodology at all: in fact, it usually is a treatise laying
out a specific course of study in a particular subject. Yet even
these treatises are not entirely devoid of philosophical significance, for this sort of course-outlining, when applied to higher
subjects such as theology or law, might have serious consequences
for the subjects themselves. Before we pass to the higher facul-

[25] *Ibid.*, p. 116.

ties, it might be well to dwell for a moment upon the relation of Humanist educational reforms to the quadrivium, that other branch of the arts curriculum.

METHOD IN THE QUADRIVIUM: THE RECOVERY OF GREEK MATHEMATICAL WORKS

Arithmetic, geometry, music, and astronomy—these were the traditional subjects presumed to make up part of the intellectual equipment of any free man. Boethius and others had transmitted them, albeit inadequately, from Roman education to the Middle Ages. Or the four, astronomy was perhaps the most seriously studied by medieval students; geometry was strictly subordinate to it, while the other two theoretical disciplines seldom received prolonged attention in the arts curriculum. The quadrivium had indeed been diligently studied at Oxford in the fourteenth century, and some works in geometry, "calculation," and statics were the result of this interest. Yet generally speaking it was only toward the end of the fifteenth century and the beginning or middle of the sixteenth that mathematics began to assume an autonomous role in European universities and to become an independent subject studied for its own sake.

In mathematics, the usual Humanist emphasis on recovery of the sources—in this case exclusively Greek—of the discipline was very beneficial. Such recovery presupposed a knowledge of the Greek language as well as of mathematics, and this linguistic sophistication was the contribution of Humanism. In addition, mathematics in the educational programs of the day received an impetus from the Humanist reevaluation of the arts curriculum, which tended to emphasize mathematics at the expense of logic. For methodology this emergence of the Greek sources of mathematics created a need to distinguish clearly between mathematical and nonmathematical senses of "analysis." Because analysis was one of the traditional four Platonic methods of dialectic, and the root of Aristotle's *Analytics* as well, the Greek commentators, as we have observed, brought the geometrical version into their discussions of these topics. The geometrical sense of "analysis" had been incorporated into traditional methodology at least as early as the second century, and it continued to appear, although not without transformation, in the methodology of later commentators, Peripatetic and Platonic, until Byzantine times. Both Arab and Latin commentators and philosophers took over this tradition, the Latins using the terms *resolutio* and *compositio* for the two methods. But these medieval Latin versions were so distant from their mathematical origin, and so bound up with metaphysical and even theological ideas, that they can scarcely be regarded as keeping alive the spirit of Greek geometry. It was not until the detailed description given by Pappus was published, in the Latin translation made by Federigo Commandino,[26] that we can again speak of the influence of Greek geometry upon general philosophical methodology. This classical and exact description began to have an influence upon philosophy, notably upon Galileo; but since it was published only in 1589, not many of the writers we meet in the sixteenth century have as yet had a chance to absorb it. The geometrical sense of the terms "analysis" and "synthesis" began to gain currency, replacing the medieval *resolutio* and *compositio* used by Commandino to translate them. In fact, the very replacement of these Latin words by the Greek in subsequent philosophical and scientific usage is un-

[26] This translation was so important for the later period that it may be well to give it in full: "Locus, qui vocatur ἀναλύομενος, hoc est, resolutus, O Hermodore fili, ut summatim dicam, propria quaedam est materia post communium elementorum constitutionem, iis parata, qui in geometricis sibi comparare volunt vim ac facultatem inveniendi problemata quae ipsis proponuntur: atque huius tantummodo utilitatis gratia inventa est. Scripserunt autem hac de re tum Euclides, qui elementa tradit, tum Apollonius Pergaeus, tum Aristaeus senior. Quae quidem per resolutionem et compositionem procedit. *Resolutio* igitur est via a quaesito tamquam concesso, per ea quae deinceps consequuntur ad aliquod concessum in compositione; in resolutione enim id quod quaeritur tamquam factum ponentes, quid ex hoc contingat, consideramus: et rursum illius antecedens, quousque ita progredientes incidamus in aliquod iam cognitum, vel quod sit e numero principiorum. Et huiusmodi processum *resolutionem* appellamus, veluti ex contrario factam solutionem. In *compositione* autem per conversionem ponentes tamquam iam factum in quod postremum in resolutione sumpsimus; atque hic ordinantes secundum naturam ea antecedentia, quae illic consequentia erant; et mutua illorum facta compositione ad quaesiti finem pervenimus, et hic modus vocatur *compositio.*" *Pappi Alexandrini mathematicae collectiones a Federico Commandino Urbinate in Latinum conversae, et commentariis illustratae* (Venice, 1589), ff. 157v-58r.

questionably due to the fact that the Greek words were now associated very precisely with their geometrical usage, and thus were considered superior to the medieval Latin terms, with their more extensive yet vaguer connotations.

For this contribution, obviously, the Humanists can take only a small share of credit. They contributed more by encouragement from the sidelines than by actual participation in the formation of new ideas or the revival of fruitful old ones. They simply helped to furnish the materials which more original minds could work upon. Yet they also helped to promote mathematical studies in the schools.

HUMANIST PROMOTION OF MATHEMATICS IN THE SCHOOLS

As one of the seven liberal arts, geometry had been part of the encyclopedic training of the Greek boy and, in theory, of the Roman. In practice, however, the mathematical studies had been neglected by the Romans, and this neglect continued to prevail, with some exceptions, throughout the medieval period. As actually taught, geometry was a very minor part of the university scholar's intellectual accomplishment: it was required primarily for the understanding of astronomy. Any master of arts could lecture on the *Sphere* of Sacrobosco without being especially trained in mathematics, although it was customary to preface astronomical teaching with the exposition of a few books of Euclid's *Elements*. In the late Renaissance mathematics began to emerge from its lowly position, with Italy far in advance of the rest of Europe in appointing permanent teachers for mathematics alone.

One might have thought that the study of mathematics, with its esoteric symbolism, would have been as distasteful to the Humanists as was Terminist logic. Yet the study of geometry and mathematics was not so foreign to the world of Humanism as one would expect from the predominantly literary character of that movement. To Humanist educational reformers, weary of the endless disputing of the Schools, the study of geometry seemed a welcome relief from the traditional quibbling of logic.[27] They liked to stress the fact that the study of geometry could be carried on in complete silence (an observation usually accompanied by commendatory references to the two years of silence said to have been imposed upon initiates in the Pythagorean school). Furthermore, the Humanists vastly preferred the geometrical application of the *Organon* to its use in argumentation. Conversely, they often stressed the usefulness of a knowledge of geometry to the student of Aristotle's logic, with the implication that geometrical exercises were much more rewarding than syllogistic argumentation. As a preeminently useful art, geometry could properly take its place in the curriculum beside rhetoric and a dialectic purged of Terminist quibbling.

The famous Alsatian Humanist Johann Sturm (1507-89), rector first of the school and then the university at Strasbourg, emphasized the value of a knowledge of geometry to the student who wished to understand Aristotle's dialectical works. Conrad Dasypodius, or Rauchfuss (c.1532-1600), a teacher of mathematics in Sturm's university, was convinced that practice in Euclidean demonstration would give his pupils greater insight into Aristotle's theory of demonstration.[28]

About the same time, the study of algebra was introduced from Italy into Germany by a Viennese circle called the *Sodalitas litteraria Danubiana*: the Humanist Conrad Celtis was active in this group. Celtis also hoped to include two professorships in mathematics in his new Poets College at the University of Vienna. Again, Melanchthon was very sympathetic to the study of mathematics; the statutes at Wittenberg had expressly emphasized the value of mathematics for a knowledge of Aristotle before

---

[27] Rudolph Agricola attributed the neglect of mathematics in his time to its unsuitability to serve as the basis for noisy disputations. See his *De inventione dialectica* ... (Paris, 1529), p. 146.

[28] "Annis viginti sex nostri Gymnasii consuetudo fuit, ut qui ex classibus ad publicas lectiones promoventur, primum audiant Euclidis librum, quo praecepta τῆς ἀποδείξεως exercere, et ad usum aliquem accommodare possint; siquidem nemo facilius vim et efficatiam [efficacitatem?] eorum, quae in libro de demonstratione explicatur, aut etiam ab ipso Aristotele in suo *Organo* traduntur, intelliget, quam qui in pulverem descenderit geometricum." Preface to Dasypodius' Greek and Latin edition of Euclid (Strasbourg, 1564).

Melanchthon came there, but his encouragement meant much. Finally, the Jesuits, who were the most determined if not the most sensitive Humanists of all, gave considerable prominence to mathematics in their course of instruction.[29]

Peter Ramus' activities as a dilettante and sponsor of mathematical research have not received the recognition they deserve. In addition to writing some very elementary texts in geometry and arithmetic, Ramus was active in searching out manuscripts of Greek mathematical works and in encouraging the study of geometry among his friends and protégés. He left money to endow a chair exclusively for mathematics at Paris, and he addressed an open plea to universities and princes to found similar chairs throughout Europe, pointing out quite correctly that the foremost mathematicians of his day did not hold chairs in the subject. Ramus emphasized the loss to philosophers from their neglect of Euclid, and wished for some Apollo to revive the study of the art of geometry at the University of Paris.[30] Ramus' own attempt at reviving the study of geometry, his textbook on the subject, was a pitiful performance, for it omitted the proofs and simply presented the theorems. Yet in extenuation of this it must be remarked that the proofs in the *Elements*, in Ramus' day, were usually considered to be scholia, or parts of a commentary, upon the text, written by a certain Theon (the fourth century A.D.

[29] For the details of the rise of mathematics to respectable status in the university curriculum, and incidentally for the part played therein by Humanists, see Siegmund Günther, *Geschichte des mathematischen Unterrichts im deutschen Mittelalter bis zum Jahre 1525* (Berlin, 1887), esp. Chap. 4, "Der Aufschwung der Mathematik zum selbständigen akademischen Nominalfach," pp. 219-86. For the role of Celtis, see Lewis W. Spitz, *Conrad Celtis: The German Arch-Humanist* (Cambridge, Mass., 1957), pp. 55-71.

[30] "Est vero in Academia Parisiensi tantaque discentium multitudine dolendum tam nobilis disciplinae studia sic iacere, ut non modo Geometriae usus nullus in tot philosophorum scholis exerceatur, sed ne ars quidem ipsa tota discatur. Multum enim est et magnum, si quis philosophiae magister aliquot Euclidis libros praelegerit, tanquam gustasse aliquid eius artis sit satis, non tota cognoscenda sit, imo non totius fructus et usus quaerendus et tractandus sit, et hic Geometras Aristoteleos esse valde cupio, ut se putent Geometriam ἁπλῶς ἐπίστασθαι, cum non solum generalia praecepta utcunque intellexerint, sed multo magis cum in exemplis singularibus quamplurimis exercuerint, Apollineque aliquo rursus esset opus ad hominum nostrorum ignaviam castigandam." Petrus Ramus, *Aristotelicae animadversiones liber nonus et decimus in Posteriora Analytica* (Paris, 1553), pp. 106-7.

editor of the *Elements*), who had commented upon Euclid in this rather laborious fashion. The authenticity of the proofs was not generally conceded until somewhat later in the century. When Peter Ramus omitted the proofs from his edition of Euclid, then, he was simply dropping, so he thought, an unnecessary commentary with which the student need not be burdened!

Ramus was certainly right: the study of Euclid was indeed neglected by the Aristotelians of Paris. But in Italy the study of mathematics had serious consequences for philosophy and for methodology also. For the Aristotelian theory of demonstration was undergoing a searching examination which was to create in the minds of many students a serious doubt as to the applicability of Aristotle's scientific method to mathematics. Although this development was only very indirectly fostered by Humanism, it may, for the sake of convenience, be considered in this chapter.

THE INFLUENCE OF THE NEW INTEREST IN MATHEMATICS UPON THE ARISTOTELIAN THEORY OF SCIENTIFIC DEMONSTRATION

The loss in antiquity of Aristotle's work upon mathematics deprived the Peripatetic tradition of a text upon which to base lectures on the philosophy of mathematics. This fact, coupled with the lack of commentators on the *Posterior Analytics* who were also competent geometers, meant that Aristotle's theory of scientific demonstration, in the medieval schools, was somewhat divorced from the mathematical sciences that had inspired it. True, there were Scholastics such as Roger Bacon who deplored this state of affairs, but their comments amount to little more than wistful recognition of the desirability of improvement.

The professionalization of mathematical teaching and the recovery of Greek mathematical texts, on the other hand, exerted a considerable and immediate influence on the interpretations of Aristotle's views concerning the method of demonstration. The most earnest students of Aristotle's *Posterior Analytics* had long felt themselves handicapped by too little familiarity with Euclid, and this feeling was readily exploited by editors of the mathematical works of the Greeks. Many sixteenth-century editions of these works are prefaced by the solemn warning that unless the student be acquainted with geometry, Aristotle's theory of scientific demonstration must remain unintelligible. One could interpret such strictures as special pleading designed by the editors to induce Aristotelians or other students to buy their goods—as is certainly the case when great benefits are promised to the student of law from his study of geometry. Yet students in other faculties could be so addressed with greater plausibility. Medical practitioners, for instance, had long been closely associated with the study of mathematics,[31] chiefly in connection with the cultivation of "useful" astrological lore. Mathematical ability was considered, in theory at least, to be a *sine qua non* for the successful pursuit of the healing art. Galen was frequently quoted on the usefulness of a knowledge of geometry in medical practice, and his advice was enthusiastically repeated by editors anxious to gain a wide audience for their editions of Euclid.

There were some ancient writers who dealt with the subject of mathematical demonstration from a philosophical point of view —notably Proclus, whose analysis of scientific demonstration is fundamentally Aristotelian, in spite of his generally Platonistic orientation. Proclus' commentaries on the first book of Euclid furnished the Renaissance with a mine of information on the historical development of geometry and mathematics in antiquity as well as considerable food for philosophical thought. They were the basis for a course given by Francesco Barozzi (fl. 1550-90) at Padua in 1560.[32] Although Proclus' commentaries[33] could

[31] See the lengthy list of medical men from the period who were also mathematicians, compiled by David Eugene Smith, "Medicine and Mathematics in the Sixteenth Century," *Annals of Medical History* (Summer, 1917), pp. 125-40.

[32] Barocius also translated the work into Latin: *Procli Diadochi Lycii philosophi Platonici ac mathematici probatissimi in primum Euclidis Elementorum librum commentariorum ad universam mathematicam disciplinam principium eruditionis tradentium libri IIII* (Padua, 1560).

[33] The fact that a great deal of historical information about Greek mathematics can be found in Proclus' commentaries, and also some serious analysis of geometry and its methods of proof, should impose limitations on the wide acceptance that Edward Strong's otherwise trenchant attack on Renaissance Platonism, *Procedures and Metaphysics* (Berkeley, 1936), has gained. In this work, which is primarily a

undoubtedly inspire speculation on the mystical properties of numbers, they contained also a wealth of observation on the nature of mathematical demonstration and exercised a very appreciable influence on mathematical writers of the late Renaissance.

In the minds of scholars and mathematicians of the Renaissance, Plato was the champion of mathematical study. Almost every writer who discussed geometry and demonstration managed to refer at one time or another to the "inscription on Plato's door": "Let no one unskilled in geometry enter." This curious fragment, repeated so often that even unwary modern students take it to be genuine, is actually a very late anecdote: it can be found in the commentary of Philoponus (sixth century A.D.) on the *De anima*, and in several other sources even farther away in time from Plato.[34] Yet in the sense that Platonists had been actively interested in methods drawn from geometry, this scholarly belief in the Platonic endorsement of mathematical study was quite justified. Almost all of the entries concerning geometric analysis in the commentaries find their way, as we have

---

campaign against Edwin A. Burtt's *The Metaphysical Foundations of Modern Physical Science* (London, 1925), Strong examined what he called the "metamathematics" of the Platonic-Pythagorean tradition, carefully avoiding all but the most mystical and fantastic speculations to be found in Nicomachus, Theon, and Proclus —with the result that the prestige of Renaissance Platonism suffered a severe setback: it became, in the eyes of Strong's readers, a form of primitive superstition not much superior to voodoo. Yet Proclus' commentary on Euclid contains much sober reflection on the role of axioms and postulates in geometry, and "metamathematics" of this sort was widely discussed during the Renaissance and later by men who were actively engaged in the extension of mathematical knowledge, as for example, Sir Isaac Barrow. Granted that Proclus derives most of this sober reflection from the Aristotelian tradition and from the Stoic Geminus (see Karl Tittel, *De Gemini Stoici studiis mathematicis quaestiones philologiae* [Leipzig, 1895]), still it seems somewhat unfair to condemn him for passing on mystical Pythagorean doctrines and yet not balance the ledger by giving him credit for more valuable contributions.

Actually, the metamathematics of the period (in other words, the prevailing theory of mathematical proof and scientific demonstration), which was basically Aristotelian, is hardly touched upon in Strong's study. Girolamo Cardano's treatise on dialectic, in which he struggles to reconcile Euclidean methods of proof with Aristotle's theory of scientific demonstration, is not mentioned, for example.

[34] The reference in Philoponus may be found in CAG, XV, 117. A similar reference is in Elias' commentary on the *Categories*, CAG, XVIII[1], 118. A Byzantine writer, Tzetzes, of the twelfth century, wrote a verse incorporating this supposedly Platonic inscription: see his *Variarum historiarum liber . . .* (Basel, [1546]), p. 161.

said, by means of one of the four "dialectical methods of Plato."
Hence it was quite in keeping for Commandino, in his edition
of Euclid, to praise that writer for having known how to use
these four dialectical methods in his *Elements*.[35]

The chief philosophical issue raised by the revival of mathematical studies, however, was whether the actual procedure of
geometers in proving theorems and solving problems could be
reconciled with Aristotle's description of a demonstrated science.
The central difficulty faced by those who thought it could be so
reconciled was the role of the syllogism. If the syllogism as Aristotle had developed it was the instrument par excellence of science, how was one to explain the fact that the proofs of Euclid
are not sequences of syllogisms but "linear proofs," to use the
ancient phrase? Aristotle's *Posterior Analytics* is clearly not an
Axiomatik in the modern sense,[36] yet Renaissance scholars were
eager to torture it into one.

A gallant but hopeless attempt to salvage Aristotle's theory as
Axiomatik was made by a few loyal mathematicians. Conrad
Dasypodius, who was teaching mathematics at Strasbourg from
1562, attempted to cast the proofs of Euclid (or rather, as he
thought, those appended to Euclid's theorems by Theon) into
syllogistic form.[37] If any of his brighter pupils followed this

---

[35] "In hac igitur elementari institutione Euclidem quis non summopere admiretur
propter ordinem et electionem eorum quae per elementa distribuit theorematum
atque problematum? Non enim omnia assumpsit, quae poterat dicere, sed ea duntaxat
quae elementari tradere potuit ordine. Adhuc autem varios syllogismorum modos
usurpavit, alios quidem a causis fidem accipientes, alios vero a signis profectos,
omnes necessarios et certos atque ad scientiam accommodatos [this much by way
of salute to the Aristotelian theory of demonstration], omnes praeterea dialecticas
vias ac rationes: Dividentem in formarum inventionibus, Diffinientem in essen-
tialibus rationibus, Demonstrantem vero in professibus, qui a principiis ad quaesita
fiunt. Denique Resolventem in iis qui a quaesitis ad principia fiunt regressibus."
Euclides Elementorum libri XV . . . , ed. Fredericus Commandinus (Pesaro, 1577),
prolegomena. The same defense of mathematics as exemplifying the four Platonic
methods of dialectic may be found in Proclus (Leipzig, 1873), pp. 42-43 and p. 69.
Commandinus may well have taken his ideas from Proclus.

[36] Heinrich Scholz, "Die Axiomatik der Alten," *Blätter für deutsche Philosophie,*
IV (1930-31), 259-78. Scholz points out that Aristotle's theory deals not with the
properties of an axiom system but with "die Lehre von den Bestandteilen einer
strengen, d.i. am Paradigma der Mathematik orientierten Wissenschaft."

[37] Dasypodius undertook this dreary task with the aid of a colleague named
Christian Herlinus (died 1562), also a teacher of mathematics. The result was

attempt carefully enough, Dasypodius may have defeated his
own purpose, for it is hard to see what possible benefit could
come to either mathematician or theoretician of science from this
trivial confrontation of geometry and the *Posterior Analytics*.
Christopher Clavius (1537-1612), the great Jesuit mathematician,
also started out to present Euclid in syllogistic form, but soon
gave up the attempt as useless.[38]

Nevertheless, the examination of Aristotelian principles of
demonstration by their application to Euclidean geometry offered
possibilities of a better understanding of Aristotle's thought than,
say, examples taken from physics, and could lead to constructive
criticism of his theory of scientific demonstration. Such examination had been undertaken in antiquity by the learned and
polymath Alexandrian commentators on Aristotle. These writers
were receiving increasing attention from scholars during the Renaissance, especially in Italy, and from them new insight into the
relations between Aristotle and geometry was gained. One finds
increasing use of geometrical examples in Aristotelian commentaries of the sixteenth century,[39] a trend that was definitely en-
couraged by the reading of these Greek writers who lived after
Euclid and hence possessed the elements of geometry as we
know them.

Strangely enough, the mathematicians apparently entertained
a greater respect for Aristotle as a theoretician of mathematics
than did Peripatetic logicians. At Padua in the middle of the
century, there was a standing dispute as to whether geometrical
proofs conformed to Aristotle's requirements of an ideal science

---

entitled *Analyseis geometricae sex librorum Euclidis* ... (n.p., 1566). See Moritz
Cantor, *Vorlesungen über Geschichte der Mathematik* (Leipzig, 1892), II, 510.

[38] Christophorus Clavius, *Euclidis Elementorum libri XV* (Rome, 1574). After
giving a syllogistic analysis of the first problem in Euclid, Clavius says: "Non aliter
resolve poterunt omnes aliae propositiones non solum Euclidis, verum etiam caete-
rorum Mathematicorum." He then adds: "Negligunt tamen Mathematici resolutionem istam in suis demonstrationibus, eo quod brevius ac facilius sine ea demon-
strent id quod proponitur, ut perspicuum esse potest ex superiori demonstratione"
(ff. 22ʳ-22ᵛ).

[39] A teacher at Padua, Petrus Catena (1501-77), compiled a work giving the
references to mathematics in Aristotle in considerable detail: *Universa loca in logicam
Aristotelis in mathematicas disciplinas hoc novum opus declarat* (Venice, 1556).

at all. A very strong current of opinion, represented by Alessandro Piccolomini (1508-78), held that "most powerful demonstrations" as outlined by Aristotle are not to be found in mathematics.[40] Barozzi upheld the converse and answered Piccolomini's arguments one by one in his work on the certitude of mathematics.[41]

The opinion that mathematics did not fulfill Aristotle's requirements for a valid science was voiced also by a Portuguese Jesuit, Benedictus Pererius (1535-1610)—"no mean Peripatetic," as Sir Isaac Barrow was to call him. His view[42] was widely quoted. The Englishman John Case (died 1600), who thought that examples of demonstration should come from mathematics, yet conceded that there was room for controversy as to whether they conformed to strict Aristotelian requirements or not.[43]

The traditional view itself was indeed not free from ambiguity. Are mathematical "middles" causal? Must the property which is the causal middle be a part of the definitions of the subject of demonstration or of its passion? The questions raised by such

[40] *Alexandri Piccolominei . . . Commentarium de certitudine mathematicarum disciplinarum, in quo de resolutione, diffinitione, et demonstratione, necnon de materia, et in fine logicae facultatis quamplura continentur, ad rem ipsam, tum mathematicam, tum logicam, maxime pertinentia* (Venice, 1565). This book was first published in Rome, 1547.

[41] Barozzi's reply is to be found in *Francisci Barocii Patritii Veneti Opusculum, in quo una oratio, et duae quaestiones, altera de certitudine et altera de medietate mathematicarum continentur* (Padua, 1560). This work of Barozzi shows the extent to which he relied on Proclus and the Greek commentators.

[42] This strangely authoritative opinion was given in a work on physics: Benedictus Pererius, *De communibus omnium rerum naturalium principiis et affectionibus, libri quindecim* (Cologne, 1595): "Multorum est opinio, illud genus demonstrationis potissime, quod traditur in I. *Posteriorum* aut nusquam aut certe in disciplinis mathematicis potissimum inveniri" (p. 119). Pererius dismisses this view: "Caeterum licet haec opinio sit pervulgata et a multis recepta, mihi tamen nullo modo probari potest: censeo enim demonstrationem potissimam quae depingitur ab Aristotele I. *Posteriorum* aut nullo modo, aut vix reperiri in scientiis mathematicis" (p. 120).

[43] " Res plane trivialis, ac nullius fere momenti quibusdam videtur, in quaestionem vocare, an Mathematici veris demonstrationibus perpetuo utantur: hoc (inquiunt) nihil aliud est, quam dubitare, an ullae Mathematicae sint scientiae. Horum pace id dicam, rem nullam vel incertius moveri, vel spinosius tractari in hac arte ab interpretibus: nam etsi exempla Aristotelis plerunque earum artium fluunt, etsi conclusiones firmissimae et perspicua praecepta inde colliguntur, non est tamen res tam extra omnem aleam litis et controversiae, quin possit lancibus rationis subtilius ponderari." John Case, *Summa veterum interpretum . . .* (London, 1584), pp. 193-94.

considerations are complex and require for their solution extensive scholarship and mathematical sophistication. It was not until the next century that a man like Isaac Barrow could combine these merits and produce a consistent and plausible interpretation of Aristotle—but by this time Aristotle's analysis had given way to that of Descartes. The Cartesian analysis, which, in its influence, acted more as a psychological guide to research than an objective *Axiomatik*, had then swept the field, and students were no longer interested in saving Aristotle. What is more, the actual course of mathematical research during this period had already begun to take a different turn: the stern spirit of rigorous proof epitomized in the *Elements* of Euclid gave way to the free play of mathematical imagination.[44] It was not until the nineteenth century that rigor—and a much more sophisticated rigor—again attracted mathematical minds.

HUMANISTIC METHOD IN FACULTIES OTHER THAN THE ARTS

As Humanists or Humanistically trained scholars began to infiltrate the faculties of medicine, law, and theology toward the end of the fifteenth and the beginning of the sixteenth century, they took with them the new ideas of educational method which had developed in relation to lower studies. The pattern of study in all these fields was roughly the same: a standard text (Roman law in civil law, the Bible and Church Fathers in theology, Galen and Hippocrates in medicine), with an accumulation of centuries of glosses, commentaries, and selections—the whole to be mastered in each case by means of *lectiones* and *disputationes*.

---

[44] "While Greek geometry retained an important place, the Greek ideal of axiomatic crystallization and systematic deduction disappeared in the seventeenth and eighteenth centuries. Logically precise reasoning starting from clear definitions and non-contradictory, 'evident' axioms, seemed immaterial to the new pioneers of mathematical science. In a veritable orgy of intuitive guesswork, of cogent reasoning interwoven with nonsensical mysticism, with a blind confidence in the superhuman power of formal procedure, they conquered a mathematical world of immense riches. Gradually the ecstasy of progress gave way to a spirit of critical self-control." Richard Courant and Herbert Robbins, *What Is Mathematics?* (Oxford, 1941), p. xvi.

Therefore it was possible for the Humanists to advance similar criticisms in respect to teaching in each of these subjects. Bulky commentaries were condemned for their barbarous Latinity, and the student was sent to the sources in their original Greek, Latin, or Hebrew. With printed editions plentiful, slow and painful readings for dictation could be dispensed with. Disputations, the Humanists maintained, could be reduced to a minimum, and the time thus gained devoted to the reading of classical authors in the field.

Besides these obvious and well-known features of the Humanists' attack, there were more fundamental ones, to examine which would lead us from explicit discussions of method into the implicit application of methods of study and thinking. In each field, for instance, there was a standard system of thought to be saved from contradiction when it threatened, generally by the technique of making distinctions far down the line of development. This way of avoiding embarrassing contradictions had been pursued to the point of diminishing returns by the Schoolmen, and its usefulness had almost completely disappeared. The alternative way out of these difficulties—that of revamping the first principles—was one that became more obvious during the Renaissance. As scholars gained an increasingly intimate knowledge of the philosophical sects of ancient Greece, the possibility that philosophical systems might have wholly different basic assumptions and principles became more and more apparent. This opened the door to the possibility of replacing or reconstructing the first principles within other fields as well. But these questions are much more fundamental than the ones explicitly dealt with by Renaissance writers, and we must leave their consideration to the student of seventeenth-century thought—that period in which first principles were to be so thoroughly challenged.

THE RISE OF LEGAL METHODOLOGY

Some works on the method of studying law were written during the Middle Ages, chiefly in Italy. We have an amusing little letter[45] full of advice to prospective law students, written in the thirteenth century by Martinus de Fano. Several fifteenth-century works on the "mode of studying" law were frequently reprinted in the sixteenth, such as the *De modo studendi et vita doctorum* of Johannes Baptista de Caccialupis (born c.1420), or the *De modo studendi in utroque jure* of Johannes Jacobus Canis (died 1490), professor of law at Padua, where his treatise was published in 1476. By the sixteenth century, treatises of this genre[46] were beginning to be called "methods" of studying law, thus bringing their terminology up to date.

In the tremendously complex study of law as it was carried on at the time, these guides to study were no doubt of some service. Yet it was not long before the whole method of the glossators upon which this study was based was to be challenged by the Humanists. Early Humanists manifested considerable enmity toward the jurists of the day, an enmity not altogether free from professional jealousy, for professors of law were usually the best-paid and most-sought-after teachers on the medieval scene. Some scathing criticisms of the study of law were made by Lorenzo Valla (1406-57) and by a German Humanist, Heinrich Bebel (1472-c.1516), who had studied law in his youth but subsequently felt the attraction of the classics and turned to the teaching of Humanities at Tübingen. It was not long, however, before this purely destructive criticism began to give way to what might be called a Humanist method of legal interpretation in a movement led by Angelo Poliziano (1454-94), Ulrich Zasius (1461-1535), Guillaume Budé (1467-1540), and, most famous of all, Andrea Alciati (1492-1550). These writers advocated and practiced a philological approach to the study of the sources of law; their method was known as the *mos Gallicus* because it became the vogue in French law schools. The traditional system

---

[45] This work has been published by Lodovico Frati, "L'epistola *De regimine et modo studendi* di Martino da Fano," *Studi e memorie per la storia dell' Università di Bologna,* VI (1921), 21-29.

[46] An Italian exile named Matthaeus Gribaldus (c. 1500-1564) wrote such a treatise, to which he gave the title *De methodo ac ratione studendi libri tres* (Lyons, 1541).

inherited from the glossators received, in the sixteenth century, the name *mos Italicus*, in order to distinguish it from its new rival.[47]

The treatise of Gribaldus[48] bearing the "modern" title *De methodo ac ratione studendi* was, actually, a defense of the traditional *mos Italicus*. It illustrates the complexity of the exegetic approach of the glossators and gives some indication of why the study of law required so many years to complete. The assembling of authoritative legal opinions, which began to be known as *loci communes* during this period, played a not inconsiderable part in this process.[49]

The Humanist philological and historical examination of the sources of law entered into lively competition with this highly ritualized and elaborate medieval method, producing incidentally a split between theoretical and practical jurisprudence, for philological competence did not necessarily equip a lawyer to handle everyday cases. According to Stintzing, however,

the issue between the *mos Gallicus* and the *mos Italicus* was not based on external mechanical questions alone, for the exegetic methods of traditional legal study could quite easily have been reconciled with the requirements of the Humanists, namely, that scientific work in law proceed by means of better Latin; that it handle the authorities with greater independence of judgment; and that it moderate its dialectical subtleties and make greater application of antiquarian learning.[50]

What actually precipitated the most lively discussion of method in legal circles was not this opposition of teaching methods but the question as to whether it was possible to complete Cicero's

---

[47] In the following account I have drawn upon Roderick von Stintzing's *Geschichte der deutschen Rechtswissenschaft* (Munich and Leipzig, 1880-84), esp. Chap. 3 on Humanism and Reformation, and Chap. 4 on scientific methods up to the seventeenth century. Stintzing undertook to carry on the history of Savigny, which is sketchy and bibliographic in its treatment of the later period.

[48] See footnote 46.

[49] Stintzing attributes the importance of these legal florilegia, which correspond to the *Sentences* of Peter the Lombard in the study of theology, to the necessity for some mnemonic aid in mastering such an unsystematic mass as medieval law had become. *Geschichte*, pp. 114-18.

[50] Stintzing, *Geschichte*, p. 139 (my translation).

project, announced in the *De Oratore*,[51] of reducing law to an art. This question directed the attention of jurists to the fundamentally unsystematic character of their discipline and stimulated a reexamination of the body of law. The question as to whether law as then known constituted an art according to Cicero's criteria naturally aroused great interest in Humanist legal circles, for Cicero was the prince of Latin eloquence; moreover, the rediscovery of this work of his in 1422 had been a Humanist triumph.

Once the Ciceronian ideal of reducing civil law to an art had been clearly grasped, there arose a dispute as to whether such a project were feasible, or indeed whether it had not already been achieved in the *Digests* of Justinian. The order of the *Pandects* and the *Codex* was examined from this methodical standpoint: if it were found wanting in systematic arrangement, the further question arose whether it was not justified, indeed required, to present the civil law in another order. Thus arose the great controversary over *Method* which occupied the younger jurists of the sixteenth century.[52]

The task of the legal methodologist during this period was not clearly defined: the needs of scientific research and of the school were not sharply separated. In general, the requirements of school instruction predominated. Christopher Hegendorf (1500-1540), who taught both law and literature in German universities,

---

[51] Cicero's program for reducing law to an art was described in the *De Oratore*, I, 42; it is referred to by Aulus Gellius, *Noctes Atticae*, I, 22. The *De Oratore* is of considerable interest. Cicero has remarked that the subject matters of all the other arts (music, geometry, astrology, grammar, and dialectic) had once been scattered and dispersed until ordered by "art." There is need of some art from another field which would "glue together" matters disconnected and broken up, and which would bind them together *by a fixed procedure:* "Adhibita est igitur ars quaedam extrinsecus ex alio genere quodam, quod sibi totum philosophi adsumunt, quae rem dissolutam divolsamque conglutinaret et *ratione quadam* constringeret." The method which Cicero then proposes (he would have produced such an art himself if granted sufficient leisure) certainly reflects the methodology of his time, most probably as it was discussed in the Academy. First, the end of the art must be established, then the method of division applied and certain genera and species defined within the purpose of the art. Then, Cicero says, you will have a perfect art of civil law, great and fruitful rather than difficult and obscure.
[52] Stintzing, *Geschichte*, pp. 140-41. "Es war die Frage nach der '*Methodus*,' wie man die systematische Darstellung zu nennen pflegte. Wie lebhaft diese Frage seit dem zweiten Jahrzehnt des 16. Jahrhunderts die jüngeren Juristen beschäftigte, zeigen uns ihre Briefe."

complained[53] of the fact that students in the other higher faculties could avail themselves of curricula and plans, but not the law student.

The existence of huge and unusable legal commentaries was attributed, in typical Humanist fashion, to lack of proper instruction in Latin speech on the part of the commentators. It would seem a rather unfair accusation, since some of the products of Humanist legal scholarship, such as Budé's 'Annotations on the Pandects,' although no doubt written in better Latin, are quite as bulky as the medieval commentaries. But such criticism maintained that faulty grammar gave rise to ambiguities that had to be cleared up by the commentaries. Such was the position of Franciscus Duarenus (1509-59), teacher of law at Bourges and disciple of Alciati.[54] Duarenus also accuses the law professors of his time of being ignorant of the method and art of teaching, which, together with propriety of speech, is a prerequisite of sound teaching. In the application of the law to single cases, one has need of practice (*usus*), just, as, conversely, without way and method, experience is useless: both practice and method are essential.[55] Duarenus attacks those who think they can acquire

---

[53] See Hegendorf's letter "De compendiaria discendi iura civilia ratione," reprinted in the appendix to a work entitled *Methodica iuris utriusque traditio* ... (Lyons, 1562), pp. 998-1008. This appendix contains a number of legal works on method. Hegendorf's correspondent had been complaining of the lack of a planned curriculum in law, and Hegendorf endorses his complaint: "Nam alios ad Theologiam animum adiicere, alios medicinae studio se tradere, tertios iurisprudentiae nomen dare. Verum hoc tibi displicere aiebas, quod cum tam theologiae quam medicinae studiosis multae adeo, et certae professionem utranque feliciter auspicandae viae a doctissimis quibusque et Theologis et Medicis praescriptae sint, nullus inter Iurisconsultos nostri seculi certam iura civilia ingrediundi methodum iuventuti praemonstraret" (p. 998). Hegendorf, of course, intends to fill this gap. Hegendorf was the author of a work on legal dialectic for the use of young men destined for the law, which he says is going to supplement the treatises of *loci* which do not deal with dialectic in general: *Dialecticae legalis libri quinque.* (Antwerp, 1534).

[54] See Duarenus' letter in the above-mentioned *Methodica iuris utriusque traditio*, pp. 1008-23. After complaining of the lack of proper instruction in Latin, he continues: "Caeterum ista corrupte loquendi ac scribendi consuetudo quos errores quasque contentiones pariat, tam facile mihi esset hic demonstrare, quam liquido confirmare possum, ingentem illam commentariorum molem, qua totum pene ius obrutum est, magna ex parte ex subtilibus et otiosis altercationibus, quas puri sermonis contemptus et ignoratio peperit, natam esse" (pp. 1011-12).

[55] "Sed quia instituti nostri ratio fusius haec disseri non patitur, ad reliqua iuris

facility in law by amassing a huge library of law books, while neglecting method, and illustrates the danger in this by a story from Galen concerning a medical practitioner who lost his books and hence his skill at compounding drugs, and so died of the plague.[56]

Both the criticism of the existing law from the standpoint of its unsystematic nature and the criticism of existing instruction in law thus owe something to the Humanists. To them also we can indirectly trace the compilation of compendia and collections of commonplaces of law, which here as in other fields smoothed the transition from medieval commentaries to modern systematic treatises.[57]

DISCUSSIONS OF METHODOLOGY IN THE MEDICAL SCHOOLS

Students and teachers of medicine in the universities of Europe had been debating the subject of method for centuries, for two of the standard authorities in medicine, Galen and Averroes, were logicians as well as medical men, and their writings are full of problems in logic and method which the conscientious student

professorum vitia atque errata iam nostra festinat oratio, in quibus illud non minimum est, quod methodus, et ars docendi non minus quam sermonis proprietas apud eos contempta iacet, licet utraque res ad docendum aeque sit necessaria. Nam ut praeclare inquit Cicero, non solum aliquid scire artis est, sed est quaedam ars etiam docendi, in qua Servium Sulpitium valde exercitatum fuisse, ideoque caeteris excelluisse Iurisconsultis, idem autor est. Fieri enim non potest, ut sine ea methodo, quam Aristoteles, Galenus, et alii eruditissimi viri docuerunt, quaque in scriptis suis nunquam non usi sunt, quicquam recte doceatur. At in istorum doctrina, Dii boni, quam confusanea, et (ut vere dicam) monstrosa sunt omnia. Miscentur et confunduntur, quae oportebat, secerni, et quae natura coniungi postulat, seiunguntur ac distrahuntur, etc." *Ibid.,* p. 1012.

[56] "Verum ut certius atque expeditius boni et aequi artem ad negotia singula accommodare queamus, adhibendus est usus, sine quo disciplinae fructus omnis perit: ut vice versa absque methodo et via minimum valet: alterius sic altera poscit opem res et coniurat amice. Iis igitur qui ad perfectionem huius artis consequendam acervum ingentem librorum sibi parant, periculum est, ne idem quod illi medico eveniat, quem Galenus scribit, cum nullam unquam methodum componendorum pharmacorum didicisset, amissis libris, quibus multae huius modi compositiones descriptae erant, tabe confectum periisse." *Ibid.,* p. 1019.

[57] It should be mentioned that Ramism later had some influence upon this legal methodology; but in Stintzing's opinion, the concern with method in law antedated this influence of Ramus, at least in Germany. See his *Geschichte,* p. 148.

felt he had to master. Medical students received from their training in the arts a grounding in Aristotelian philosophy before entering upon their medical studies, or they made its acquaintance during their medical studies. Hence they were already thoroughly familiar with the *Posterior Analytics*. To the Aristotelian "methodology" and to their reading of Galen, there must be added a third influence, that of the mathematical sciences. We have already had occasion to note the popularity of mathematical studies among medical men in the Renaissance. To these studies they owed an acquaintance with the geometrical methods described by Euclid and Pappus, and also some knowledge of Ptolemy's views on epistemology.[58] In addition, it was not at all unusual for scholars to move from the teaching of philosophy or logic to that of medicine or mathematics, and this ease of academic locomotion accounts for the similarity of discussion of method in these three fields. It also helps account for Galen's tremendous influence even with nonmedical writers.

As heirs of three methodological traditions, then, medical men were in the forefront of the methodological controversies of the day. Almost to a man, medical teachers were champions of the strict Aristotelian theory of science as explicated by Galen. It is chiefly from their ranks that the Aristotelian defense against the Humanist innovations in logic and method came. There occurred no split among these medical teachers comparable to that which developed between Humanist and traditionalist teachers of law.

Most of the controversy over method in medicine turned upon the interpretation of the opening passage of Galen's *Ars parva*.[59] As a required text in medical schools, this little compendium of the medical art had been the object of countless commentaries, mostly the by-product of lectures given by teachers in medical schools. The preface to Galen's work became perhaps one of the

[58] Girolamo Cardano (1501-76) was representative of the medico-mathematical trend of his time. He lists five authorities for the practice of dialectic in his treatise "Dialectica": "Haec autem ex his accipere convenit auctoribus, quos maxime in huiusmodi praestitisse animadvertimus, quorum primus est Aristoteles, secundus Hippocrates, tertius Galenus, quartus Euclides, quintus Ptolemaeus." Hieronymus Cardanus, *Opera omnia* (10 vols., Lyons, 1663), I, 293.
[59] See pp. 16-22 and 45-46.

most controversial passages in the entire medical and even philosophical corpus, with the possible exception of the "active intellect" passage in Aristotle's *De anima*. The very first sentence presented an exegetic problem for commentators and often resulted in an excursion into general methodology, supplemented by the *Posterior Analytics* and by whatever other traditions the commentator happened to be familiar with. The Arab commentators on Galen had identified the three "orderly teaching doctrines" mentioned in the first sentence with Aristotle's theory of demonstration,[60] to the complete confusion of the original sense of the passage, which is obscure enough in the Greek, reflecting as it does the eclectic methodology—Platonic, Aristotelian, and Stoic—of Galen's time. Galen's philosophical and medical reputation reached its highest point in the sixteenth century, when at least a dozen editions of his complete works were published, as well as numerous commentaries on single works. The *Ars parva* alone received at least thirty commentaries dedicated exclusively to it during the century,[61] while consideration of Galen's views on the three ordered ways of teaching, popularly but incorrectly known as the three "methods" of Galen, may be found in virtually every philosophical discussion of order and method in the arts and sciences from that period.

The greatest development of doctrine on method took place in the schools of northern Italy, especially in Padua and Bologna. A number of medical teachers who commented upon Galen and other medical writers became so well known that they received nicknames—the "Conciliator" (Petrus de Abano, died 1316), the "Plusquam Commentator" (Torrigiano, or Drusianus, 1270-

---

[60] See John H. Randall, Jr., "The Development of Scientific Method in the School of Padua," JHI, I (1940), 177-206, for the history and details of this development.

[61] Justus Niedling, *Die mittelalterlichen and frühneuzeitlichen Kommentare zur Techne des Galenos* (Paderborn, 1924), contains a list of commentators on the work from the time of Honein ben Ishaq to the sixteenth century. The sixteenth-century commentators comprise scholars from all of Europe, including Spain and Portugal.

For the place of Galen's *Ars parva* in the medical curriculum, see Donald Campbell, "The Medical Curriculum of the Universities of Europe in the Sixteenth Century, with Special Reference to the Arabist Tradition," *Science, Medicine, and History: Essays on the Evolution of Scientific Thought and Medical Practice* (2 vols., Oxford, 1953), I, 357-67. (The volumes are dedicated to Charles Singer.)

c. 1350), and so on. These teachers, whose doctrines developed chiefly out of their commentaries on the *Ars parva* of Galen, have been explored in a pioneer study by John H. Randall, Jr. The main sources of their thought were Aristotle, Galen, the Arab Haly Abbas (tenth century A.D.), and Averroes, whose views they combined in various ways to produce theories of demonstration or of teaching. Knowing how complex the methodological tradition is, we must look carefully at this branch of it in order to determine just when usage otherwise apparently unfamiliar and not native to Italians began to develop there. The earliest writer discussed by Randall, the above-mentioned Petrus de Abano, does not speak of Galen's "methods" at all: he refers to Galen's way of teaching as *ordinatae doctrinae*. Nor does Hugo of Siena (1376-1439), who has recently received a thorough biographical and historical study,[62] speak of "method," if we may safely judge from the excerpts of his writings published.

Thus at the start of the fifteenth century, although methodology of a fairly complex sort was being discussed by these medical theoreticians of science, *methodus* had not yet become a technical term. It may be supposed that the earlier translations of Galen (those of Constantine the African, who died in 1087) did not use the term, and that only when the word had become established much later in newer translations of Galen directly from the Greek, in the sixteenth or perhaps even in the late fifteenth century, did Galen's three ways of teaching come to be known as the "three methods of Galen." At any rate, by the middle of the century, these "three methods" were famous: they were discussed and argued and debated over not merely in medical lectures and treatises but in general discussions of method by logicians as well. Naturally the fact that (1) Galen did not discuss μέϑοδος in the passage usually cited (the beginning of the *Ars parva*) but (2) did use the word, in a number of other senses, in other works

---

[62] Dean Putnam Lockwood, *Ugo Benzi, Medieval Philosopher and Physician, 1376-1439* (Chicago, 1951), pp. 39-40. In Appendix 7, entitled "Ugo's Theories on scientific method—further elucidations," Lockwood presents the only supplementary material to be uncovered since Randall's initial study of this methodological tradition.

raised great difficulties for those methodologists who wished to develop their doctrines in faithful reliance upon Galen. Humanistically trained teachers of medicine untangled some of the confusion, at the expense of reducing Galen from a theoretician of science to a theoretician of medical education (which of course he was as well). Such difficulties of interpretation explain why it became necessary in the late Renaissance for loyal yet honest Aristotelians such as Zabarella to strike out on their own and develop a doctrine which, although obviously not Aristotle's, could easily have been.

LEONICENO: HUMANIST EXEGESIS OF GALEN

Since the discussion of Galen was predominantly an exegetic one, Humanist scholarship could and did have a considerable part to play in it. The influence of Humanism upon this medical methodology may be seen in the writings of Niccolò Leoniceno (1428-1524), who, although young enough to be a contemporary and friend of Pico and Poliziano, lived into the sixteenth century in his old age. Leoniceno taught medicine and Greek philosophy for many years at the University of Ferrara. His initial schooling was acquired from the well-known Humanist teacher and student of Vittorino, Ognibene, under whom he made remarkable progress in Greek and Latin. It is to his precocious and conspicuous skill in these languages [63] that Leoniceno owed his great fame as a scholar and expositor of Galen and Hippocrates.

In his treatise on Galen's three ordered ways of teaching, [64] Leoniceno sweeps away the confusion that had been caused by the correlation of Galen's "way of teaching in order" (διδασκαλίαι

---

[63] See the remarkable tributes of Scaliger and Erasmus quoted by Domenico Vitaliani, *Della vita e delle opere di Nicolò Leoniceno Vicentino* (Verona, 1892), pp. 200-1, especially that of Scaliger: "Primus [Leonicenus] philosophiam et medicinam ipsam cum humanioribus litteris coniunxit: primus nos docuit, homines qui sine bonis litteris medicinam tractant esse similes iis qui in alieno foro litigant."

[64] "Nicolai Leoniceni de tribus doctrinis ordinatis secundum Galeni sententiam," which occupies ff. 13ʳ-24ᵛ in a volume of treatises whose title begins, *Nicolai Leoniceni in libros Galeni greca in latinam linguam a se translatos prefatio communis . . .* [Venice, 1508].

τάξεως ἐχόμεναι) with various forms of Aristotelian demonstration and with the four methods (*modi*) of Platonic dialectic. These "modes" of teaching had been introduced into the text of the *Ars parva*, he maintains, only by neglecting the stress Galen put on the phrase "in order" (τάξεως ἐχόμεναι). This allowed the commentators to launch into general treatments of demonstration and dialectic, whereas Galen had been talking just about ordered procedures in teaching. The Latin commentators on Galen all agree that the resolutive manner of teaching mentioned in the introduction to the *Ars parva* is a form of demonstration. Yet the Greek commentators distinguish explicitly between the resolutive method and demonstration or the other methods.[65] Leoniceno takes his stand with the Greeks on this point and holds as a result that the *four* modes of teaching of the Greek commentators cannot possibly be identified with Galen's *three* ways of teaching in order.[66] The three orders Galen speaks of differ not in respect to certitude, as do the modes of dialectic, but only in respect to their suitability for certain teaching purposes: the third order, for example, is useful for teaching a whole art *sub compendio*, being easily committed to memory.[67]

[65] Leoniceno reviews the four dialectical methods as found in Platonically influenced Greek writers and commentators, including Ammonius, Philoponus, Joannes Damascenus, Alexander of Aphrodisias, "Alcinous," and Proclus—an impressive and scholarly survey. Having passed their respective doctrines in review, he continues: "Haec sunt quae graeci auctores non minus Platonicae quam Aristotelicae sectae familiares de quattuor doctrinarum modis et variis resolutionum significatis concordi fere sententia scripsere. Illud autem in eorum scriptis diligens lector animadvertet omnes eos quos commemoravimus auctores resolutivam doctrinam demonstrativae ac reliquis duabus tanquam ab illis diversam opposuisse. Latini autem expositores Galeni in hoc omnes conveniunt, quod doctrina resolutiva de qua Galenus loquitur in prohemio *Artis parvae* sit doctrina demonstrativa." *Ibid.,* f. 14ᵛ.

[66] "Quod autem tres doctrinae ordinatae non sint docendi modi tali argumento colligitur. Doctrinae ordinariae sive ordines doctrinarum secundum Galenum sunt tantum tres: modi autem doctrinales iuxta antiquos philosophos sunt plures quam tres ad minimum quattuor, ergo modi doctrinales non doctrinae ordinatae de quibus Galenus loquitur. Ordines autem sub quibus unaquaeque scientia doceri potest esse tantummodo tres ita probatur: scientia quae docetur aut eodem ordine docetur quo invenitur et primum in mente constituitur: et hic ordo docendi vocatur 'resolutorius,' vel ordine converso, et hic ordo vocatur 'compositorius'.... Si quis vero diffiniat scientiam quam intendit docere et in docendo sequatur ordinem partium diffinitionis, hic doctrinam facit diffinitivam quam se facturum promittit Galenus in prohemio *Artis parvae. Ibid.,* f. 19ʳ-19ᵛ.

[67] *Ibid.,* f. 21ʳ.

Leoniceno's conclusions were more or less traditional, but the manner in which he reached them was characteristic of the more Humanistic philosophizing of the sixteenth century. He examines Galen's other works and compares the observations on method in them with the *Ars parva* passage; he takes seriously Galen's intention of writing the *Ars parva* itself in the third, or compendious, order. That these "ordered ways" of Galen's were not modes of philosophizing or methods of dialectic but ways of teaching was a point that needed to be emphasized. Leoniceno confessed that "it was not easy to try to abolish from the minds of men accustomed to hearing them the inveterate opinions of those highly regarded in our time, not merely in medicine but in all of philosophy as well." Leoniceno considered that his opinion gave a very easy explication of this question, whereas the manner in which it had been hitherto treated in universities had given rise only to perplexing and unsolvable difficulties.[68]

MANARDI CONTINUES THE HUMANIST EXEGESIS OF GALEN

Much the same sort of linguistic and textual analysis was applied by Leoniceno's successor in the chair of medicine at Ferrara, Giovanni Manardi (1462-1536). Manardi focused on the key word in the opening of the *Ars parva*:

The word "doctrine" has a wide application and signifies different things. Sometimes it expresses the habit of mind by which someone is called learned, as when we say that Hippocrates and Galen were men "of excellent doctrine." Sometimes it means the very act and practice of teaching, which is the meaning Galen uses when he says (in the first book of the *De alimentis*) that the "best doctrine" is that which is carried on *viva voce,* and in the *De optima doctrina,* where he says that "doctrine" consists in making something clear to the intellect, when someone who understands a subject makes it clearly intelligible by reducing himself to the duller understanding of the person (he is teaching). At other times it means method, i.e., a certain way and procedure, by which we can find things that are hidden or can teach others: it is in this sense that the Peripatetics have held that there are "four doctrines"—definitive, divisive,

[68] *Ibid.,* f. 24v.

resolutive, and demonstrative. And Averroes in the preface to the *Physics* explores the kinds of "Aristotelian doctrine." Sometimes it means a mode of writing and transmitting some art, in which last sense Galen takes the word, both in this passage and in his exposition of the first Aphorism [of Hippocrates], where he tells what "doctrine" is aphoristic.[69]

Because they failed to beware of the ambiguity of this term, the commentators have been seriously misled, says Manardi.[70] Galen intends to say in the *Ars parva* passage that there are only three ways in which an art can be taught in an orderly fashion.[71]

TRIVERIUS OF THE MEDICAL FACULTY OF LOUVAIN

The resemblance of Galen's third or compendious way of teaching to the "short art" or what we have called artistic method was not lost upon Manardi's readers. One of them, Jeremias Triverius or Drivere (1504-54), professor of medicine at Louvain, remarked upon the relative poverty and worthlessness of present-day compendia as compared with those of the ancients.

Now Galen also held that the definitive way is more suitable for memory and for brevity (*compendium*): indeed he explained the reason for the one but hid the reason for the other—or rather it is obscure in itself. Therefore we must discriminate all the kinds of prolixity and brevity, for there are many of them. First of all, he who does not understand a subject very well is prolix. For how can he teach briefly if he only knows the subject in a cloudy fashion? Another is when a person knows the subject quite well and has his thoughts on the tip of his tongue but cannot find the words: and so he too is unable to express anything briefly but wanders around aimlessly. Moreover these forms of prolixity and brevity do not arise from the nature of the doctrine itself but from the aptitude of the teacher—or rather his lack of knowledge. Whence it comes about that the Ancients had a twofold short cut over us for the purpose of brevity: a supply of words and a thorough knowledge of things themselves. Far different is the manner of those who write compendia today: they omit the more detailed and all the best problems and breeze through the more general aspects of their subject, already known to all, with a light touch, so that there is neither much art nor much utility to their

[69] Joannes Manardus, *In artem Galeni medicinalem luculenta expositio* ... (Basel, 1529), pp. 101-2.
[70] *Ibid.*, p. 103.   [71] *Ibid.*, p. 113.

work. The fourth mode of brevity is that of those who hurry on to the conclusions of an art but omit the reasons.[72]

Triverius quotes at length from the two previously mentioned writers, but he does not follow them slavishly.

In common with these men [Leoniceno and Manardi] we begin our commentary with the dialectical methods, which are as many in number as there are passages. There are a lot of them, but four stand out: Definition, Division, Demonstration, and Resolution. Now anyone who has some knowledge of dialectical matters knows what Definition, Division, and Demonstration are. There is no general agreement, however, so far as I can see, on Resolution. Some identify it with Division. Others regard it as contrary [to Division], considering that Division divides a genus into species, a whole into parts, whereas Resolution collects a whole out of parts, genus out of species, species out of individuals. And since each one is entitled to his opinion, I am now maintaining that Resolution is contrary to Demonstration. For Resolution proceeds from effect and signs to the cause, Demonstration from cause to effect. From these it seems to me, three modes or orders (for there is no difference) are drawn.[73]

Triverius goes on to identify Galen's three ways of teaching with the first three of the Platonic dialectical methods, those of resolution, demonstration, and definition, respectively. He omitted division, deeming it to be unsuitable for teaching.[74]

Although these three writers by no means exhaust the roster of medical men who composed commentaries on Galen's *Ars parva* and presented version of the famous "three ways of teaching," it should be clear that certain features common to them might also be expected to appear in other writers. It was no longer possible, thanks to Humanist criticism, to correlate in rather arbitrary fashion the "ways of teaching" and the varieties of demonstration, as had been fashionable with medical writers since the Arabs. A much closer concordance of doctrine, and not merely the use of a similar word, must be found to justify such correlation. In short, the influence of Humanism in this medical methodology resembles its influence in other fields: doctrines which purported to rest on authority must be shown by conclusive linguistic and

[72] Jeremias Triverius, *In Texnhn* [sic] *Galeni clarissimi commentarii* (Lyons, 1547), pp. 21-22.
[73] *Ibid.*, p. 14.   [74] *Ibid.*

textual grounds to be supported by a passage in the sources, in the original language. This meant the shifting of philosophical discussion from the presentation and refutation of arguments to the scholarly examination of classical passages. Medieval exposition, which was a mixture of philosophical examination and scholarly quotation, of *ratio* and *auctoritas*, was beginning to yield to a division of labor in which the authorities were left to the scholar and reasoning to the philosopher. Much of what passed as philosophical writing in the late Renaissance was actually already in the first category, that of historical scholarship. In the particular case at hand, that of the interpretation of the first sentence of the *Ars parva*, sixteenth-century scholars were unable to arrive at a clear historical understanding of the puzzling passage—which is not surprising, since it has not received a satisfactory scholarly explication to the present day.

HUMANISM AND THE METHOD OF THEOLOGY

The impact of Humanism upon theology was great: perhaps in no other field was the study of the sources to have such momentous effects for human history. Along with active innovations in the presentation and content of theology there went an explicit discussion of methodology in that subject which, although not as lively as simular discussions in other fields, is still of considerable interest.

When Desiderius Erasmus (1467-1536) wrote a prescription for study in theology, he called it first a *Methodus*, the implication being that his guide would save the time and trouble of candidates in that subject. He called by this name one of the prefatory treatises to his edition of the New Testament, printed at Basel in 1516. Later this section was enlarged and called a *Ratio seu methodus compendio perveniendi ad veram theologiam.*[75] This work, with its modest title, was much more than a course of study for candidates in theology, although its author

---

[75] First printed with this longer title in his edition of the New Testament which was published at Basel, 1519. It was later published separately.

professed only to set forth "a certain method and rationale" of theological study.[76] He realized that even this was a large task but hoped that his remarks would be useful to candidates in divinity, serving not only to keep them from losing their way but also to expedite the passage to knowledge, so that they might arrive more quickly and with less labor at their goal. How completely in the tradition of Humanist pedagogy this work was appears from a comparison of it with other treatises of Erasmus presenting methods in typically Humanist subjects: his *De ratione studii* (1511), *De conscribendis epistolis* (1522), and *De pueris statim ac liberaliter instituendis* (1529). As a treatise on pedagogical methodology, his *Ratio seu methodus* belongs to the group which considers the course of instruction as a whole, corresponding roughly to those Humanist treatises on the same subject in law. This reform of theological method could not fail to have important repercussions.

MELANCHTHON'S LOCI COMMUNES

For Philip Melanchthon (1497-1560), on the other hand, a method of theology was not a course of study but a *compendium*, eliminating useless questions and explaining things with the utmost simplicity. Melanchthon's method took the form of a listing of theological "commonplaces."[77] As he told King Henry the Eighth in the preface to one of the editions of his *Loci*

---

[76] "Magnum quidem est ad theologiae studium animos hominum inflammare, sed absolutioris artificis est huiusce caelestis studii viam ac methodum tradere, non dicam ut dignum est (quid enim potest humana industria, quod rebus divinis ulla ex parte respondeat?), sed sic, ut labor hic noster mediocrem afferat utilitatem sacrosanctae theologiae candidatis. Non minima negotii pars est adeundi negotii viam nosse. Et satis festinat, qui nusquam aberrat a via. Saepe et sumptum duplicat et laborem, qui crebris erroribus ac longis ambagibus tandem eo pervenit, quo destinarat, si tamen pervenire contingat. Porro qui compendiariam quoque viam indicat, is gemino beneficio iuvat studiosum: primum ut maturius quo tendit pertingat, deinde ut minore labore sumptuque quod sequitur assequatur." *Desiderius Erasmus Roterodamus Ausgewählte Werke*, ed. Hajo Holborn (Munich, 1933), p. 177.

[77] For the relation of Melanchthon's "method" in this work to that of Agricola and Erasmus, see Paul Joachimsen, "Loci communes: Eine Untersuchung zur Geistesgeschichte des Humanismus und der Reformation," *Luther-Jahrbuch*, VIII (1926), 27-97.

communes theologici,[78] in teaching it is a great advantage to "have at one's command the main points distributed by order and procedure and contracted into a method." But Melanchthon by no means considered his method an innovation: the same method, he tells us, was used by John the Damascene among the Greek Fathers and by Peter Lombard among the Latins. So great is the difficulty of composing such a method that it often occurred to Melanchthon that it was a task not for one man but for a synod of the best and most learned. His main purposes in methodizing the doctrines of Christian theology were to facilitate their teaching and to aid in combating "impious opinions."

Melanchthon's collection of theological commonplaces called forth rival collections from Catholic writers. One of Peter Ramus' early opponents from the theological faculty at Paris, a Benedictine named Joachim Perionius or Péron (died c.1559), wrote a theological topics intended to refute the heresies of the day.[79] This writer had also translated the *Topics* of Aristotle into Latin, with commentaries to which he added a consideration of Cicero's *Topics* as well. The Spanish Dominican Melchior Cano (1523-60) also wrote theological commonplaces, but insisted that his work was not a collection of what were popularly called *loci communes* but of *loci* plain and simple, providing an arsenal of arguments on theological subjects.[80]

For we do not promise that we shall dispute in the work about "commonplaces," which customarily deal with a whole subject, or with the subheadings of important subjects, such as justification, grace, sin, faith, and so on (which are also currently called *loci communes*)—as many of our persuasion do, and of the Lutherans not only Philip Melanchthon but also Calvin—but, just as Aristotle in his *Topics* proposed "commonplaces" as seats and marks of arguments from which all argumentation could be found for any disputation: so we propose certain peculiar theological *loci* as homes of all theological arguments, from which theologians may find all their arguments, both for supporting and for refuting.

[78] CR, Vol. XXI, cols. 333-34.
[79] Ioachimus Perionius, *Topicorum Theologicorum libri duo, quorum in posteriore de iis omnibus agitur, quae hodie ab haereticis defenduntur* (Paris, 1549).
[80] Melchior Canus, *Opera . . .* (Bassano, 1776), p. 4. The first edition of Cano's theological commonplaces appeared in 1562 at Salamanca.

ZANCHIUS AND STRIGELIUS: MORE PROTESTANT METHODOLOGY

The assembling of *loci* thus practiced, with slight variations, by Protestants and Catholics alike was christened the "compositive method" by Hieronymus Zanchius (1516-90), an Italian who left Italy on becoming a Protestant and taught theology in Strasbourg and Heidelberg. He was one of the Protestants who took up the discussions of method in theology after Melanchthon.[81] The counterpart of this compositive method was, according to Zanchius,[82] the resolutive method, by which we examine Scriptural passages bearing on the *loci* we have selected and examine them in their context. In transmitting theological commonplaces, Zanchius recommended following six rules, which represent a sort of Protestant adaptation of the Scholastic manner of argumentation in theology.

Another Lutheran theologian, Victorinus Strigelius (1524-69), prefaced his edition of Melanchthon's *Loci communes theologici* with some remarks on method that reflect the general methodology current at his time. He first distinguished a general method, which pertains to the whole body of doctrine, and a special method, by which single parts of any art are explained. The general method is threefold and has been presented by Galen in the *Liber de arte medendi*. After a lengthy description of Galen's three methods, Strigelius dismisses them as not relevant to the exposition of sacred matters: the historical series alone suffices, i.e., the actual sequence of events as recorded in the Bible and epitomized in the first four chapters of Genesis. Of special method there are four forms: (1) that proposed by Melanchthon in

---

[81] "Auch sonst begann man um dieselbe Zeit, gründlicher als Melanchthon es in seiner Dialektik und Rhetorik getan hatte, über die theologische Methode zu reflectiren. Eigentümlicher und zielbewusster jedoch, als was Strigel und Flacius über diese gesagt haben, sind Zanchis Erörterungen über synthetische und analytische Methode in der Theologie." Otto Ritschl, *Dogmengeschichte des Protestantismus* (2 vols., Leipzig, 1908), I, 175.

[82] "Duae sunt praecipue docendi rationes seu methodi: συνθετικὴ καὶ ἀναλυτική, hoc est, compositiva et resolutiva. Compositiva utimur proprie in locis communibus colligendis et tradendis, Resolutiva in Scripturis explicandis." Hieronymus Zanchius, *Praefatiuncula in locos communes, cur priori loco de sacris scripturis agendum sit, et quae methodus servanda," *Opera theologica* (Geneva, 1619), p. 319. This work was written shortly after 1568.

his *Erotemata*, (2) what may be called the "anatomical" method, in which a subject is considered with respect to each of the ten Aristotelian categories, (3) geometrical method, making use of hypothesis or *deductio ad impossibile*, and finally (4) the "arbitrary" method (something of a contradiction in terms). All of these are of use in theology. Strigelius continues with some general remarks on the best way of learning the doctrines of the Church.[83]

The same three traditional Galenic methods had appeared in the methodological advice of Matthias Flacius (1520-75), a colleague and bitter rival of Strigelius at Jena. Flacius recommended the synthetic method strongly, although the analytic method might also be found useful in theology. The third method, that of definition, is, according to this writer, artifical rather than natural. Flacius considered a knowledge of method very useful to anyone in thinking, speaking, and writing, and warmly recommended his own textbook on the subject to his readers.[84]

Clearly most of the doctrines presented by these writers are borrowed from the traditional Galenic-Aristotelian stream of methodology and do not represent innovations of Humanism. Along with this borrowed discussion, however, there went a development which again stemmed from the ancient Stoic definition of an art. We have already noticed that this definition, as found in Lucian's dialogue *On the Parasitic Art*, was seized upon by Melanchthon, who laid especial stress upon the criterion of "usefulness" which that definition set up for any art. It also contained the word σύστημα, which in Zeno's usage was doubtless a very concrete sort of term, often used by the Greeks for groups of physical entities, such as a formation of soldiers. The word *systema*, now Latinized, became a favorite *terminus technicus* with Protestant theologians of the sixteenth century, being used in titles in place of the less meaningful *summa*, *corpus*, and *loci communes* to denote the whole set of doctrines of the Christian faith. Although Melanchthon's theological commonplaces had

[83] Victorinus Strigelius, *Loci theologici*... (Naples, 1581), pp. 14-17.
[84] Matthias Flacius, "De ratione cognoscendi sacras literas tractatus I," *Clavis scripturae*... (Jena, 1674), pp. 56-59.

made no pretense at completeness, the notion gradually grew that
the *corpus doctrinae* formed a "system" in which each article led
on to all the rest and formed an "integral body or perfect and
absolute system of Christian doctrine," as one Protestant theologian put it.[85] Melanchthon's popularizing of the word "system"
led to its use in theological titles and subsequently to its development as an abstract concept,[86] which it had not been in the
Greek. A Danish student of Melanchthon's who taught theology
at Copenhagen, Niels Hemmingsen (1513-1600), wrote a book
on method in which the first part was devoted to a general discussion of particular and universal methods, while the second
part dealt with theological method.[87]

Throughout the late Renaissance the connection in common
usage between "system," "art," "compendium," and "method"
was very close, although their relationships were never explicitly
developed by any one writer. Certainly to some extent their use
(especially that of "method") in titles of pedagogical works
reflected Humanist dissatisfaction with aimless and disorderly
presentations of subject matter. In England, however, the
Humanists found themselves on the other side of the fence from
the producers of compendia and abbreviations of the arts. Here
the more leisurely study of the classics was not congenial to the
production of timesaving manuals, such as those turned out by
Ramus. Perhaps also the democratic motivation of Ramus, who
wished to make education accessible to all, was lacking in the

---

[85] Leonard Hütter, quoted in Latin by Otto Ritschl in his *System und systematische
Methode in der Geschichte des wissenschaftlichen Sprachgebrauchs und der philosophischen Methodologie,* Programm (Bonn, 1906). Ritschl's study is very per-
ceptive and linguistically acute, although he limits his focus strictly to the definitions
of an art found in Lucian and Cicero. Also he does not appreciate the close tie
between the concept of an art and that of a method in antiquity. It is nevertheless
a very useful study and contains much of interest on the concept of method in
theology and in general philosophy of the sixteenth century and later.

[86] Especially by Bartholomew Keckermann; see p. 219 below.

[87] Nicolaus Hemmingius, *De methodis libri duo; quorum prior quidem omnium
methodorum universalium et particularium, quarum usus est in philosophia, brevem
ac dilucidam declarationem, posterior vero ecclesiasten sive methodum theologicam
interpretandi concionandique continet* (Leipzig, 1570). Unfortunately I have not
been able to consult this work, mentioned by Wundt and Höffding. Hemmingius
also wrote a "scientific method of natural law."

English Humanists of the time. Roger Ascham (1515-68) complained bitterly of the harm done to the study of theology by "epitomes." [88]

In his preface to Robert Greene's *Arcadia* (first published in 1589), Thomas Nashe (1567-1601) cites with favor a number of more serious scholars, including Cheke and Ascham, "all which have either by their private readings or publique workes repurged the errors of Arts, expelde from their purities, and set forth before our eyes, a more perfect Methode of Studie. But how ill their preceptes have prospered with our idle Age, that leave the fountains of the sciences, to follow the rivers of Knowledge, their over-fraught Studies, with trifling Compendiaries, maie testifie." Nashe complained that "those yeares which should bee employed in Aristotle, are expired in Epitomes," produced by "men opprest with a greater penuries of Art," who "pound their capacitie in barren Compendiums, and bound their base humors in the beggarly straits of a hungry Analysis." [89]

In Germany as well, voices of protest were raised against the

---

[88] "*Epitome.* This is a way of studie, belonging rather to matter than to wordes, to memorie than to utterance, to them that be learned alreadie, and hath small place at all amonges yong scholars in Grammar scholes. . . .

"*Epitome* is good privatelie for himselfe that doth worke it, but ill commonlye for all other that use other mens labor therein; a silie poor kind of studie, not unlike to the doing of those poore folke, which neyther till nor sowe nor reape themselves, but gleane by stelth, upon other mens growndes. Soch, have emptie barnes for deare yeares.

"Grammar scholes have fewe *Epitomes* to hurt them. . . . [A. lists some of these.] *Epitome* hurteth more in the universities and studie of Philosophie; but most of all in Divinity it selfe.

"In deede bookes of commonplaces be verie necessarie to induce a man into an orderlie generall knowledge, how to referre orderlie all that he readeth *ad certa rerum capita,* and not wander in studie. And to that end did P. Lombardus, the master of sentences, and Ph. Melanchthon in our daies write two notable bookes of common places.

"But to dwell in *Epitomes* and bookes of common places, and not to binde himselfe dailie by orderlie studie, to reade with all diligence, principallie the holyest Scripture and withall the best Doctors, and so to learne to make trewe difference betwixt the authorities of the one and the Counsell of the other, maketh so many seeming and sonburnt ministers as we have, whose learning is gotten in a sommer heat and washed away with a Christmas snow againe." Roger Ascham, *The Scholemaster* (London, 1570), ff. 42ᵛ-43ʳ.

[89] Thomas Nashe, "To the Gentlemen Students of Both Universities," in *Life and Complete Works in Prose and Verse of Robert Greene, M.A.,* ed. A. B. Grosart (n.p., 1881), pp. 18-19.

popularizing or oversimplification of philosophy by means of compendia.[90]

Many scholars in the seventeenth century shared this aversion for compendia and brief arts, which seemed to be endangering the serious mastery of subject matter. Dissatisfaction with the epitomizing trend is reflected in one of the "peccant humours" which, according to Francis Bacon (1561-1626), obstruct the advancement of learning:

> Another error, of a diverse nature from all the former, is the over-early and peremptory reduction of knowledge into arts and methods; from which time, commonly, sciences receive small or no augmentation. But as young men, when they knit and shape perfectly, do seldom grow to a further stature: so knowledge, while it is in aphorisms and observations, it is in growth; but when it once is comprehended in exact methods, it may perchance be further polished and illustrated, and accommodated for use and practice; but it increaseth no more in bulk and substance.[91]

Obviously a reaction had set in. The need for fuller treatment of subjects, including philosophy, was patent to all. The impetus had been given to produce more than just commentaries on Aristotle or epitomes and résumés of his conclusions divested of the reasoning that led to them. Seventeenth-century thinkers were ready to launch out on their own and to relegate their sources to the footnotes.

The influence of Humanism on philosophy proper will be dealt with in the second part of this study. We have already stressed the fact that this influence is felt rather indirectly in philosophy. This applies as well to the discussion of methodology.

Humanist scholarship demanded that a classical text, whether in literature or philosophy, be viewed in its linguistic and historical context. We find a relatively new antagonism to the use of short passages from the authorities cited without regard to the context or taken from commentators. Francesco Patrizzi (1529-97)

---

[90] See the quotation from Polycarpus Lyserus or Leyser (1552-1610) given by Jakob Brucker, *Historia critica philosophiae*... (6 vols., Leipzig, 1742-47), IV, 248-49.

[91] *The Works of Francis Bacon,* ed. J. Spedding and R. L. Ellis (London, 1887), III, 292. (*The Advancement of Learning* was first published in 1605.)

announced that the only clear, legitimate, genuine, and germane
Method is that Aristotle himself should explain his own opinion,
and furthermore that this opinion should be construed from all
the relevant passages in his works that deal with the subject, not
just from one or two.[92] This legitimate method was indeed
beginning to be practiced widely during the century, and the
results, in the form of a better understanding of the thought of
antiquity, were obvious.

All the subjects that made up academic philosophy (i.e., those
subjects dealt with by Aristotle in the *Organon* and in the
Nicomachean Ethics, Metaphysics, and natural philosophy) could
and did give rise to methodological discussions. In lecturing or
commenting upon these treatises, teachers of Aristotelian philosophy were now forced to defend their interpretations on
scholarly as well as on philosophical grounds, owing to the insistence of Humanists on pursuing wisdom to its sources in Greek
philosophy. In Part Two we shall examine Renaissance methodology, and in so doing shall have an opportunity to evaluate the
influence of the recovery of Greek sources upon it and to observe
the emergence of methodologies purportedly independent of Aristotle and the ancients.

[92] Franciscus Patritius, *Discussionum peripateticarum tomi IV* ... (Basel, 1581),
p. 173.

PART TWO

Chapter 4. THE METHODOLOGY OF THE DIALECTICIANS OF THE RENAISSANCE

We may begin our examination of the methodological controversies of the Renaissance with the doctrine of the "dialecticians"—those Humanistically oriented writers who emphasized the finding part of dialectic and its utility in speaking and reasoning. The tradition of *inventio,* or methodical guidance to the finding of arguments upon any desired subject, stems from the *Topics* of Aristotle, although obviously it had its origin in the practice of his predecessors. It had long been part of the stock of logical knowledge available to students of Aristotle in the Middle Ages. When the Humanists took up this part of logic, therefore, it was no new thing—but the emphasis they put upon its use was. Since the technique for finding arguments was useful in speechmaking as well as in philosophical inquiry, it had already been adopted, in diluted form, by the Latin rhetoricians: Cicero wrote a handbook on the subject. The Humanists, above all Rudolph Agricola, turned to these Latin antecedents with enthusiasm, for the subject of *inventio* seemed to offer an escape from the dry argumentation of the Scholastics, and to make of dialectic a useful and rewarding study.

This topical tradition has always been scorned by historians of logic because of its close association with rhetoric—a subject long out of fashion. But a more tolerant scholarly approach will find, I believe, that this practice of arranging standard topics for discussing any subject, barren and futile as it may seem to us, had a useful transitional role to play in the development of such disciplines as law and theology.

The character of the Renaissance interest in the *Topics* is itself indicative of a trend in attitude on the part of students of philosophy, for within a predominantly dialectical philosophical (and scientific) tradition, the finding of arguments corresponds to a methodology of research in a more empirically-minded tradition. It was a way of bringing new information or viewpoints into philosophical discussion. The Middle Ages had considered the *Topics* primarily as a guide to debate, as a set of rules for helping to overthrow an opponent in disputation. When the *Topics* begins, however vaguely, to be considered a guide to objective research, it is obvious that a considerable shift in values has come about.

The two methodological traditions, that of the "scientific" commentators and that of the "artistic" Humanists, came to grips in logic or dialectic. This subject could be regarded variously as an art or as a science, but it could also be considered the instrument of *all* the arts and sciences, "having the way," as the famous medieval definition (following Aristotle) put it, "to the principles of all methods." Consequently, when the Humanist dialecticians produced their textbooks with sections on method or on the methodical examination of "simple themes," traditionalists felt compelled to defend their own doctrine against innovation and to present the more strict and (so they felt) more Aristotelian doctrine of "scientific" or demonstrative method. Each camp produced a flood of textbooks in logic stressing the *Topics* or the *Posterior Analytics* according to their general philosophical orientation.

Now of course the methodology of the commentators, that slow-growing and carefully conserved organism, antedates the Humanist revolt. It represents a comprehensive intellectual structure to which each writer added, or from which he subtracted, some small fragment of doctrine. Each of these commentators, medical or philosophical, takes for granted a host of others who went before him; and these must be studied if we are to understand what he contributes to the whole picture.

Not so with the new doctrine of method which the Humanists took up during the early part of the sixteenth century. This was a fresh fabrication—still out of materials furnished by Aristotle, to be sure—but nonetheless not directly dependent upon medieval antecedents or upon those from late antiquity. Thus the dialecticians make a good starting point for our inquiries, representing a trend that begins during our period. To the other school of methodological thought, the scientific, we cannot give such thorough attention, for its examination would carry us back into the thirteenth century. We shall devote some time to it, for it is part of the methodological controversy of the day, and the two trends were by no means compartmentalized into schools completely independent of each other, but were in active contact. Yet it must be understood that we cannot do full justice to the traditional methodology in the space at our command.[1] We now turn to these writers on dialectic.

THE DEVELOPMENT OF METHOD AS A TOPIC IN DIALECTICAL TEXT-BOOKS

"Thus the Dialecticians have adopted this word *methodus* for the most correct order of explication." So wrote Melanchthon in his own textbook, entitled *Erotemata dialectices*, in 1547. Unfortunately he did not name any of these dialecticians, which leaves us with the problem of identifying them from among a wide array of candidates.[2] It had become customary to call "dialecticians" writers who stood in the tradition of Humanist revolt against Scholastic logic,[3] the revolt that began with

[1] Crombie's work on Grosseteste (see Bibliography) provides a good background for this discussion, as does the article by Randall on the school of Padua.

[2] Among the possibilities are Georgius Trapezuntius (1396-1485), author of a somewhat anti-Terminist textbook, *De re dialectica* (Cologne, 1536); Joachim Ringelsbergh (c.1499-c.1536), who wrote an introductory text with the title *Dialectica* (Paris, 1540) strongly recommended by Erasmus; Franciscus Titelmannus (1497-1537) of Louvain, *Dialecticae considerationis libri sex* (Paris, 1539), frequently quoted and rather more traditional than the others; Joannes Visorius (d. 1568), *Ingeniosa nec minus elegans ad dialectices candidatos methodus* (Paris, 1534); Joannes Caesarius (c.1468-1550), one of the first German Humanists to teach Greek in his native country, *Dialectica* (Venice, 1559); Erasmus Sarcerius (1501-59), German preacher and author of a *Dialectica* (Marburg, 1537); Gulielmus Lapidanus (fl. c.1550), *Methodus dialectices* (Lyons, 1543); and Ioachimus Perionius (see p. 109), *De dialectica libri tres* (Lugduni, 1551).

[3] For a good description of this revolt in its major outlines, see Ernst Cassirer, *Das Erkenntnisproblem in der Philosophie und Wissenschaft der neueren Zeit*, Vol. I (Berlin, 1906), Section III, "Die Auflösung der scholastischen Logik," pp. 122-47.

Lorenzo Valla and included Rudolph Agricola, Luis Vives, and Peter Ramus as its representatives in other nations of Europe. Of these well-known figures only one, Peter Ramus, took a part in the controversies over method, and we shall see that the term did not originate with him, for it was already in the air when he wrote, as he expressly says. Valla, in his famous outburst against Scholastic logic, did not discuss the subject, nor did Agricola and Vives, however trenchant their attacks on medieval teaching and education practices may have been. The difficulties of tracing this doctrine to its source or sources, then, are multiplied, for the books of the lesser writers are scarce nowadays. In the works I have been able to examine, there are few clues to the origins of the new concept of method. Occasionally we are told that an author has succeeded in presenting his doctrine "methodically," and the word is given in Greek.[4]

Pending thorough examination of these works, which are so hard to find in this country, we must defer to the judgment of the historian of logic. Carl von Prantl suggested that the sections on method in sixteenth-century textbooks of logic or dialectic had their precedent in the books of Johann Sturm, whom we have had occasion to discuss previously (see pp. 23, 72, 84), and Jodocus Willichius or Wilcke (1501-c.1555), who taught Greek and Latin literature as well as medicine at various German universities, including Erfurt and Frankfurt-an-der-Oder.[5]

[4] By Hermannus Raianus, the obscure but not at all uninteresting editor of Caesarius' dialectical textbook mentioned above: "Denique Caesarius post Aristotelem μετοδικῶς [sic] huius artis praecepta plenissime tradit; quae res mirifice discentium memoriam juvat" (Dedicatory epistle). Although this epistle was written in 1559, after *methodus* had become a common slogan, it does give some indication of the general feeling of the time that "method" was a Greek concept.

[5] Carl von Prantl, in discussing the conclusion of Ramus' *Dialecticae partitiones* of 1543, notes that the section on method here has antecedents in these two writers: "Den Schluss bilden Erörterungen über 'methodus,' welche den Keim der später von Ramus gegebenen ausführlichen Behandlung dieses relativ neuen Abschnittes der Logik enthalten. Aber auch ihrerseits auf Vorbilder, bei Sturm, welcher aus aristotelischen Stellen schöpfte, und bei Jod. Willich hinweisen." "Ueber Petrus Ramus," *Sitzungsberichte,* BAW, *Philos.-phil.-hist. Kl.,* II (1878), 113. Prantl did not reach the sixteenth century in his history of logic but was forced to break off his 'dreary recital' of medieval logic, as he called it, with the fifteenth century. We shall see when we treat of Ramus, however, that Prantl was not quite exact in his characterization with regard to this early edition of Ramus' work.

Although the two authors mentioned by Prantl do discuss the concept of method, it seems unlikely that they are the first in the Humanist tradition to consider the topic. Sturm's major work[6] contains nothing that would lead us to regard him as the first to take up the Platonic emphasis on method in the liberal arts. Elsewhere, in a preface that he wrote for a commentary on the *Physics*, Sturm defends Plato against the charge of the commentary's author, Hieronymus Zanchius (see p. 110), who had maintained that the *integrae artes* of dialectic, ethics, and physics are to be found not in Plato, but in Aristotle. Zanchius had evidently expressed the usual conviction of the period that Plato was not "methodical." Sturm remarks[7] that this *method* so much talked about nowadays can only be found in Plato, "both in general and singular courses of argument," as can that dialectical way of collocating arguments, the precepts for which are given by Aristotle in 'Book Eight' (of the *Topics,* evidently).

In a treatise on the subject of "resolving the Latin language," (1573), Sturm speaks of the threefold method of the arts, which he calls the method of division, of composition, and that by definition.[8] Sturm carefully gives the Greek equivalents for his Latin terms, as if he were drawing his doctrine from some Greek source, perhaps Galen. However, pending a closer examination

---

[6] Joannes Sturmius, *Partitionum dialecticarum libri duo* (Paris, 1539). Sturm also wrote a preface for the Strasbourg, 1540 edition of Willichius' *Erotematum dialecticae libri III,* and a preface to Melanchthon's *Dialectica* (Strasbourg, 1538), dated Feb. 1, 1538. Both of these prefaces are contained in Joannes Sturmius, *Prolegomena, hoc est praefationes in optimos quosque utriusque tum bonarum artium tum philosophiae scriptores* (Zurich, n.d.). None of these writings furnish any clues to the provenance of the novel (if it was novel) doctrine of method. I have not been able to locate the major work of Willichius, his *Erotemata dialectica,* published at Frankfurt-an-der-Oder in 1535.

[7] "Methodum igitur, quae hodie in omnium est ore et usurpatur a paucis, in Platone dicimus et in universis inesse, et in singulis argumentationibus haerere, et dialecticam illam collocandorum argumentorum viam, de qua apud Aristotelem libro octavo praecepta exposita sunt, in nullo qui hodie extant, ne quidem in ipso Aristotele, excepto Platone, apparere, cum in omnibus sermonibus, tum in illis praecipue qui ἐριστικοί et πειραστικοί nominantur." Joannes Sturmius, *Prolegomena . . . ,* pp. 136-37. The first sentence suggests to me that discussion of method was already very much in the air in Sturm's time.

[8] Joannes Sturmius, "Linguae Latinae resolvendae ratio," in *Institutionis literatae . . .* (Thorn, 1586), p. 511. See Walter J. Ong, *Ramus, Method, and the Decay of Dialogue* (Cambridge, Mass., 1958), p. 233.

of this influential educator, we must simply content ourselves with noting that Ramus undoubtedly owed much to the actual classroom methods of Johann Sturm, and perhaps also something to his theoretical discussion of method.

Indications given in a work of the other author, Jodocus Willichius, suggest that his doctrine of method resembled Melanchthon's, which we shall discuss shortly, and which corresponds to the "dialectical way of collocating arguments" mentioned by Sturm. Willichius' treatise is rather sketchy; it is concerned with formative studies in any of the arts. When an incomplex theme is "methodically" explicated, according to Willichius,[9] it is subjected to a certain sequence of questions, the first four of which are drawn from Aristotle's *Posterior Analytics* (89^b23): the that, the why, whether the thing exists, and what it is. These are questions "by which the ways of science and art are transmitted," remarks Willichius. It is this addition that opens the door to the kind of artistic methodology which the sixteenth century drew from Greek sources and inserted into the text of Aristotle.

Inadequate as our evidence is, then, we may hazard a few guesses as to the origin of this dialectical methodology. From the reading of Plato, these Humanistically trained students of logic and dialectic began to understand the importance attributed to "method" by Socrates in the dialogues and to try to derive precepts for this method from Aristotle. Not finding any clearcut doctrine of dialectical method in the Philosopher, they were forced to concoct a doctrine from what elements they could muster and to foist it upon Aristotle as the way of treating a subject "methodically." Basically, then, this "method" of the dialecticians seems to have been an adaptation—a caricature, if you will—of the dialectical method of Plato, as adapted by Aris-

---

[9] "Fit autem cum locus communis, seu ut saepe diximus, thema simplex, quod est ἄνευ συμπλοκῆς, id est incomplexum methodicos explicatur. Verum methodus nobis hic est artificiosa et compendiaria vel discendi vel docendi per certas quaestiones ratio. Quaestiones vero sunt Aristoteli ζητούμενα, et quatuor numerantur, quibus scientiae et artis viae traduntur, ut sunt τὸ ὅτι, τὸ διότι, εἰ ἐστίν, τί ἐστιν." Jodocus Willichius, *De formando studio in quolibet artium* ... (n.p. 1564), p. 147. The example which Willichius then gives, of how to discuss the nature of law, follows not this program but the conventional list of rhetorical loci.

totle in Greek and by Cicero and Boethius in Latin. Method, for these sixteenth-century students, was still a way of discussing a subject, as it was for the Greeks, although now bound by strict and over-simplified rules far removed from the free play of Socratic dialectic or the careful intellectual weighing of Aristotle. Naturally such doctrine tended to assimilate itself to the language of Latin rhetoric and to borrow terms from that tradition.

With the earlier dialecticians, however, method was a part of *inventio*, and hence disturbed traditional logicians very little, for they were more interested in *obligations* and *consequences* and devoted little attention to the *Topics*. As we shall see, Peter Ramus altered this scheme by putting method very definitely into the judging part of dialectic, where, as *secundum iudicium*, it threatened to displace the syllogism altogether. This explains why the storms of methodological controversy centered over the head of the Parisian revolutionary, whose single method was a threat to the whole of traditional logic.

MELANCHTHON: ARTIFEX METHODI

However much he may owe to his obscure predecessors, there can be no doubt that Philip Melanchthon (1497-1560) was one of the first writers on the subject of method to gain wide influence. As a man who was instrumental in the reform of both church and school, Melanchthon inherited the reforming zeal of the Protestants in theology and the Humanists in education. He regarded John the Damascene and Peter the Lombard as his predecessors in theological method, but for method in general he looked to Aristotle as the most reliable guide. Aristotle alone was the true *artifex methodi* (a phrase later applied in turn to Melanchthon himself): the trait that most recommends his writings to the serious student, aside from the truth of the doctrines expressed therein, is their methodical character. Aristotle does not stray from the subject, but proceeds in orderly fashion to explain his true opinions.[10]

[10] See the numerous laudatory remarks about Aristotle and his method in the *Corpus Reformatorum:* for example, XI, 349; III, 362; and XI, 654-55.

Method and correct speech are essential to the student (thus far the Humanist speaking): from philosophy and from long practice, he will gain the methodical habit which is essential and which is especially useful in religious controversies.[11] When Melanchthon speaks of the "habit" of calling all things back to method, he obviously has in mind the Greek definition of method[12] as found in Philoponus. Students and teachers alike should strive to cultivate this habit. The educational motivation was very strong in Melanchthon; even his definition of dialectic[13] stressed the teaching aspect of that art.

Method requires that a subject, whether it is being taught or investigated, should be dealt with by asking the following questions about it in this order: (1) what does the word signify? (2) does the thing signified exist? (3) what is the thing? (4) what are its parts? (5) what are its species? (6) what are its causes? (7) what are its effects? (8) what things are "adjacent" to it? (9) what things are "cognate" to it? and finally (10) what things are repugnant to it?[14] These questions, as Melanchthon tells us, are derived from the four which Aristotle outlines in the *Posterior Analytics* (the same passage from which Willichius drew his doc-

[11] Deinde duae res sunt, ad quas comparandas opus est magna et varia doctrina et longa exercitatione in multis artibus, videlicet, methodus et forma orationis. Nemo enim fieri artifex methodi potest, nisi bene et rite assuefactus in Philosophia, et quidem in hoc genere philosophiae, quod alienum est a Sophistica, quod veritatem ordine et recta via inquirit et patefacit. Qui in eo studio bene assuefacti ἕξιν sibi paraverunt revocandi omnia ad methodum, quae intelligere aut tradere aliis cupiunt, hi norunt etiam in disputationibus religionis informare methodos, evolvere intricata, dissipata contrahere, obscuris et ambiguis addere lumen." These remarks are from an oration on philosophy given in 1536, CR, XI, 280-81.

[12] Which he quotes elsewhere; see p. 70.

[13] Dialectica est ars seu via, recte, ordine, et perspicue docendi, quod sit recte definiendo, dividendo, argumenta vera connectendo, et male cohaerentia seu falsa retexendo et refutando." *Erotemata Dialectica,* CR, XIII, 513. This work appeared in three different forms, the first of which was published in Leipzig in 1520. The present form first appeared in Wittenberg in 1547. Once again, the inaccessibility of earlier editions prevents us from determining whether doctrines of method appeared in the earlier versions of this work.

[14] "Quot sint methodi quaestiones? Cum de una voce dicendum est, viam monstrant hae decem quaestiones. Prima, quid vocabulum significet. Secunda, an sit res. Tertia, quid sit res. Quarta, quae sint rei partes. Quinta, quae sint species. Sexta, quae causae. Septima, qui effectus. Octava, quae adiacentia. Nona, quae cognata. Decima, quae pugnantia." CR, XIII, 573.

trine), with six more added by him (from the Topical tradition). This rather superficial doctrine is hardly sufficient to justify the reputation which Melanchthon himself soon gained as *artifex methodi*. In Melanchthon's series of questions, mélange though it be, one may still discern traces of the Hippocratic-Socratic method of examining a subject. Such Platonic parentage is discernible in many writers of the Humanistic tradition. Had Melanchthon supported his doctrine by any extended and probing analysis of the Platonic dialogues or of the practice of Aristotle, he might have deserved the reputation he acquired as a theoretician of method. Actually, his reputation as a champion of method seems to have rested upon his own oral teaching and upon the methodical form of exposition which he used in his many textbooks rather than upon any theoretical explication of method.[15] Melanchthon belongs far over toward the Humanistic and pedagogical end of the methodological spectrum. To him method was a way of teaching, and it was method of this sort for which he himself became famous. Yet he had the greatest respect for the Aristotelian theory of science—without being deeply versed in it—and regarded Aristotle as the master of method. The rhetorical and pedagogical motivation of his dialectic placed him close to Ramus, and thus these two writers formed the standard fare of those who opposed the traditional Aristotelian-Galenic theory of scientific method, the self-styled "Philippo-Ramists." Yet there were differences in treatment that justify our considering the famous single method of Ramus in a separate chapter, for Melanchthon still dealt with method in the finding part of

---

[15] A question that incidentally arises is the extent of Galen's influence upon Melanchthon's methodology. So far as I can see, the only doctrine of Galen that Melanchthon may have adopted was the reliance upon *ennoiai koinai* or "common notions" as the bases of morality and of the sciences. See Wilhelm Dilthey, "Weltanschauung und Analyse des Menschen seit Renaissance und Reformation," *Gesammelte Schriften* (7 vols., Leipzig and Berlin, 1921-27), II, 173-86. This essentially Stoic belief in common notions was widespread among Renaissance Aristotelians: it was reinforced by the fact that the axioms of geometry were called *ennoiai koinai* by Euclid, and hence were considered to be the foundation of demonstrative procedure.

dialectic, while Ramus' signal, and most controversial, innovation was the placing of method into judgment.

Chapter 5. THE SINGLE METHOD OF PETER RAMUS

It is surely no accident that the other outstanding methodologist of the arts, Peter Ramus (1515-72), was also an adherent of reformed religion, and also deeply interested in the reform of education. And, it must be added, his grasp of the scientific methodology of Aristotle and Galen was just as superficial as Melanchthon's. Yet, unlike the preceptor of Germany, Ramus did not retain a respect for the syllogism as the sole instrument of demonstrative science; instead he campaigned with telling effect against its preeminent place in the Scholastic scheme, hoping to replace it with the rhetorical examples called for by his own dialectic. The success which this campaign gained won for Ramus his reputation as the archenemy of Aristotle—a reputation which tends to obscure the real historical significance of his doctrine. One cannot hope to judge this significance accurately unless the historical context of Ramus' innovations is known in detail. For example, we shall see that his doctrine of a single method, central as it became in the controversies that followed its proclamation, was formulated in opposition not only to Aristotle and Galen but to certain other popular conceptions of method in his day, such as those of the "dialecticians." By his widely diffused writings, in which he attacked these methodologies in detail, Ramus did much to publicize the notion of method and to make the subject central in the philosophical differences of the Renaissance. He stood alone, proud and defiant, with a doctrine that seems the very acme of banality to us, but which struck his contemporaries as original and indeed revolutionary.

As a young man of twenty-eight,[1] Ramus published two books
that challenged the Aristotelianism of his day—one a textbook
embodying his own innovations in dialectic, the other an attack
upon Aristotle's logic. These two books aroused a furor of resentment in the University of Paris which resulted in their being
banned from the kingdom of France. They constituted an impu-
dent challenge to the Aristotelianism of the Renaissance, and
they contained the substance of Ramus' doctrine in logic, which
received much elaboration but little change in subsequent editions.[2]

Because of the meagerness of Ramus' contributions to logic
(or strictly speaking, to dialectic) in these works, modern scholars
are apt to overlook the details of his critique of Aristotle and
Galen, which in fact made these attacks significant for his contemporaries. It has been suggested by a historian of logic[3] that
Ramus was not at all a pathbreaker in most of the logical reforms
he advocated. He was by no means the first to fuse rhetoric and
logic, or to depart from Scholastic logic, or to emphasize the
practical use of logic, or to use the vernacular in writing on logic,
or to question the authenticity of Aristotle's works. Furthermore,
this fact was well known to his contemporaries—who, after all,
could read Valla and Agricola and Vives as well as we can. Yet
his writings, especially those in which Ramus advocated a "single

---

[1] For a thorough examination of Ramus' life and doctrine, see Walter J. Ong,
S. J., *Ramus, Method, and the Decay of Dialogue* (Cambridge, Mass., 1958), which
replaces the nineteenth-century work by Charles Waddington, *Ramus (Pierre de la
Ramée): sa vie, ses écrits et ses opinions* (Paris, 1855). Father Ong's book contains
a wealth of bibliographic information as well as extensive insights into the background of Ramus' logic in the Renaissance. Also worth consulting is Perry Miller's
sympathetic account of Ramist doctrine in *The New England Mind* (Cambridge,
Mass., 1939).

[2] Neglect of bibliographic precision has caused much confusion in the interpretation of Peter Ramus and his doctrine. The two books of his which caused
the initial trouble appeared in the same month—September, 1543—in the same
format. But the textbook on dialectic had appeared earlier with the title *Dialecticae
partitiones*. The titles of the two books are *Petri Rami Veromandui Dialecticae
institutiones ...* (Paris, 1543) and *Petri Rami Vermandui Aristotelicae animadversiones ...* (Paris, 1543). For an infallible guide to the mazes of Ramist bibliography, see Walter J. Ong, *Ramus and Talon Inventory* (Cambridge, Mass., 1958).

[3] Carl von Prantl, "Ueber Petrus Ramus," *Sitzungsberichte der philosophisch-
philologischen und historischen Classe*, BAW, Band II, Heft II (1878), pp. 157-69.

method," stirred up a tremendous controversy in Europe that lasted for generations. We are thus driven to the conclusion that it was not so much the novelty of his conclusions that gained Ramus notoriety in his time, but the force and skill with which he expressed them and the success of the teaching which put his doctrines into practice. We must examine his works in some detail, then, not only in order to gain some idea of what Ramus advocated, but also in order to see what sort of methodology he was attacking and how he went about his task.

RAMUS' EARLIEST WORK ON LOGIC

When we examine the first manifesto of Ramist logic, the 'Dialectical Institutions,' in the light of the later history of Ramus' method and the vigor with which he defended his doctrine, we are surprised to find that "method" does not figure as an essential term in his vocabulary. Having made the traditional dialectical distinction between invention and judgment, Ramus divides the latter into three parts: syllogism, collocation, and the "conjunction of all the arts and relation of them to God." The second step in judgment, which he here calls *collocatio*,[4] is the *methodus* for which he later battled so strenuously.

Ramus draws his doctrine here expressly from Plato; he quotes the passage from the *Philebus* concerning the way of investigating, teaching, and learning as being the "gift of the gods to men" and even uses the methodological language of Cicero—but he does not yet speak of *method* himself.[5] Ramus states further

---

[4] "Primus dialectici iudicii gradus hactenus expositus est: secundus (qui sequitur) *Collocationem* tradit: et ordinem multorum et variorum argumentorum cohaerentium inter se, et perpetua velut catena vinctorum, ad unumque certum finem relatorum: cuius dispositionis partes duae principes sunt, *definitio distributioque:* res enim primum universa definienda et explananda: deinde in partes diducenda est: tertium membrum in hac collocatione nullum est: quod de rebus quid vetat Socratem in Protarcho [?], Philoeboque copiosissime disputantem audire?" *Petri Rami Veromandui Dialecticae institutiones ...* (Paris, 1543), f. 27ᵣ.

[5] Ramus quotes from the *Philebus* a passage which ends: "Dii ergo (ut diximus) hanc nobis investigandi, discendi, docendi, viam ostenderunt.' Haec ille [Plato] in *Philoebo:* ubi etiam docet, quemadmodum observatione contraria doctrinae primo collectae sunt, et repertae. Iubet igitur Socrates in rebus (quae dissipatae sunt et

that he has used this Platonic way of explicating an art himself, in presenting the art of dialectic, by starting from its end, and then examining its parts and their function.

Evidently Ramus had not yet made up his mind to join issue with the Galenists by calling his second grade of judgment *method*. In the companion volume of 'Aristotelian Observations,' Ramus pointed out that Aristotle had no satisfactory doctrine of "second judgment" in his logical writings. He maintains that Aristotle discussed this "second judgment" in all the books except the ones in which he ought to have dealt with the subject, namely, the *Organon*. Furthermore, he questions Aristotle's veracity in saying that the ancients had developed no such doctrine—since Prometheus, who lived two thousands years before him, had seen this way of second judgment, Zeno had taught it, Hippocrates had practiced it, and Plato himself had confirmed it.[6]

In the same work, Ramus attacks briefly the medical methodologists,[7] in a section which he was to expand to great lengths in subsequent editions of the book. He blames the confusion of the medical methodologists upon Aristotle's failure to deal with second judgment in its proper place, and says that this led to false doctrines concerning the methodical establishment of an art—doctrines that are misleading medical men.

GOVEANUS' ATTACK ON RAMUS

How Ramus was led to call his second judgment "method" and in so doing to throw down the gauntlet to the Galenists may be

divulsae) conglutinendis et *certa ratione* (quemadmodum Crassus interpretatur) constringendis, ut finis primum definiatur, demonstreturque; deinde genera proponantur; generum partes subiiciantur; nec prius illa progressio quiescat, quam ad infinita individuorum partium multitudinem pervenerit." *Ibid.*, f. 28r.

[6] *Ibid.*, ff. 61v-62r.

[7] ... hic enim morbus tuus [that is, Aristotle's neglect] Medicos etiam fefellit, ut sanitatem putarent: hanc itaque pestem seculi novorum principia malorum pepererunt: cum docuerunt modo similitudinem et dissimilitudinem ad methodicam cuiuslibet artis constitutionem sufficere, modo praeter compositionem et divisionem faciendis artibus nullam viam esse, modo utraque coniungi, modo trium methodorum genera, primum compositionem et divisionem, secundum consequentium et pugnantium cognitionem, tertium rerum inter se mutationem, in maioris et minoris et aequalis et similis ratione, etc." *Ibid.*, ff. 62v-63r.

seen very clearly from a defense of Aristotle against Ramus
published in December of the same year 1543 by Antonius
Goveanus (c.1505-1565), a Portuguese who taught humanities
at Paris and Bordeaux but made his reputation chiefly as a writer
on law, which he studied at Toulouse. Goveanus thus falls into
a category which we shall see represented very frequently in the
sixteenth century: that of the Humanist Aristotelians. One of
the earliest of Ramus' adversaries, Goveanus remarks[8] that
Ramus calls "second judgment" what the Greeks call *methodos*,
the procedure for transmitting the arts, and he asks why Aristotle
should be expected to have taught it in the *Organon*, which is
concerned only with the precepts of reasoning. Goveanus protests
his willingness to diverge from the views of Aristotle if it can be
shown that Aristotle was wrong, but he sees no reason to charge
him with neglecting method when he was concerned only with
giving precepts for reasoning. Furthermore, since Ramus apparently has offered nothing on method, Goveanus proposes to
make up for the omission by paraphrasing Galen's views on the
subject—which he proceeds to do.

RAMUS PRESENTS HIS DEFENSE

From reactions such as this we can understand why it was that
Ramus later called his "second judgment" *method* and why he

---

[8] *Secundum iudicium* credo vocas [addressing Ramus] rationem artium traden-
darum quam Graeci μέθοδον appellant: eam in suo *Organo*, ubi disserendi duntaxat praecepta dantur, cur doceat Aristoteles? Aliud *disserere* est, aliud *artem
aliquam* tradere: alia itaque rei illius, alia huius praecepta sunt, neque eadem
utrius rei ratio est. Siquid praetermissum ab Aristotele est, quod ad disserendi
rationem pertinet, profer, reprehende, flagitium Aristoteles agnoscam, tuam laudabo,
suspiciam, admirabor diligentiam. Neque enim ita me Aristoteli addixi, ut illius aut
errata defenderem, aut negligentiam excusarem, neque ita a te unquam opinione
dissensi, ut si quid aut invenisses per te, aut acceptum ab alio melius tractando et
explicando fecisses, meritam tibi laudem supprimere voluerim.... Nihil necesse est,
Rame, cum disserendi traduntur praecepta, rationem explicandarum artium ex-
poni. De qua quoniam nihil mihi dicere videris, ipse quae a Galeno hac de
re scripta sunt, dicam. 'Tres omnino viae sunt, quibus artes aut inveniuntur aut
explicantur: resolutione finis in mediis inveniuntur, compositione, et definiendo explicantur... etc.'" Antonius Goveanus, "Pro Aristotele responsio adversus Petri
Rami calumnias," in *Opera iuridica, philologica, philosophica* (Rotterdam, 1766),
pp. 810-11. The work was first published separately at Paris in 1543.

undertook to defend it with more elaborate arguments against the doctrine of the Galenists. His most thorough treatment of the subject is found in the 1553 edition of the *Aristotelicae animadversiones*.[9] In the preface to this work, Ramus announces that he is going to defend his elementary textbook on dialectic as conforming to "Aristotelian principles." However, as the defense proceeds, it becomes clear that the Aristotelian principle Ramus chooses as a guide is one that fits his own conception of method, in which the syllogism plays little part. Ramus' method, as we shall see, dictates that the more general and prior by nature should precede in the exposition of any art or science. Instead of the chain of continuous development which this method requires, Aristotle offers us a "science" that consists of a chain that links back on itself: the syllogism.[10]

Aristotle seems to call the syllogism the single *artifex* and teacher of every science and art.[11] This is no doubt due to his pride in having invented the syllogism,[12] and yet certainly arts were discovered before this means of demonstration was found, as we can see from Plato, who mentions definitions, divisions, causal propositions, and examples as means of constituting arts, but does not mention syllogisms. And yet Aristotle seems to attribute the making of all arts and sciences to the demonstrative syllogism. Ramus, on the other hand, thinks that the valid method which he advocates can be drawn from Aristotle's logical

---

[9] Many editions of this work appeared, in which Ramus made changes in his position (a habit for which he was chided by his contemporaries). Prantl notes that the 1553 edition of the work contains the most detailed exposition of method: it is this edition that I have used, and subsequent references will be to its pages (the pagination is extremely confused). The 1553 edition actually contains only Books IX and X of the subsequent editions, which eventually comprise twenty books covering the entire *Organon*. See Ong, *Ramus and Talon Inventory*, p. 60. For a complete picture of Ramus' development—if it can be called that—it would be necessary to take into account the later editions, in which the section on method is somewhat curtailed. See Prantl, "Ueber Petrus Ramus," BAW, II (1878), 167.

[10] "At Aristoteles hic [in *Analyticis Posterioribus*] videtur neque nominatim neque de industria sibi proposuisse hanc methodum, atque hanc universam totius artis et disciplinae seriem tanquam perpetuam longioris cuiusdam catenae continuationem: sed syllogismum demonstrationum eius catenae velut annulum quendam saepius in sese replicatum, ex quo scientia omnis efficiatur." *Aristotelicarum animadversionum liber nonus et decimus in Posteriora Analytica* (Paris, 1553), p. 2.

[11] *Ibid.*   [12] *Ibid.*, pp. 2-3.

works. Therefore, in his observations on Aristotle's *Posterior Analytics*, Ramus proposes to sift out the useful and legitimate, and present only those doctrines which may be put to use in teaching, learning, or practicing any discipline or art.[13] The true method of Aristotle requires that the prior and more general precede:[14] if this is lacking in any science or discipline, then so is method. Although the precept that the prior by nature and the more general should precede in any art might appear simple, there is nothing harder than to apply it consistently.[15]

It is to this method that Aristotle owes his superiority over all other philosophers, and by it he himself may be surpassed, if by anything. Ramus' major complaint is that the *Organon* itself is not methodically disposed, hence not designed for use.[16] Part of the blame for this lack of method in the *Organon* must fall upon those Aristotelians who composed the *Organon* as we now have it: they were ignorant of method.[17] The chief cause of error of these interpreters of Aristotle was that they neglected the use of logic and its method: instead of producing examples to which logic applies, they turned it to disputation and quarreling.[18] (This is a typically Humanist reproach, in that the alternative to such disputation and quarreling is conceived to be the production of examples, which are especially effective in teaching). Ramus then takes issue with views, which he attributes to the Greek commentators, concerning the two methods used in the practical arts: *analysis*, by which the means to the end of an art are

---

[13] *Ibid.*, p. 10.

[14] ... sed tamen intelligo ab Aristotele methodum, et artis formam rursus hic informari, ut in arte praecedunt absolute naturaque sua priora et notiora, id est, generalia et universalia, unde specialia et singularia absolute naturaque sua posteriora et ignotiora discantur et sciantur. Nam si scientia et doctrina ex absolute prioribus et natura notioribus progrediatur, certe si in una doctrina multae definitiones, partitiones, demonstrationes fuerint, generaliores et universaliores, id est, per se, naturamque priores et notiores praecedent. Cum igitur haec doctoris praecepta didiceris, interrogatus de methode et ordine collocandae artis, respondebis a prioribus absolute progrediendum esse." *Ibid.*, p. 41.

[15] "Ex omnibus enim logicae artis partibus nulla praeceptis brevior, usu autem et exercitatione et opere nulla maior, nulla difficilior. Quomodo sunt artes collocandae? Notiora praecedant, ait haec methodus, sic uno verbo tanta res comprehenditur, et tamen nihil adhuc philosophis, magistris artium et doctoribus difficilius unquam quicquam fuit." *Ibid.*, pp. 41-42.

[16] *Ibid.*, p. 42.   [17] *Ibid.*, p. 47.   [18] *Ibid.*, p. 48.

excogitated, and *genesis,* in which the end is actually pursued by those means. This first method, which the commentators call *analysis,* is valid, since it proceeds from the general, prior, and more known by nature; however, when the commentators say that it is by this method that the arts are found, Ramus demurs, for arts take their origin, as Aristotle teaches, from the senses, and ascend from the induction of singular facts to the specific, and from the specific to the general. Hence the commentators are wrong in attributing the finding of the arts to this analysis.[19]

Ramus here enters upon a detailed critique of these doctrines of the Greek commentators, challenging incidentally the order in which they arranged the works of the *Organon,* according to their ideas of the way in which an art (in this case, logic) should proceed:

Whence we may see how many errors lurk in one comment of the interpreters, errors by which the logic of Aristotle, already sufficiently obscure in itself, has been made even more obscure and difficult. These imprudent men propose the true rule of method under the name 'analysis,' but they falsely refer it to the finding of the arts, give a false example, and oppose it to "genesis"; thus false rules generate an example both false and unsound. But if these interpreters had really wished to know the logic of Aristotle, they would never have made analysis prior to genesis but the converse, as Aristotle did in the first book of the *Prior*

---

[19] "Porphyrius, Ammonius, Philoponus, Simplicius, et reliqui qui logicam (quam nunc Aristotelis nomine tenemus) non ex Aristotelis principiis perpendere et componere, sed qualemcunque acceperant, pro suo arbitratu tradere voluerunt, duas vias in descensu ascensuque finxerunt, rectam alteram, alteram inversam, *analysim* et *genesim* nominant: ut per analysim finem primo deinde fini proxima, postremo reliqua ut erunt propinqua vel remota, ita prius posteriusque cogitemus; per genesim contra opus ordinemus ex eo loco, ubi analysis desierat, tandemque eam concludamus, ubi analysis incoeperat, analysis denique a crassissimis maximeque compositis descendet ad simplicia, genesis contra a simplicibus ad composita perveniet. In quo multiplex et varius est error. . . . Haec rerum per tales gradus subductio methodus est Aristotelica, quam sequor et laudo. . . . Dicunt artes hac via inveniri: hoc Aristotelicae philosophiae contrarium est; non approbo, non laudo. Omnium enim artium inventio et observatio licet summum artis finem propositum habeat, a sensibus oritur, et inductione singularium ascendit ad specialia: a specialium inductione ad generalia, ut decimo quarto capite huius Aristoteles docebit. Error interpretum hic primus est, quod huius ἀναλύσεως nomine talem artium inventionem confingunt. Dicunt finem logicae esse demonstrationem. . . . In quo, toto caelo aberrant. Ex Aristotelis autem loco male intellecto, . . . demonstrationem logicae finem fecerunt. At finis est bene disserere, quod prima logicae definitione comprehenditur et comprehendi oportere Aristoteles ipse docet. . . ." *Ibid.,* pp. 48-50.

Analytics.... These interpreters not only failed to apply the art of logic; they did not even understand the art they presumed to interpret.[20]

The space Ramus devotes to the Greek commentators shows to what an extent the views of these writers of late antiquity had entered into the mainstream of Aristotelian interpretation. It may be assumed that he was directing his comments chiefly to those Italian Aristotelians who had made a particular point of interpreting Aristotle by means of the Greek commentators, although Ramus never mentions explicitly any of his contemporaries who did this.

RAMUS ANALYZES GALEN'S METHODS

Having disposed of the Greek commentators with their doctrine of analysis and genesis, Ramus next turns to Galen, "who championed the same pair of methods and many others besides." Ramus objects to having the authority of Galen brought against him—a man who clearly expressed the scorn he felt for those who followed one sect rather than the Truth and who, like himself, demanded that the arts be made useful.[21] Galen had required that the rule of truth in all philosophy should be experience and certain demonstration alone, not the opinion of any man. Ramus admits that Galen surpassed all the other commentators on Aristotle, and he especially admires his free and sincere zeal for philosophy. He cites with respect Galen's practice of censuring those ancient philosophers who foolishly believed whatever they heard or read without bothering to inquire into its empirical truth.[22] It must be admitted that Ramus did share to a considerable extent Galen's attitude of bold independence. How superficial is the modern view that attributes to Galen the role of a "dead hand" weighing down tradition-bound medical men and philosophers, and disregards completely the inspiration they found in him toward a fresh consideration of received doctrines! Ramus then begins his examination of the methods recommended by Galen, pointing out that Galen uses sometimes

---

[20] *Ibid.*, p. 50ᵛ.   [21] *Ibid.*, p. 51ᵛ.   [22] *Ibid.*, pp. 51ʳ-51ᵛ.

"method," sometimes "theory," and sometimes "way of teaching in order" for this concept.[23] Ramus suggests that his readers adopt as a standard general definition of method that given by Galen in his treatise 'On the Opinions of Hippocrates and Plato,' where Galen maintains that a person who sets out to seek the truth on any subject possesses a method if he knows what must come first in his search, then second, and so on.[24] If this is Galen's concept of method, observes Ramus, then he discusses it everywhere in his writings. Ramus singles out four descriptions of particular methods that seem to satisfy this criterion: three of them occur in the above-mentioned work, the other in the *Ars medica*. Actually what Ramus is dealing with in this passage is not what might truly be called Galen's method. For as we have seen, Galen advocated a whole philosophical program embracing what he considered valid in the methods of Hippocrates, Plato, Aristotle, and the Stoics. Ramus was incapable of handling such a large assignment in the history of philosophy—although, to his credit, he did recognize the Platonic origin of much of Galen's discussion.

The first method that Ramus finds in Galen's treatise 'On the Opinions of Hippocrates and Plato,' he describes as follows:

The first concerns the comparison of similar and dissimilar [things], the accurate cognition of which seems to be sufficient and suitable in itself, in Galen's view, so much does he extol this method—and here you will see that he is speaking of our method. This passage occurs at the beginning of the book where Galen is interpreting the [following] passage of Hippocrates on similitude and dissimilitude:[25] . . . . "It is possible for all to learn whether things are similar or dissimilar, beginning from the largest and the easiest, from what is known completely in every way, which we may see and hear, and which we may perceive by sight and smell and taste and mind, by means of which we know.". . . This saying of Hippocrates is the true way and gives the same method Aristotle advocates

---

[23] "At quanvis Galenus talis tantusque philosophus in quamplurimis rebus fuerit, attamen quid de methodis docuerit, animadvertamus. Appellat modo μέθοδον, modo θεωρίαν, ut Simplicius, modo διδασκαλίαν τάξεως.   Verba mittamus, rem teneamus." *Ibid.*, p. 51ᵛ.

[24] The passage occurs on pp. 730-31 of Müller's edition of Galen, *De placitis Hippocratis et Platonis* (Leipzig, 1874).

[25] Ramus here quotes the Greek text of Galen given on pp. 732-33 of the Müller edition cited above, and follows it with a Latin translation (as is his practice throughout this particular edition of the *Aristotelicae animadversiones*).

and which we follow from Aristotle: we must begin from those things which are in most common usage and are most readily applied (as Galen rightly interprets), and which are, moreover, most known both to sense and mind—that is, as Aristotle says, both absolutely by nature and to us and our senses. . . . But Galen did not notice the form of artificial disposition in this passage of Hippocrates, but took the question to which the method was applied by Hippocrates for discussion and solution as the method itself.

Technically, says Ramus, this is not a method at all but an *argument*, of splendid use in its proper place, but not advanced by Hippocrates as a way of ordering and disposing an art. Through carelessness Galen has accepted as a method something that neither is nor was intended to be one: Ramus dismisses the whole notion as the "scholastic dream of some teacher."[26]

The second of Galen's methods—drawn by him from the *Phaedrus*—consists of a pair of methods necessary for establishing an art, which Galen calls the divisive and the synthetic.[27] Here again Ramus argues that Plato was expounding a single method similar to his own: in constituting or finding an art, to be sure, one must proceed from the collection and division of experiences ("as Plato and his pupil Aristotle taught"), but in teaching an art, one must proceed from that which is more general, prior by nature, and closer to the cause. Ramus maintains, not very convincingly, that these methods correspond to the "analysis" and "genesis" of the Greek commentators, especially Simplicius. Galen had quoted a section of the *Phaedrus* (265D) to show that Plato favored these two methods, but Ramus argues that these are parts of one method, since Plato later refers to them in one breath as "collections and divisions." Futhermore, they are the same as Ramus' own method.[28] The same sort of criticism is applied by Ramus to a passage Galen had cited from the *Philebus*: "But Plato here again says that all arts must be deduced from the most general through the intermediates to the most special, and from the unity of the *summum genus* to the multitude of infinite singulars—in spite of the fact that they may

---

[26] *Aristotelicarum animadversionum liber nonus et decimus*, pp. 52ʳ-52ᵛ.
[27] *Ibid.*, p. 53ʳ.   [28] *Ibid.*, pp. 54ʳ-54ᵛ.

have been found by the contrary way, by means of observation and experience of the most special."[29] Moreover, Plato's writings can furnish no valid example of this so-called double method of Galen's; Ramus appeals to all philosophers to compare the doctrine of Plato with the dogma and opinions of Galen. If they do this, they will recognize the latter for what they are: scholastic foolishness.[30]

For his third possible method, Ramus takes up a passage from the same chapter,[31] in which Galen has set forth three classifications of method, whose invention he again attributes to Plato.[32] The first classification, that of composition and division, has been dealt with before, and the fact that Galen here presents it as a single method proves Ramus' contention that they were indeed just one. Yet it is impossible for a single art to be instituted by both kinds of order. The second classification, that of utilizing the knowledge of consequences and repugnances, Ramus dismisses by remarking again that it is just one of the dialectical arguments or *topoi*, not a method.[33] Similarly, the last classification offered by Galen, that of the comparison of mutual things, greater, equal, and similar, does not constitute a method but an argument: for it does not tell the person composing an art what should come first, second, and so on. These arguments, which may be of great use in invention, are of no use in disposition, which is, on Ramus' showing, the concern of method.

Finally, Ramus comes[34] to the traditional "three methods" of Galen, those ways of teaching with order presented at the start of the *Ars parva*. According to Galen the first method, that of "analysis," is the one by which all arts are found and constituted; in the *De medicae artis constitutione* he celebrates it not only by precept but also by example. Ramus thinks that Simplicius followed Galen in this method, calling "analysis" by the same name but using "genesis" for Galen's "diaeresis."[35] Analysis is indeed

---

[29] *Ibid.*, p. 54v.   [30] *Ibid.*, p. 55r.
[31] Galen, *De placitis Hippocratis et Platonis*, ed. Kühn, V. 796-97.
[32] *Aristotelicarum animadversionum, liber nonus et decimus*, p. 55v.
[33] *Ibid.*, p. 56r.   [34] *Ibid.*, p. 56v.   [35] *Ibid.*, p. 57r.

superior in respect of dignity; however, the arts are not found by
this method but by induction from singular facts, as Plato, Aristotle, and Galen himself elsewhere maintain.[36] Ramus challenges
not only Galen's modesty in claiming to be the inventor of this
method but his memory as well, for he had just quoted passages
from Plato to the same effect.[37] The second method, that of
composition, has already been disposed of by Ramus when considering that return way which corresponds to division: it is
invalid because by its dictates the more specific would precede the
more general, to the utter confusion of the art.[38] The third
method, that of definition, gives no guidance as to what should
come first, second, and so on in the disposition of an art, and
hence is not a genuine method by Galen's own criterion.[39] Having
disposed of the particular suggestions to be found in Galen,
Ramus asserts that experience, use, and utility of all precepts
and doctrines—which Galen called the sole master—all recommend the single method which he himself advocates, based upon
the experience, use, and utility of grammar, rhetoric, logic, mathematics, and philosophy.[40]

Here Ramus concludes his examination of the methodology of
Hippocrates, Plato, Aristotle, and Galen, the net result of which
is to show that they all agree in recommending a single method
which Ramus himself endorses, and that all the other methods
which they may seem to recommend are inventions of the school-
masters or delusions of their inventors. We may judge the
method of Galen best by studying his own usage, not the miscel-
laneous methodology that he took over from the "scholastic
dreams of inane methods and untried comments of the teachers"
rather than from true and excellent examples. The reason for
devoting this much space to the subject of method, says Ramus,
is that only by the restitution of the true method can the logic of
the *Organon,* so rich and fertile, be rescued from the confusion
into which it has fallen. Thus Ramus considers that by the use

---

[36] *Ibid.,* pp. 57ᵛ-58ʳ.   [37] *Ibid.,* p. 58ʳ.   [38] *Ibid.*   [39] *Ibid.,* p. 58ᵛ.
[40] *Ibid.,* p. 60ᵛ.

of the true (Aristotelian) method he has produced the compendium of logic so much sought after by the men of his time—selecting from a confused mass the necessary, syngeneous and universal
documents of logic, so that the prior precedes and the posterior
by nature follows.[41]

METHOD IN RAMUS' TEXTBOOK OF DIALECTIC

The textbook with which Ramus proposed to fill this need was
his 'Dialectical Institutions.'[42] It is indeed a compendium, com-
pressing into a small space the whole of the *Organon*, with a very
prominent place given to the *Topics*, as one might expect. The
topics comprise the finding part of dialectic, while syllogism and
method form the disposing part. Reasoning has no other function
than these two—finding and disposing.[43] Disposition ("the suitable collocation of things found") is a part of doctrine obviously
of great service for strengthening the memory, so that one and
the same teaching deals with two major powers of the soul,
intelligence and memory. If disposition deals with only one
argument, it will be a syllogism; if with many, method.[44] The
disposition of many arguments is of two sorts, one a method of
doctrine, the other of prudence. The *methodus doctrinae* is that
set forth in his 'Aristotelian Observations': the disposition of
many things, from universal and general principles to the subordinate and singular parts, by means of which the whole subject
may be more easily taught and perceived. All that is required for
the methodical disposition of doctrine is that the general and
universal (e.g., a definition or some sort of comprehensive

[41] *Ibid.*, page unnumbered, between p. 60 and p. 61.
[42] The account which follows is based upon an early form of the work: Petrus
Ramus, *Institutionum dialecticarum libri III* ... (Paris, 1547), a copy of which I
used in the library of Teachers College, Columbia University. Walter Ong lists
this edition on page 51 of his *Ramus and Talon Inventory* as the fourth of seventeen printed editions of the work.
[43] "Dialecticae artis partes duae sunt, Inventio et Dispositio: posita enim quaes-
tione, de qua disserendum, sit, probationes et argumenta quaeruntur; deinde iis via
et ordine dispositis, quaestio ipsa explicatur; tertia mentis actio in disserendo nulla
est." Ramus, *Institutionum dialecticarum*, pp. 2-3.
[44] *Ibid.*, p. 77.

summary) should precede in teaching; the special explication of the parts should follow; the definition of single parts and their illustration by suitable examples should be last.[45] Ramus again states his opposition to the doctrines he opposed in the other work, remarking that there is no need of the precepts of finding here, nor of the syllogism. For all things have been found and all the parts proved true and examined.[46] On the other hand, the second sort of disposition (the "method of prudence") cautions us to give due consideration to the conditions of persons, things, times, and places, and depends upon a man's natural judgment and prudence: it is not a matter of art at all.[47]

Ramus' pronouncements on the subject of method proceed generally according to the method of dichotomies for which Ramists later became notorious. Ramus himself does not seem to have specifically defended this practice, so reminiscent of the *Sophist* dialogue. Almost the only time that Ramus divides anything into more than two parts is when he gives the general requirements for mastery of the arts of reasoning: in this one case he follows the ancient trichotomy of "nature, art, and exercise." When the student of dialectic has mastered the precepts of the art and fixed them firmly in his mind, he must exercise his newly acquired art in two ways: by "analysis" (the exploration of disputations already made) and by "genesis" (the production of new disputations).[48] All sorts of disputations, in orators and poets as well as in philosophers, should be weighed by the law of method: faulty ones as well as praiseworthy, just as Socrates in the Platonic dialogues takes the speech of Lysias to task because it defines nothing and divides nothing. An immense obscurity arises from such confusion of things. One can see how universal this fault is. For one who leads a willing person by a hidden way is just as much at fault as he who leads someone resisting by an open way. Nor need we here recall, Ramus adds, that the term "method" is on everyone's lips but no one uses the true method. In explaining disciplines there is one

---

[45] *Ibid.*, pp. 122-23.   [46] *Ibid.*, p. 124.   [47] *Ibid.*, p.129.   [48] *Ibid.*, p.136.

simple way, from general to species, from whole to parts—a way that has scarcely ever been observed in the course of centuries.[49]

SUMMARY

This constitutes the whole of Ramus' methodology. One can see how this doctrine might sweep that part of Europe which was not tied to traditional logic and methods, for it is simple to grasp, without nuances or subtleties of any kind, and apparently offers a significant alternative to the overcomplex methodologizing which writers in the Aristotelian tradition had developed. From the authorities whom Ramus attacks and reduces to advocates of his single method, we can see how diversified was the material upon which the medical and philosophical Aristotelians were relying for support. Actually, they were in possession of the materials for a thorough understanding of Greek methodology, and it may be that Ramus sensed the historical connection between the analytic method of Hippocrates, Socrates' dialectical method, Aristotle's scientific methodology, and Galen's adaptation of them all. But Ramus' own analysis was a tendentious leveling of all to one common denominator—always proceeding from the general and more known whole, to the specific and less known parts.

The disposition of the rules of an art has little to do with the later conceptions of scientific method. But in calling for examples of method and in setting up the criterion of usefulness, Ramus introduced (though he was not the first to do so) useful antidotes to the smug and abstract methodologizing of Scholastic Aristotelians. This challenge was then taken up by traditionalists who believed sincerely that Aristotle practiced what he preached —and that the methods he advocated were exceedingly subtle and not to be reduced to the single method espoused by Ramus.

---

[49] *Ibid.*, pp. 160-61. It is interesting to compare one sentence from this passage ("Minime vero necesse est hoc loco commemorare, quam omnes methodi nomen in ore habeant, quamque vera methodo utatur fere nemo") with the similar passage from Ramus' teacher, Johann Sturm: "Methodum igitur, quae hodie in omnium est ore et usurpatur a paucis, etc.," quoted on p. 123, n. 7.

Chapter 6. THE REACTION TO THE METHODOLOGIES OF RAMUS AND THE DIALECTICIANS

The methodological "reform" of Ramus stirred up a tremendous reaction among European scholars. "At least Ramus' industry was this much help to the republic of logic," observed an English writer on logic, "that it aroused good minds to pursue the subject of method more diligently."[1] Melanchthon's doctrines of method could be accepted by many academic Aristotelians because he represented a Humanistic outlook congenial to their own: like him they were willing to recognize in Aristotle the most methodical form and highest development of Greek philosophy while conceding that the Aristotelian treatises could not rival Plato's dialogues as literary works. Melanchthon's methodology, in other words, could be absorbed into the mainstream of Aristotelian thought. But Ramus, with his replacement of the *Posterior Analytics* altogether, was a challenge to be reckoned with by all who claimed to be true Peripatetics. And the challenge was taken up at once, by Goveanus and Perionius.

CARPENTARIUS: THE MOST DETERMINED OPPONENT OF RAMUS

But the most notorious of the counterattacks against Ramus was that of Jacobus Carpentarius or Jacques Charpentier (1524-74), a colleague at the University of Paris and Ramus' chief academic rival. So bitter was the rivalry between these two men that Carpentarius has even been suspected, although on very dubious grounds, of playing a part in Ramus' death in the St. Bartholomew's Eve Massacre of the Huguenots in 1572. Carpen-

---

[1] Robert Sanderson, in his *Logicae artis compendium* (Oxford, 1618), p. 122.

tarius carried on a lengthy personal feud with Ramus as a result
of various clashes. In 1554 Carpentarius published his observations
on Ramus' textbook of dialectic.[2] In this work, Carpentarius' remarks on method are not lengthy, yet they contain in essence the
approach he was to employ later, pointing out nuances over which
Ramus had run roughshod and calling for a more scholarly treatment of the individual authors cited to support his views. Ad-
dressing himself to Ramus, he quotes a passage from the 'Dialectical Institutions' and points out that Ramus had overlooked several
methods. Carpentarius maintains that Ramus should not have
neglected the Platonic method of *synagogé*, by which the mind
forms universal notions collected from the observation of many
singular things. Surely this would furnish that counsel for acting
required by Ramus of an art—and a very important one at that,
for it exhibits the use of natural reason at its most acute.[3]

Carpentarius then takes his older colleague to task for saying
that Aristotle employed only one method; he cites passages from
the various works of Aristotle to show that the Stagirite used
many different methods. Usually Carpentarius quotes the brief
remarks that Aristotle makes on method at the start of his consideration of a subject, e.g., those in the *Politics*, the *Physics*, the
Parts of Animals, and the *Posterior Analytics*. He shows considerable scholarly insight in his discussion of these passages.
Carpentarius notes, justly enough, that in recommending the
analysis of passages in ancient authors as exercise Ramus has
sent his students on a wild goose chase, for he has systematically
rejected all those who might have served as models of good
method—Cicero and Plato, Quintilian, Galen, Euclid, and Aristotle. In closing, Carpentarius makes the interesting charge that
Ramus puts forth as his own simply what he learned from his
masters: Valla, Agricola, Agrippa, and Vives.[4] (Johann Sturm,

---

[2] I cite from the edition which appeared in the following year: Jacobus Carpentarius, *Animadversiones in libros tres dialecticarum institutionum Petri Rami*
(Paris, 1555). On this edition, see Walter J. Ong, *Ramus and Talon Inventory*
(Cambridge, Mass., 1958), pp. 498-99.
[3] Carpentarius, *Animadversiones*, p. 35r.
[4] *Ibid.*, pp. 38r-38v.

who might very well have been added to this list, is not mentioned.)

Ten years later Carpentarius followed up this initial assault with a more detailed 'Disputation on Method,'[5] which he incorporated later into his 'Comparison of Plato with Aristotle,'[6] a work in that conciliating trend which, as we have had occasion to notice, was a prominent feature of the period. In this later work, Carpentarius emerges as a capable scholar, displaying considerable knowledge of ancient philosophy. He gives the impression of having devoted much more thorough attention to the reading of the original texts than Ramus, even though he was perhaps not as familiar with Greek as was his enemy.[7] We have previously noted how skillfully Carpentarius characterized the *Epitome* of Albinus as a mixture of Platonic, Aristotelian, and even Stoic doctrine.

Once again the general tenor of Carpentarius' answer to the insistence of Ramus upon a single method in all the arts and sciences is that there are many methods, not just one.

There is no single Method for investigating and explaining that which has already been found, nor are all parts of the same art treated by the same method in the continuity of teaching. Nor is that which we call "analytic" suitable only for the teaching of things found, but is necessary for the diverse manners of analysis, for constituting the arts in the mind when it is a matter of investigating them.[8]

As a step toward clearing up the verbal confusion introduced by Ramus' reduction of all methods to one, Carpentarius tries to distinguish the senses in which the ancient writers used the words "analysis," "genesis," "diaeresis," and "synthesis," all of which

[5] It first appeared as *Disputatio de methodo, quod unica non sit, contra Thessalum, Academiae Parisiensis methodicum . . .* (Paris, 1564). "Thessalus" was Carpentarius' scornful name for Ramus: Thessalus was the rival of Galen who offered an accelerated course in medicine.

[6] *Platonis cum Aristotele in universa philosophia comparatio, quae hoc commentario in Alcinoi institutionem ad eiusdem Platonis doctrinam explicatur* (Paris, 1573). The treatise on method occupies pp. 48-76 of this work.

[7] In the unpaged preface to his 'Comparison of Plato with Aristotle,' Carpentarius remarks that his knowledge of Greek is good enough to enable him to catch errors in Ficino's translations of the Platonists, but not good enough to enable him to remedy them.

[8] *Platonis cum Aristotele in universa philosophia comparatio,* p. 75.

appeared frequently in the discussions of method. Then, in the multiplicity of meanings that result from this examination of ancient usage, Carpentarius asks whether it is possible to maintain, against Aristotle and indeed all antiquity, that one method is to be constituted in all arts.[9]

The critical acumen of Carpentarius is shown especially in his discussion of "analysis" in Aristotle, which he regards as derived from geometrical usage; he points out the references in the *Ethics* to the similarity between a person deliberating and a geometer analyzing a problem. The inscription of the *Prior Analytics* and the *Posterior Analytics*, Carpentarius thinks, is also taken from geometrical usage, because those works contain the rule of treating all arts exactly. By this inscription Aristotle indicates that the geometers are to be greatly imitated as the most exact artificers and true "methodics."[10]

Carpentarius takes Ramus to task for neglecting the method by which arts are originally investigated at the expense of the manner in which an art already discovered is disposed. He points out[11] that the definition of method that Ramus cites from Galen refers to the original inquiry. In order to avoid any misunderstanding over terms, Carpentarius selects a definition of the term from Galen to which he is sure Ramus will agree (although it differs from the one Ramus had offered): "Method is the institution of a way or order in many things pertaining to the subject or art yet not obtaining the same grade in it."[12]

---

[9] *Ibid.*, p. 50.

[10] "Analysis, ut intelligi potest ex Aristotelis capite tertio libri tertii *Ethicorum*, pertinet ad Geometrarum descriptiones: in eisque significat revocationem eius de quo quaeritur ad principia in suo genere omnino prima, per ea quae intermedia sunt. In quibus nullus gradus sine vitio praetermitti potest. Hinc ab eodem translata ad artem demonstrandi; quam inde 'Analyticam' appellavit. Ut in explicatione eius, quae artium omnium exacte tractandarum regulam continet, vel sola inscriptione indicaret se maxime Geometras imitari: ut exactissimos artifices et valde Methodicos. . . ." *Ibid.*, p. 51.

[11] *Ibid.*, p. 54. Carpentarius cites Galen's definition of method in *De methodo medendi* (Kühn, X, 31), in which to find something by method is opposed to finding it by chance, so that we are told what should come first in our inquiry, what second, and so on.

[12] "In qua disputatione, ne in verbo magis quam in re laboremus, constituamus quid Methodi nomine significetur: ut ad id tanquam ad regulam nos in hac dis-

Carpentarius first observes that Ramus had introduced his long discussion of method as a comment upon Aristotle's distinction of the *a priori* and the *a posteriori* methods in the *Posterior Analytics*, noting that these surely apply not just to the disposition but to the investigation of the subject of an art as well. Carpentarius considers this distinction very important in philosophy, but will not deal with it in this place. Ramus should have discussed method in the part of his logic that concerns Invention —unless he intended to suggest that the order of the *loci* which he listed in that part of his dialectic should be followed by a person investigating an art. But not a word appears of this sort of method.[13] Ramus tries to avoid criticism by calling his method a *methodus doctrinae*, but even as a method of teaching his doctrine is oversimplified and inadequate: here too Carpentarius would maintain that there are various methods, or rather a more complex single method with different parts.[14]

Noting that Ramus has claimed Hippocrates, Plato, Aristotle, and Galen as champions of his single method, Carpentarius observes that Ramus thus sanctions an analytic method that embraces all of the various meanings given to "analysis" by these writers.[15] This means that Ramus, in order to make his doctrine consistent, has to show, by example as well as by declaration, that each of the four "analytic" methods recommended by these writers proceeds always from the more general and universal. Carpentarius takes the illustrations that Ramus had used (from physics, grammar, arithmetic, and geometry) and shows that he was guilty of inconsistency in his treatment of them.[16] Thus the method proposed by Ramus fails to satisfy Galen's criterion, since it offers conflicting advice as to what parts of a discipline should

---

putatione referamus. 'Sit vero haec, in multis ad eandem rem sive artem pertinentibus, nec tamen eandem gradum in hac obtinentibus, viae sive ordinis institutio.' " *Platonis cum Aristotele in universa philosophia comparatio,* p. 53. The passage in Galen comes from the *De placitis Hippocratis et Platonis.*

[13] *Platonis cum Aristotele in universa philosophia comparatio,* pp. 57-59.

[14] "Quam tu Methodum doctrinae appellas, ut eam significes rebus docendis magis quam inveniendis esse accommodatam. Hanc, inquam, doctrinae Methodum unicam esse vis: ego vero multiplicem, eiusque partes inter se differentes esse contendo." *Ibid.,* p. 60.

[15] *Ibid.,* p. 62.   [16] *Ibid.,* p. 64.

come first: it gives no guidance for instituting an art out of the "many things pertaining to the subject of art but not obtaining the same grade in it."

Carpentarius agrees with Ramus that method deserves a pre-eminent place in philosophical inquiry. Not only has it not been in practice long, but the precepts of the art are most difficult to explain. Carpentarius does not agree that Aristotle's method could be surpassed, but holds that it ought to be followed. The *ars disserendi* was brought by Aristotle to its present state, in which it can truly be called the art of the other arts, not only the art of explicating them when the matter has already been found but also of investigating and constituting them. Although he approves of the division of method into a method of exact doctrine and one of common prudence, Carpentarius deplores the substitution of examples from poets and orators for those from the most serious philosophers.[17]

Carpentarius refutes Ramus' attack on the distinction between "analysis" and "genesis," in which Ramus had maintained that the commentators were wrong in making analysis prior to genesis. For in ethical deliberation the analysis of the end must certainly precede the active pursuit of that end by the means chosen. And in respect to the arts, if we call "genesis" the ascent from singulars and their observation, then that analysis by which men are aroused to the investigation of these must precede. Possibly what deceived Ramus was the fact that he equated "genesis" with the synthesis (*synagogé*) of Plato's *Phaedrus* and "analysis" with Plato's *diaeresis* in the same dialogue. In this case genesis must indeed precede analysis, for the collection of the idea out of single instances must precede its intellectual analysis.[18] The confusion in which Ramus finds himself can only be due to his neglect of the different meanings of words such as "analysis": if he wishes to give the word a new sense, then he should not take the ancients to task for using it in a sense other than his.[19]

The subject matter of any art or science may be said to be a whole in two senses: as an integral whole composed of member

[17] *Ibid.*, p. 66.   [18] *Ibid.*, pp. 69-70.   [19] *Ibid.*, p. 70.

parts, or as a universal which comprises many species within its scope. If we call the composition of the integral whole out of its parts "genesis," and the distribution of a genus into its species "analysis," clearly these two methods are both applicable to a single art, and yet they are different. But they are methods satisfying Galen's criterion.[20] Both of these methods find a place in teaching, especially in the writing of compendia of arts, for men need to be stimulated to the study of an art by an analysis that sets up the end to be achieved, and they then need a genetic account of how that end is to be reached. Certainly Galen followed some such procedure in the *Ars parva*, which is not written by a third method, but is a compendious mixture of the other two methods.[21] Men are aroused to the finding of arts by analysis, but in the observation of precepts they follow genesis, which Carpentarius, with Galen, might also call *synthesis*.[22]

CARPENTARIUS' MERITS AS A CRITIC AND SCHOLAR

Carpentarius limits his attack on the Ramist methodology to an examination of the authorities from which Ramus drew his doctrine: Plato, Aristotle, and Galen. This procedure was certainly justified in view of the heavy reliance Ramus placed upon the testimony of the ancients (in spite of his professed independence in philosophizing). From a purely scholarly standpoint, it must be conceded that Carpentarius was much more astute than his opponent in selecting references to method in the works of clas-

---

[20] *Ibid.*, pp. 71-72.

[21] "...Praesertim in artium compendiis, in quibus ad hominum studia excitanda si e primo loco posito, eoque aliqua definitione concluso, artes ipsas Analytice constituimus, deinde in eisdem a primis elementis breviter expositis, ad id quod maximum est, per Genesin ascendimus.... Hoc vero quicunque facere instituunt, ab earum artium quas tradere volunt definitione incipiant est necesse. Non quod ab hac artis compositio progredi debeat, in quam ipsa potius desinit: sed quia Analyseos, quae Genesin praecedit, caput illa continet. Quod quidem in fine est positum; a quo optima artis definitio duci debet. Et certe Galenus in *Arte medica*, quae *parva*, id est, compendiaria, appellatur, id ipsum quod disputo secutus videtur: in eo ordine quem definitionis esse ait. Quoniam hic non tam fortasse novam Methodi speciem continet a duabus prioribus omnino diversam, quam duarum in unam collectionem quandam compendiariam." *Ibid.*, p. 73.

[22] *Ibid.*, p. 69.

sical philosophy and in explicating them. Although he made no use of the usual Humanist authorities on method—Quintilian, Cicero, and the Stoics—Carpentarius' approach was not very much different from that of the methodologists of the arts: the fact that he used the Platonic dialogues to such advantage reveals this affinity.

Carpentarius recognized that much of what passed for Galen's methodology was in actual fact not scientific methodology at all but was concerned with the transmission or teaching of an "already-constituted" discipline. Yet he was not at all concerned to reconstruct the actual scientific methodology of Galen, although the work 'On the Method of Healing' alone could have furnished ample material for such a reconstruction. He gives instead what might be called a very Platonic version of the methodology of both Aristotle and Galen.

On our intellectual scale, then, Carpentarius ranks halfway between the two extremes of methodological doctrine. Although he was combating the Humanist trend of Ramist methodology, with its exclusive concern for the transmission of the arts rather than their investigation or demonstration, his own philosophical technique was strictly Humanistic, not in the traditional style of the commentators. In his explication of Galen and Aristotle, he managed to separate the pedagogical from the scientific motive and thus to oppose the Humanist methodology in which these were combined or in which the scientific motive was altogether submerged. It may be added that his understanding of Plato was unquestionably broader and sounder than his opponent's. Yet his whole position was essentially a defensive one and yielded little in the way of fresh analysis.

THE INDIGNANT REACTION OF A MEDICAL ARISTOTELIAN: BARTOLO-MEO VIOTTI

In the work of Bartolomeo Viotti, or Viottus (died 1568), a little-known professor of medicine at the war-torn university in Turin, we may glimpse something of the resentment aroused among more traditional teachers of logic and medicine by Ramus and his fellow methodologists. Viotti's book 'On Demonstration'[23] was the product, so he tells us, of a lifelong concern with sound demonstration in medicine. The treatise was prompted by his deep concern over the baleful influence of the dialecticians, who pretended to be good Aristotelians, but who in reality were weakening the general respect for true science. By their emphasis on reasoning on both sides of propositions, they had undermined confidence in all the arts, including medicine.

This treatise is in the form of a dialogue, a rather unusual form for an Aristotelian to adopt. Viotti proposed[24] to set out the method of demonstration, which it is the function of logic to teach. Reversing the complaint of Ramus, he complains that the dialecticians have made "reasoning with probability" or "inferring probable conclusions" the end of the art of dialectic, rather than demonstration. He compares the dialecticians of his day to Favorinus, the teacher whom Galen had attacked as offering both sides of all questions and letting his pupils take their own choice as to which side to adopt.[25] Those who teach the "dialectic of probabilities" affirm that they can teach how to argue with equal persuasiveness for and against any proposition, and can offer as positive doctrine only that infamous dictum: "This one thing we know, that we know nothing." Among the writers of these pernicious volumes on dialectic he lists Melanchthon and Rudolph Agricola. Ramus, although he receives his share of unfavorable attention in the body of the text, is not mentioned here. The dialogue is only incidentally a refutation of Ramus or the other dialecticians, for it purports to be a presentation of Viotti's own views of demonstration. But the antidialectical bias which was instrumental in the composition of the work is evident throughout.

[23] Bartolomaeus Viottus, *De demonstratione libri quinque* (Paris, 1560).

[24] "Scientiam autem perfectam, omnium iudicio, vel nullam habemus, vel eam per demonstrationem acquirimus. Non itaque parvi momenti est demonstrandi ratio, quae nos ad scientiam et veritatem conducit. Hanc vero methodum docere praecipue est Logici scopus." *Ibid.*, dedicatory epistle.

[25] See Galen's *De optima doctrinae genere*, in *Scripta Minora*, ed. Johann Marquardt (Leipzig, 1884), p. 83.

When these perverters of logic write about demonstration,
their conclusions are so sterile and jejune that what they say is
more pernicious than if they had kept silence on the subject
altogether and left it to others. As it is, they corrupt the youth
and lead them to Pyrrhonian and Academic scepticism.[26] It may
be remarked that even such a sworn opponent of the dialecticians
as Viotti does not deny their study a place in the Aristotelian
scheme, nor does he accuse them of "confusing logic with
rhetoric": his major complaint is that they do not deal *adequately*
with demonstration. (Modern students of the period sometimes
tend to forget that the dialecticians acknowledged demonstration
as a subject at all.)

Part of the blame for this revival of Pyrrhonian doubts must
be laid, according to Viotti, upon Aristotle himself, for Aristotle
contrived to hide his meaning so that it is extremely difficult to
extricate it from his treatises. In the opinion of the commentators,
his writings are obscure because they were addressed to lecture
audiences, not to readers. Viotti thinks rather that they are obscure because Aristotle, greedy of fame, deliberately wrote so
that his opinion could be construed either way, as in the question
of the immortality of the soul and in the subject matter of the
Posterior Analytics.[27] The possibility that true demonstration according to Aristotle's precepts may not even exist has been so
much bruited about recently that for many years no one has dared
to put this art into use and practice. "Wherefore, leaving aside
Aristotle's astuteness and skill at hiding his opinions, we present
what has been well said by Galen, Themistius, Philoponus, Averroes, and others, for easy application; and following the way
shown by them, we add something of our own." It would be
ungrateful to suppose that nature, the parent of all, had poured
upon Aristotle all talent and had rendered all of posterity sterile
and ineffectual.[28]

With this pronunciamento, Viotti launches into his exposition
of the method of demonstration which, in the dialectic of its de-

---

[26] *De demonstratione libri quinque*, Preface.
[27] *Ibid.*   [28] *Ibid.*

velopment, almost approaches the Greek. His exposition deals almost entirely with the ideas of Aristotle and Galen on the subject. We may note that although he has professed nothing but scorn for the dialectical tradition of assembling *loci,* his own contribution consists of a peculiar adaptation of the method of the *loci* to demonstration: he lists five "demonstratory *loci"*— axioms, postulates, definitions, causes, and effects—from which specific arguments may be drawn in demonstration. Among these *loci* are the axioms or "dignities," which correspond very closely to Melanchthon's *ennoiai koinai,* and, as in his case, are derived mostly from the theories of Galen. The inner light which nature has implanted in all of us is what enables us to recognize these axioms as true. No method, no way, no rationale has been found which replaces this inner light. All certitude of demonstration derives from it.[29] These demonstratory *loci* alone can furnish arguments for science: dialectical *loci* such as the dialecticians offer are unable to generate anything but opinion.

Viotti quotes Galen as extensively as does any writer of the period. He confesses that if Galen's fifteen books on demonstration still existed, he would not have undertaken the labor of writing the present book.[30] Since Viotti frequently quotes passages from Galen (usually in the translation of Thomas Linacre) in which the ancient physician speaks of "the methods I have handed down in the work on demonstration," we must assume that he was familiar with Galen's usage,[31] and perhaps

[29] "Adeo id in dignitate est evidens, ut ex ipsa nominis expositione statim innotescat, ἀξίωμα enim seu *dignitas* seu *proloquium* seu *maxima,* est propositio universalis adeo manifesta ut ex sola vocum cognitione omnibus innotescat, nulla addita probatione. Non sic se res habet de aliis principiis, nam illa necessum non est quemlibet docendum ex solo naturae lumine habere, sed ab eo qui demonstrandum aliquid suscepit, etiamsi non demonstrari, explicari tamen et probari debent priusquam ponantur, et assumantur tamquam principia manifesta: ut quasi qui videt acutius, alium cui visus sit hebetior, ad videndum adducere videatur. Ob id postulata et definitiones *positiones* vocarunt, quia ponantur tamquam manifesta. Dignitatem vero, quia digna sit cui fides habeatur, citra probationem, 'Omne totum maius esse sua parte' dignitas est, a qua demonstrationes geometricae apud Euclidem dependent, necessum est enim quemlibet docendum hanc habere: docendum inquam in iis, quae ab illius cognitione dependent, habere a seipso intelligo solo lumine adiutum, quin omnibus natura tribuit sensus et intellectum." *Ibid.,* p. 170.
[30] *Ibid.,* Preface.
[31] For example, Viotti speaks of the necessity for explaining the "notion" or

was influenced to speak of the true method from his reading of
that author. Certainly he does not accept the common view of
medical men that the three ways of teaching at the start of the
Ars parva represent Galen's "method" of science. He rejects the
identification of these three ways of teaching with various forms
of demonstration on the grounds that not all arts and sciences
make use of the forms of demonstration. Viotti thinks that it is
false to say that a procedure which goes from first elements or
causes to the end of the discipline or from final end to the first
elements constitutes *demonstration*. For in other works Galen
gives examples of these two orders drawn from the mechanical
arts, which surely do not make use of demonstration. Medicine,
on this showing, would be a "most powerful" science, never
frustrated of its end—which is false. Also the end and those
things into which it is proximately divided would reciprocate—
which is completely false, for it is one thing to divide or resolve
correctly and quite another to demonstrate correctly.[32] In another
work, Viotti maintains that medical expositions must follow the
path laid out by Galen—that "methodical and logical (i.e., rational) way that starts from certain medical postulates and derives
its propositions from them."[33]

Viotti was typical of the "antidialectical" teachers of logic and
medicine, who sternly opposed any pedagogical or rhetorical innovations in their subject and kept to a close reliance on the sci-

---

common acceptance of terms, and adds: "Quam tamen summam necessariam Galenus
et verbis et observatione ostendit, ut primo *Methodi Medendi* cum scribit: 'Tecum
vero omnem sermonem conferam, ipsis usus methodis, quae in commentario de
demonstratione tradidi....' " *Ibid.*, p. 85.

[32] *Ibid.*, pp. 277-78.

[33] "Cumque Aristotele, primo *Posterioris Resolutionis*, tria sint principiorum
genera: proloquia, postulata, et definitiones. In hoc demonstrandi genere, quo
rerum facultates Medicae explicantur, etiam si principia quibus utimur dignitatum
et definitionum nomen omnia non promereantur, nemo tamen erit qui inficiari possit
quin maxima illorum principiorum pars certissima et verissima Medica postulata
sint vocanda: ̣uod si quispiam tam delicati palati est, ut etiam hoc cognitionis
genus a demonstrationis nomine reiiciendum putet, is se nihil scire fateatur, is
methodicam et λ γιχήν, hoc est, rationalem Galeni viam relinquat, Peironeorum
sectae seipsum devoveat...." Bartholomaeus Viottus, *De balneorum naturalium
viribus libri quatuor* ... (Lyons, 1552), pp. 89-90.

entific methodology of Aristotle and Galen, which they read in
the Greek, with considerable concern for its exemplification in
mathematics. In his mind a distinct concept of method had not
yet crystallized, although he was a close follower of Galen, who
spoke frequently and urgently of "method," "scientific method,"
and "logical methods." Viotti's discussion of the axioms necessary to demonstration in all disciplines resembles that of Melanchthon, although it was worked out in much more detail. Probably
if we knew more of such writings from traditional Aristotelians
of the premodern period, we would be able to see how thoroughly
Aristotle's methodology of science had become merged with that
of Galen. For example, the idea that demonstration must rest
upon certain *ennoiai koinai* that lie at the foundation of all
demonstrative disciplines (ethics and jurisprudence included) was
very commonly held, and constituted one of the basic epistemological premises against which John Locke in the seventeenth century was to direct his attack.[34]

It is astonishing to see how vividly the intellectual milieu of
Galen was recaptured by writers such as Viotti or Carpentarius,
who saw in their contemporaries the reincarnation of men whose
doctrine Galen had attacked, Thessalus and Favorinus—names
unfamiliar even to the close student of ancient thought. Galen
was studied so devotedly that his attitudes were adopted by his
sixteenth-century admirers, including his attempt to overcome
the doubts of the Pyrrhonians by the method and certitude of
mathematics. Perhaps no other writer of the period came as close
to recovering the scientific methodology of Galen as did this
obscure Savoyard teacher of medicine. Yet at the same time we
may see the influence of Humanism in his knowledge of Greek
and his frequent quotations in that language; in the dialogue
form in which he chose to present his views on such an academic
subject as demonstration; and in his adaptation of the method of
the *Topics* to strict demonstration.

[34] See the opening passage of Locke's *Essay*. It is quite impossible that Locke
is referring to Descartes when he speaks of the commonly received opinion concerning these *ennoiai koinai*.

A HUMANIST ARISTOTELIAN: JACOB SCHEGK

In roughly the same camp as Viotti was another opponent of
Ramus named Jacob Schegk or Schegkius (1511-87), teacher of
medicine and logic at the University of Tübingen,[35] with whom
Ramus entered into active conflict as the outcome of an exchange
of unsympathetic letters. Schegk had made some derogatory
remarks concerning Ramus in his work, De demonstratione libri
XV (Basel, 1564), an exhaustive scholarly examination of Aristotle's theory of science. Ramus, finding the work in Strasbourg,
wrote to its author proposing a rapprochement of views, an offer
that was indignantly rejected by Schegk. The answer to this
rejection was a 'Defense of Aristotle,' published by Ramus in
1571.

Schegk was well trained in Greek and Latin and, in fact, had
been offered in 1531 the opportunity of lecturing on Virgil and
Theognis at Tübingen. He spent the great majority of his teaching years lecturing on medicine and on logic (the Organon of
Aristotle) : at these lectures the students had the Greek text before them, while Schegk explained single sentences in Latin, with
here and there a word of German in addition.

The work on demonstration that aroused the interest of Ramus
was a commentary on the Posterior Analytics, "painfully written
after years of effort at understanding the obscure thought of
Aristotle." Through his lectures on medicine, Schegk came to
appreciate the need for thorough grounding in Aristotelian philosophy: he was not one of those who while teaching medicine
scorned philosophy. Schegk considers the teaching of Aristotelian philosophy as practiced in his time, by compendia and paltry
precept, to be destructive of sound learning.[36] He exhorts students
to study those most outstanding philosophers, Plato and Aristotle.
Schegk especially inveighs against those in universities who

---

[35] For a brief life of Schegk, see Cristoph Sigwart, "Jakob Schegk, Professor der
Philosophie und Medicin: Ein Bild aus der Geschichte der Universität Tübingen
im sechzehnten Jahrhundert," Kleine Schriften (Freiburg im Breisgau, 1889), I,
256-91. See also Charles Waddington, Ramus, sa vie, ses écrits, et ses opinions
(Paris, 1855), pp. 198-99.

[36] De demonstratione libri XV, Dedicatory epistle.

pretend to be philosophers when they are not and who attack
dialectic, wishing to substitute for it rhetoric and grammar. They
are ignorant of true dialectic, *magistra et dux scientiarum omnium*.
In denying the validity of dialectic they eliminate the only way of
distinguishing true arts from false.[37] In order to avoid falling
into Pyrrhonian doubt and scepticism, we require an art of dialectic by which to discern the true from the false.[38] The sciences
and arts have their quarrels and differences of opinion, just as in
matters of religion and politics: only dialectic can be an impartial
judge.[39] Toward this end, Schegk proposes to examine in detail
the doctrine of the *Posterior Analytics*, the most difficult of Aristotle's works, one on which he had spent many years of toil.
Schegk takes to task all of the commentators on this work—
Greek, Latin, and Arab. None of them understood it, and some
of them could not even explain what they themselves thought.[40]
He hopes to bring more light than they did to the explication of
the doctrine of the *Analytics*, although this treatise is undoubtedly obscure and oracular.[41] Galen's fifteen books on demonstration have not come down to us, but their loss is not at all equivalent to that which would have been ours had Aristotle's *Analytics* perished.[42]

Since nothing is more difficult than knowing and nothing more
excellent than knowledge, it will surely be no commonplace procedure and method that teaches us how we ought to investigate
things capable of being known, apprehended, and perceived, and
things that lie hidden. This method is certainly no less difficult,
arduous, and laborious than the sciences themselves. To be sure,
this doctrine and method is not itself a science but the instrument
of the sciences; it does not have a fixed subject matter but con-

---

[37] "Quod si artem aliquam esse negent, qua ratione quaeso hic litigator sua
veriora esse probabit, quam alterius, siquidem nulla fuerit ars, nulla methodus vera
et consentanea probandi?" *Ibid.*
[38] "Ars igitur ab ingeniosis et eruditis hominibus quaedam est constituta, qua
instructus quispiam posset in omnibus verum discernere a falso: quam Logicam
seu Dialecticam appellari in Scholis notum est." *Ibid.*
[39] *Ibid.*   [40] *Ibid.*, pp. 10-11.   [41] *Ibid.*, p. 11.
[42] *Ibid.*, No doubt Schegk added this comment by way of apology for the sub-
title of his work, which seemed to promise a restoration of the lost work of Galen.

siders the logical attributes of the things the sciences deal with;
it can be accommodated to the use of all disciplines.[43]

The work that follows is a long and laborious study dealing
with Aristotle's theory of demonstration, drawing upon Plato and
the whole of the Greek tradition for further insight. Throughout
the book Schegk campaigns against the "subverters of true
logic," occasionally offering his own views on subjects usually
dealt with by them, such as pedagogical matters. He stresses the
point that the knowledge of languages and eloquence cannot
replace a sound basis of scientific knowledge, which requires an
order of learning proceeding from principles.[44]

In the present confusion and controversy we need some instrument by
which the hidden and abstruse can be found and the separation of doubtful and conflicting opinions can be directed to a certain bound of truth.
This scale or balance is not itself a science but a certain *via et ratio
sciendi,* which Aristotle called "method," or sometimes "manner of inquiry" or "paideia." He called this art "analysis," and by its precepts we
are able to look for the unknown reasons of science, resolve the per-
plexed and ambiguous, collect the true and fitting ones, and bind them
in the complex of demonstration by the necessity and solidity of science.[45]

Method requires that all things be demonstrated in order and by suitable
principles. And that surely is an art, whose knowledge enables the pos-
sessor (as Cicero says) to produce an art out of things that do not as yet
form an art [Schegk quotes from the *De Oratore*]. Relying on this,
Aristotle not only set up the universal disciplines of philosophy, but even
corrected those disciplines corrupted by the errors of his predecessors and
brought them into order. No philosopher was more observant of his
method and hence none was more learned than he, nor indeed more exact

---

[43] *Ibid.*

[44] "Qualis sit Methodus docendi et discendi quidpiam. Quia vero hoc opere
instituimus eius, quo tractandae sunt omnes scientiae, quasi ἀναστοιχείωσιν et
ἀνάλυσιν tradere: prius non inutiliter nos aliquid opinor de Methodo docendi et
discendi scripturos: praesertim cum sint plurimi, qua via et quo ordine sit perven-
iendum ad cognitionem scientiarum, qui se nescire fateantur. De quo in praesentia
non omnia, nec ut res ipsa postulat, sed quantum satis est instituto nostro, pauca
quaedam commemorabimus. Omnis a principiis quibusdam ducitur, et quasi fundamentis extruitur scientia: et his quidem ut notissimis, ita longe verissimis. Ordo
autem non modo iuvat et promovet eruditionem, sed etiam discentibus est neces-
sarius: cum posteriora, incognitis prioribus, non possint intelligi. Sunt deinde non
nulla studia, quae magis ornant cognitionem veri in disciplinis, ut linguarum et
eloquentiae; non autem praecipue iuvant." *Ibid.,* p. 18.

[45] *Ibid.,* p. 437.

in finding and judging. Both analysis (transmitted by him most perfectly) and the use of the art are most clearly exemplified by his own philosophy. [Aristotle was] most perspicacious in hunting out the causes of natural things and in the explication of all nature—not only eager to guard the truth and fight for it, but also a very sharp disputer in refuting and confuting false opinions. And so the divine Aristotle showed us the way that leads to the science of things, by which it is even known what man's end is and what his *summum bonum;* although different people may entertain different views of it because of their ignorance of the method by which Aristotle warns us (in the *Ethics*) to proceed, lest led by false principles we should be deceived.[46]

Schegk is another of those writers who were goaded by the innovations of Ramus and others to return to the Greek text of Aristotle and to seek there the answers to the challenges of the Humanists. As the passage just quoted shows, they were forced to approach the *Posterior Analytics* by trying to find in it doctrines that would satisfactorily refute the superficial dismissal of this part of the *Organon* as useless by the "arts" methodologists. This attempt to justify Aristotle as the founder and user of a "method" seems to have been due chiefly to the threat offered to traditional Aristotelianism by the innovators.[47] But instead of falling back upon the methodology of the commentaries, Humanist Aristotelians like Schegk turned directly to the *Organon* in Greek, disregarding centuries of explication, just as the French jurists turned to their sources in Roman law and applied philological methods directly to them, disregarding the glossators. Yet Schegk is struggling toward a conception of method as the instrument for distinguishing the true from the false in *all* the sciences.

[46] *Ibid.,* pp. 441-42.
[47] See the exchange of letters between Schegk and Ramus in the collected speeches and prefaces of the latter, especially the following passage from a letter of Schegk: "Praeterea tuam Methodon in artibus ordinandis, non possum videre qualis sit, cum Aristotelis Dialecticam ignores, et Apodictica tantopere contemnas. Multi multa scribunt hodie de Methodis, ignarissimi *Analyticorum,* quos facile patior abundare in suo sensu, utinam nobis ipsis non tantum arrogaremus, et potius veterum inventa explicaremus, quam his per calumniam explosis, nostras nugas juventuti erudiendae in Philosophia obtruderemus." *Petri Rami professoris regii et Audomari Talei Collectaneae Praefationes, Epistolae, Orationes . . .* (Marburg, 1599), p. 190.

Schegk was led by his interest in establishing Aristotle as the chief methodist of science to examine geometry by the principles of the *Posterior Analytics*, being aided in his enterprise by Themistius and other commentators who illustrated Aristotle's theory of science by reference to theorems in Euclid. This examination, deliberately chosen to offset the literary and poetical interpretations of the rhetoricizing tradition, provoked Ramus' attack upon Schegk in his 'Defense of Aristotle against Jacob Schegk,'[48] in which Ramus attempted, by all sorts of appeals, to justify his own position and undermine that of Schegk. Against Schegk, Ramus maintains that mathematical examples of demonstration are completely alien to Aristotle's doctrine of proof.[49] The idea that "most powerful demonstrations" are not to be found in mathematics was not new with Ramus: it had been under discussion in Italy for some time, as we have seen.[50] After a good many pages of the invective common to disputes of the period, Ramus answers Schegk's charge that he is unmethodical. Reiterating his own definition of method, and stating once again that it is the method followed by Aristotle, Ramus proclaims that "the method that proceeds from the general is the one light of all the arts." He charges Schegk with being very obscure in his presentation of method: he never defines it satisfactorily, although he speaks constantly of Aristotle's method and calls Ramus unmethodical.[51] Schegk ought to concede that there is only one method, both logical and Aristotelian: its maxim is "Let the prior by nature precede."[52]

SUMMARY

Passages like these make it clear why Ramus' doctrine of method aroused such a storm of resentment among those who taught Aristotelian logic in universities. Not content with presenting his version of the *Topics* as a method useful in the market-place and

---

[48] Petrus Ramus, *Defensio pro Aristotele adversus Iac. Schecium* (Lausanne, 1571). [49] *Ibid.*, pp. 91-92. [50] On p. 90 above.
[51] Ramus, *Defensio pro Aristotele*, pp. 103-5. [52] *Ibid.*, p. 107.

forum as well as in the schools, Ramus claimed that it represented an application of the single method that prevailed in the presentation of any discipline, and what is more, that it was Aristotle's method and that he used no other. This was too much for the logicians, who could disregard Agricola and Melanchthon—after all, they all would have conceded that the *Topics* was useful both in logic and in rhetoric—but the sweeping elimination of what they regarded as the heart of the *Organon*, the *Posterior Analytics*, was much too arrogant. The result was a mass of polemical literature defending or attacking the "single method." The dispute raged furiously in France, Germany, and England: it seems to have disturbed Italy very little.[53]

[53] The fact that Ramus' writings were placed on the *Index* in the first class probably discouraged open consideration of his views in strongly Catholic countries such as Italy and Spain.

Chapter 7. THE ITALIAN ARISTOTELIANS

Meanwhile in Italy the tradition of the commentaries continued on its way, little disturbed by the storms of methodological controversy north of the Alps. The traditional authorities remained in esteem; it was not considered reactionary to cite Averroes or Albert the Great. Developments in the doctrine of order and method in Italy sprang from the discussion initiated by the Greek commentators and carried on by their medieval counterparts, Arab and Latin.

The fifteenth-century background of this traditional methodology is not very well known; it shares this condition with Scholasticism in general. In part this is due to the relative inaccessibility of the texts: for this period, manuscripts must be consulted as well as printed editions, while the latter, if printed prior to the magic date of 1500, are collector's items. Consequently research into fifteenth-century thought has all of the difficulties but offers little of the excitement of research into medieval thought—at least, that is the general impression scholars have, and it is very likely sound.[1] However, what we learn of writers from the early sixteenth century leads us to expect that order and method must have been under discussion during the preceding century almost as intensively as it was during the sixteenth.

AUTHORITIES INVOKED BY THE ITALIAN ARISTOTELIANS

Unquestionably a good deal of this interest must be attributed to the renewed study of the Greek commentators. In the sixteenth

---

[1] Naturally I am speaking here of the prevailing Scholastic philosophers in the universities, not of such well-known and interesting figures as Nicholas of Cusa and Marsilio Ficino.

century there were dozens of Latin translations printed of such commentators as Alexander of Aphrodisias, Philoponus, Ammonius, Themistius, Simplicius, and Eustratius—translations made almost exclusively by Italian scholars. All these Greek commentators could add fuel to the disputes over order and method, for in almost any of their works scholars could find Platonic doctrines of dialectical method mingled in uneasy company with Aristotelian methods of proof. More frequently than not, the Greek commentators could furnish material to combat the arbitrary identification of Galen's "three methods" of teaching with Aristotle's theory of scientific proof, made by the Arabs and those Latin commentators who followed them. Yet the Arabs continued to have their champions, who especially favored the interpretations of Averroes. These followers of Averroes may not have been as dogmatically loyal as Renan seemed to think,[2] but certainly the interpretations of Averroes (never, indeed, too divergent from Aristotle, except on a few points where Aristotle is not too clear himself) were given the most serious consideration throughout the Renaissance in Italy, as they had been since the last decades of the thirteenth century in schools such as Bologna. The standard texts in the methodology of the Italian Aristotelians were Aristotle (particularly the beginning of the *Physics,* the *Parts of Animals,* and the *Posterior Analytics*), Galen (especially the *Ars parva* and the *De Hippocratis et Platonis dogmatis*), the Greek commentators (especially Alexander, Simplicius, and Themistius), and Averroes.

AVERROES' COMMENTARY ON THE PHYSICS IN THE VERSION OF BUCCAFERREA

One of the most influential of Averroes' commentaries was that on the *Physics,* which contained some methodological observations on the manner in which the sciences are investigated and which became one of the standard texts on the subject. We

---

[2] Ernest Renan, *Averroès et l'Averroïsme* (Paris, 1866), pp. 362-416.

shall take as our expositor of Averroistic doctrine a famous teacher of philosophy at Bologna and Rome during the first part of the sixteenth century, Ludovicus Buccaferrea, or Ludovico Boccadiferro (c.1482-1545). In his commentary on the *Physics*, Buccaferrea follows Averroes' version of the usual sequence of introductory headings, among which is one dealing with the *via doctrinae*. Buccaferrea notes first that *doctrina* can be understood in three ways, according to Aristotle: (1) as a habit acquired by the student from the teacher, (2) as the act of teaching itself, or (3) as the instrument by means of which the habit of science is generated in the student. It is in this latter sense that Averroes speaks of the "way of doctrine."[3] According to Averroes the ways of doctrine are five: division, definition, demonstration, enthymeme, and induction.[4] Buccaferrea mentions a possible objection—that "resolution" and "composition" do not appear in this list—and disposes of it on the grounds that these are not ways of doctrine but orders of doctrine by means of which the sciences are ordered. They are not instruments used by the teacher, and therefore Averroes was not guilty of an oversight in omitting them from his ways of doctrine.[5]

Averroes' commentary on the introduction to the *Physics* was the chief text upon which the Italian Aristotelians relied in their discussion of order and method. Since demonstration appears as one of the five ways of doctrine, Averroes' views upon scientific demonstration received great attention in these discussions. Demonstration for Averroes was threefold: he distinguished demonstration of the sign, demonstration of the cause alone, and straightforward demonstration of both the cause and essence.[6] But Buccaferrea will not countenance the attempt to identify any of these as Galen's "compositive" or "resolutive methods": he thus rejects the attempt of the medical expositors to equate

---

[3] Ludovicus Buccaferreus, *Explanatio libri I. Physicorum Aristotelis . . .* (Venice, 1558), f. 13ᵛ.

[4] "Dicit igitur Averroes: Via doctrinae, id est, instrumentum tradendi scientias, est quincuplex, divisio, definitio, demonstratio, enthymema, et inductio." *Ibid.*, f. 13ʳ.

[5] *Ibid.*, f. 15ʳ.   [6] *Ibid.*, f. 13ᵛ.

Galen's three ways of teaching in one way or another with Averroes' forms of demonstration.

ZABARELLA: AN INDEPENDENT ITALIAN ARISTOTELIAN

We may see the typical features of the Italian Aristotelian tradition in the work of Jacopo Zabarella (1533-89), the most renowned teacher of logic in Europe during the sixteenth century. Zabarella understood his Greek Aristotle so well that his opinions still deserve to be quoted with respect today, but he was also influenced, as we shall try to show, by the commentators. Several of the prominent features of his theory of method—e.g., that the "order of doctrine" is taken not from the nature of things but from our better cognition, or that the "way of doctrine" proceeds from the known to the unknown—are derived not so much from Aristotle as from the Arabs, in particular Averroes.

ZABARELLA'S RELATION TO THE AVERROIST TRADITION

In order to place Zabarella's thought in its historical context, it will be helpful to examine first a work published after his death, his commentary on the *Physics*.[7] At the beginning of this work, Zabarella's remarks that the first five texts of the *Physics* constitute a brief proemium that has received many and varying interpretations.

But I believe that all these are proposed by Aristotle in this proemium: his purpose in the whole of natural philosophy; the "way of doctrine" he intends to use in the whole of science; the "order of doctrine" by which he is going to dispose the books of this science [i.e., physics]; his teaching in the first part of the *Physics,* which concerns first principles; and what is more the "way of doctrine" he will use in investigating these principles.[8]

---

[7] Jacobus Zabarella, *In libros Aristotelis Physicorum commentarii ...* (Venice, 1601). Incidentally, the Latin text used by Zabarella seems to be almost that of the "physics of the old translation" given by Lacombe, *Aristoteles Latinus* (Rome, 1939), pp. 126-27, with the interesting difference that the old translation had *scientias* for *methodos* in the first sentence.

[8] *In libros Aristotelia Physicorum commentarii,* f. 3ᵛ.

Now of the two key phrases in this explication—"way of doctrine" and "order of doctrine"—only the first can be found in the Greek text of Aristotle, who speaks here of the *way* (ὁδός) from what is prior by nature, but not of the *order* (τάξις). Hence, to justify his construing of the passage, Zabarella feels that he must explain the distinction he has introduced into it:

But in order that it may be clear how and where Aristotle does all this, we must state what the "way of doctrine" and the "order of doctrine" are. The "way" consists in a movement (*processus*) from the known to the unknown by syllogistic discourse, for where there is a necessary inference (*illatio*) of this from that by some logical means (*instrumentum*), it is called "method" or "way of doctrine." Thus among the "ways of doctrine" are included all the species of demonstration, as Averroes says—and those who think that the "way" is demonstration *a posteriori* and that the "order of doctrine" is demonstration *a priori* are mistaken. For both are "ways," since they lead us in syllogistic form from known principles by a necessary movement (*processus*) to the knowledge of an unknown conclusion.... Order, on the other hand, is neither a syllogism nor an inference (*processus illativus*) of one thing from another, but merely the suitable disposition of all parts of a science.[9]

There are only two "ways of doctrine" used in science: the principal kind is known as demonstration *propter quid*; the secondary kind is called demonstration *quia*. Aristotle will deal with the secondary kind later in the *Physics*, according to Zabarella: here in the first text he proposes the principal sort of demonstration.

Since Aristotle concludes that in natural science natural things are to be known by their principles, who can doubt that we can acquire a perfect science of things via knowledge of principles? And this truth was not unknown to the Greek commentators, as will be clear to anyone who reads Themistius, Simplicius, and Philoponus—who mention not only the demonstration *a posteriori* of which Aristotle speaks in the second text, but also the demonstration *a priori* he proposes in the first.[10]

Now while there is ample justification for distinguishing two such sorts of demonstration in the *Organon*, it must be stressed that there is little warrant in the Greek of this text for describing

[9] *Ibid.*   [10] *Ibid.*, f. 4ʳ.

Aristotle's "ways" (ὁδοί) to and from the principles as "methods." And Zabarella was certainly enough of a linguist to know that μέθοδος elsewhere in Aristotle would not bear the special weight he was putting upon it here. However shifting the senses of μέθοδος may be in Aristotle's Greek, it would hardly occur to an untutored reader of that Greek to distinguish two such complex "methods" in the way Zabarella has done.[11] Why then, does Zabarella insist on making this distinction?

A plausible explanation, I believe, can be found by considering the Greek commentaries on the *Physics*. Since Zabarella mentions Simplicius, it is highly likely that he was familiar with the quotation from Alexander of Aphrodisias that occurs in Simplicius' commentary on the very same passage of the *Physics*. Alexander had introduced the Stoic definition of μέθοδος into the discussion of this passage, which gave Simplicius the opportunity of noting that method could not be the cognition of principles but only of the science that arises *from* the principles and causes of the thing known.[12]

With this Greek background in mind, we can understand why the famous distinction between the *a priori* and the *a posteriori* should have come to be known and discussed as "methods" by Averroistic Aristotelians. For Zabarella knew perfectly well that Aristotle did not describe these procedures as μέθοδοι but as ὁδοί: in fact, he quotes the words in Greek. As we have seen, his position is that Aristotle in this text[13] is describing the secondary way of doctrine (demonstration *quia*) which we have to use in investigating the principles of physics.

---

[11] A little later, in framing Aristotle's intent in a subsequent passage in syllogistic form, Zabarella notes that Aristotle here is not dealing with things themselves but with all "methods, or sciences." He is thus aware that Aristotle often uses μέθοδος as virtually equivalent to "science" or "art"—and that in this sense there are as many methods as there are arts and sciences.

[12] See p. 47 above.

[13] The text runs as follows in the Latin translation used by Zabarella: "Innata autem est ex notioribus via, et manifestioribus ad manifestiora naturae et notiora; non enim sunt eadem, et nobis nota, et simpliciter. Quapropter necesse est adhunc modum procedere, ex immanifestioribus quidem naturae nobis autem manifestioribus ad manifestiora naturae et notiora." *In libros Aristotelis Physicorum commentarii*, f. 19v.

It now becomes possible to see what Zabarella has drawn from the text of Aristotle and what he has put into it. In the first place, Aristotle had used μέθοδος in the passage, but only in that sense in which it is practically equivalent to τέχνη, especially to a τέχνη as revealed by inquiry. This sense Zabarella neglects altogether. In the discussion of the distinction between *a priori* and *a posteriori*, he is forced to add two elements which were not in Aristotle's text. (1) Because Aristotle says that we have to begin with what is known to us and proceed to the unknown, Zabarella is able to introduce the Arab doctrine that logic gives us the principles for proceeding from that which is known to that which is unknown.[14] (2) Futhermore, by an easy transition, he is able to introduce a technical sense of μέθοδος from Simplicius' commentary on the *Physics*, as a "going forth" (*processus*) to that which can be known by some orderly way (ἡ μετὰ ὁδοῦ τινος εὐτάκτου πρόοδος ἐπὶ τὸ γνωστόν). The result is that Aristotle's two directions—toward and from the principles—became "methods" in Zabarella's hands.[15] Only by such a devious route could the Greek term μέθοδος have been introduced into Aristotelian interpretation in a sense that simply is not Aristotle's.[16]

ZABARELLA'S DOCTRINE IN THE DE METHODIS

With Zabarella's relation to the Averroist tradition in mind, let us turn to examine his own doctrines on the subject as expounded in the *De methodis*. For Zabarella, the purpose of Aristotle's logic is to hand down methods or instruments for knowing; hence his logic is called "instrumental" logic.[17] Aristotle dealt with this

[14] Carl von Prantl's *Geschichte der Logik im Abendlande* (4 vols., Leipzig, 1855-70), II, 303, n. 16, gives the views of the Arabs in the words of Albert the Great: "Logica intendit docere principia, per quae per id, quod notum est, deveniri potest in cognitionem ignoti...." Prantl notes that Alfarabi, Avicenna, and Averroes all follow this doctrine.

[15] Cf. this terminology with that used by Aquinas in discussing the same distinction (e.g., as given on p. 29 above, where *processus* certainly cannot be justified by the Greek text).

[16] Translations of the Greek commentators made by Italian or other scholars in the sixteenth century make use of the word in its Latinized form. See, for example, the Renaissance translation of Simplicius given on p. 47 above.

[17] Jacobus Zabarella, "De methodis," in *Opera logica* ... (Treviso, 1604), p. 121.

subject most diligently and "artificially" in the *Posterior Analyt-ics*.[18] With this statement, Zabarella aligns himself with those Aristotelians who rely exclusively upon the *Organon* for their doctrines of method and disregard the methodological advice to be found in other parts of the Aristotelian corpus.

Two scientific methods (*scientificae methodi*) thus emerge, no more and no less. One is most appropriately called demonstrative method: this the Greeks call κύριον ἀπόδειξιν, or ἀποδείξιν τοῦ διότι, while we are accustomed to call it "most powerful demonstration" or "demonstration *propter quid*." The other, which proceeds from effect to cause, is called "resolutive," since progress of this sort is resolutive, just as that from cause to effect is called "composition": the Greeks call this method συλλογισμὸν τοῦ ὅτι or διὰ σημεῖον; we call it "demonstration *quia*" or "syllogism from sign" or "second-grade demonstration."[19]

Since all that we can or need to know is either substance or accident, and since the resolutive method makes known the definitions of substance, and the compositive method the accidents, it is clear that these are the only two methods we need in science.[20]

Since method only proves and makes things known singly but does not dispose (Zabarella was no Ramist), we need *order* also for perfect science. Without it we might indeed gain science, but only with the greatest difficulty and trouble on the part of the learner.[21] Order, which lacks the force of inference possessed by method, has as its end our better cognition. There are two sorts of orders, the "compositive" (used in the theoretical disciplines) and the "resolutive" (used in the practical).[22] Thus both method and order are intellectual instruments by means of which we acquire the knowledge of that which is unknown from our knowledge of that which is already known—with this difference, that method must have deductive force (*vis illativa*), by means of which something is inferred from something else by necessary

---

[18] "In *Posterioribus Analyticis* . . . enim credimus Aristotelem diligentissime atque artificiosissime de methodis disseruisse. . . ." *Ibid.*, p. 121.

[19] *Ibid.*, p. 120.   [20] *Ibid.*, p. 138.   [21] *Ibid.*, pp. 138-39.

[22] *Ibid.*, pp. 95-96. The doctrine is of course entirely Scholastic and traditional.

inference.[23] (The Greek commentators had a part in making this distinction, which was not original with Zabarella.)

JUDGMENT OF ZABARELLA

Thus the net conclusion of Zabarella's methodology is that there are only two methods in scientific inquiry, and these consist of syllogisms in which one of the following conditions obtains: either the middle term is the cause of the major term (demonstration *a priori*, or the compositive method), or the major term is the cause of the middle (demonstration *a posteriori*, or the resolutive method).[24] If there were no such causal relation between the terms, there would be no necessary connection between them and hence no science could be derived from them.

Ernst Cassirer attributed considerable historical significance to Zabarella's formulation of these two methods.[25] Since Cassirer's account has gained wide currency, it might be well to dwell at this point upon the salient features of Zabarella's methodology. It should be observed that the strict science here envisaged is one in which the scientific syllogisms constructed by method are disposed by order. In first investigating a science, according to our author, we must proceed by the *a posteriori* or resolutive method, deriving causes from effects. But once we have done this, we are then in a position to develop the science in *a priori* fashion by the compositive or demonstrative method. If we already knew the principles of a particular science there would be no need of the resolutive method, and indeed this is the case in mathematics, where the principles are known per se. Zabarella expressly excludes mathematical analysis from his resolutive method, since it proceeds from the unknown to the known, which is contrary to his criterion for what constitutes a method.[26]

---

[23] "... *methodus* igitur, ut ab ordine distinguatur, vim illativam habeat necesse est, qua aliquid ex aliquibus per necessariam consequutionem colligatur." *Ibid.*, pp. 117-18.

[24] *Ibid.*, p. 120.

[25] Ernst Cassirer, *Das Erkenntnisproblem in der Philosophie und Wissenschaft der neueren Zeit* (Berlin, 1906), I, 146.

[26] Zabarella, *Opera logica...*, p. 139.

Cassirer gave to this doctrine a decidedly empirical interpretation by means of which he connected it with Galileo's experimental method. While it is certainly true that Zabarella proceeded resolutely and effectively to eliminate from Scholastic doctrine all metaphysical and neo-Platonic accretions (he devotes a great deal of space to refuting the Platonic dialectical methods outlined by Ammonius Hermiae and Eustratius), nevertheless the resulting doctrines are scarcely more empirical than other Scholastic epistemologies.[27] Of course a good deal turns upon the interpretation given to the cause-and-effect relationship, which here received what was to be the prevailing interpretation in the Aristotelian tradition, and which came to be called the "necessary connection of cause and effect." The only empirical element that can be found in this sort of discussion, it seems to me, is the advice given for finding the causal middle terms that are to serve in scientific syllogisms. One can maintain that Zabarella gave fresh and stimulating advice to researchers in their search for these middle terms only by giving to his "resolutive method" a modern or mathematical interpretation which the original language and meaning simply will not bear. It is significant that in attempts to make Zabarella a modern empiricist scholars are forced to paraphrase rather extensively and to speak of "analyzing a phenomenon" into its "components"—rather strained translations for Zabarella's very traditional and Scholastic language.

A METAPHYSICAL OPPONENT OF ZABARELLA: PICCOLOMINI

A famous debate between Zabarella and his colleague at Padua, Francesco Piccolomini (1520-1604), was occasioned chiefly by their disagreement over order in the sciences, but it involved the notion of method as well.[28] As we have seen, the juxtaposition

---

[27] To be sure, Zabarella's De regressu is rather more empiricist in tone.

[28] Piccolomini attacked Zabarella's De methodis in a section on order in the sciences that occupies pp. 17-39 of his Universa philosophia de moribus ... (Venice, 1583). Zabarella defended his views in a work (written in 1584) entitled De doctrinae ordine apologia (Venice, 1604). To this defense Piccolomini replied,

of these two concepts was a heritage of the Averroist tradition. But where Zabarella's constant effort was to purge Arab doctrine of its metaphysical trappings and reduce it to a manageable and usable epistemology, Piccolomini's interest remained frankly metaphysical. He insisted that the order of disciplines must correspond to something he calls the "order of nature," described as twofold: "one of composition, the other of intention." There are accordingly only two orders, the compositive and the resolutive, not three as the medical men, following Galen, had maintained.[29]

Since the issue in this debate concerned order rather than method, we need not enter into its details. Piccolomini accepted the current doctrine that the development of methods of knowing was the province of logic: the nature of method thus depends on our mode of knowing.[30] He also seems to have accepted implicitly the view that method requires the explanation of one thing by means of another, although so far as I can discover he did not develop any distinctive doctrine of the sort of inference required by method.[31]

Of more particular interest to us is a passage from Piccolomini's final refutation of Zabarella, for it shows how he was able, on the basis of his own particular separation of order from method, to realize that Galen's doctrine of method was not, as so many students believed, presented at the start of the *Ars parva*. This much had been recognized already by Leoniceno, but Piccolomini goes on to identify the Platonic origin of much of Galen's theory of method:

Let us consider how obviously they slip into another error, for they confirm their opinion by the authority of Galen, in the *De Platonis et Hip-*

---

after his opponent's death, with his *Comes politicus, pro recta ordinis ratione propugnator* (Venice, 1594). On this debate see Pietro Ragnisco, "Giacomo Zabarella, il filosofo. La polemica tra Francesco Piccolomini e Giacomo Zabarella nella università di Padova," *Atti del Reale Istituto Veneto di Scienze, Lettere, ed Arti,* Ser. VI, Tomo 4[2] (1885-86), pp. 1217-52. Ragnisco considers personal jealousy to have been partly responsible for the disagreement.

[29] Franciscus Piccolomineus, *Universa philosophia de moribus,* pp. 24-25.
[30] *Ibid.,* p. 21.
[31] Not even in his textbook on logic, of which I examined a 2d edition copy: Franciscus Piccolomineus, *Discursus ad universam logicam attinens* (Marburg, 1606).

pocratis decretis, IX, ii, where Galen, following Plato, says that we must "order from the more known." They infer from this that order is to be sought from our manner of knowing. But they do not notice that Galen is speaking not of order but of method taken for "way." And this is perfectly clear, for Galen in the same book proposes to deal with that method by which the true is distinguished from the false, by the comparison of similar and dissimilar—as is obvious from Galen's words and from the title. It is of this method taken as a way that Plato speaks in the *Phaedrus* and *Philebus.* For who doubts that when we are considering how we tell the true from the false by means of the comparison of similar and dissimilar, this is relevant not to order but to way? Just as that opinion of Plato mentioned by Galen in the same chapter pertains to the way of knowing, where he quotes Plato as asserting that justice in our souls is to be explained and elucidated by means of justice in the whole republic and its parts as being the more known—for that way is taken from analogy. Because the grades of internal faculties of our soul constitute an internal but hidden republic, so to speak, in which internal justice has its place and shines forth through the justice of the whole external republic, according to a certain analogy of the kind Plato frequently uses. Analogy however belongs not to order but to way, as all agree.[32]

This examination of Galen is merely an incidental refutation of those who based their conception of order on Galen's *Ars parva.* Piccolomini's own thinking was built on the discussion of order in the fifth book of Aristotle's *Metaphysics* and on certain Scholastic sources.[33]

It might seem to a modern reader that the doctrines of Zabarella and Piccolomini were not very much different. To be sure, Zabarella could not accept Piccolomini's attempt to rescue Galen's definitive way of teaching as a mixture of the other two orders, but the two writers agree in essence on the traditional two orders, compositive and resolutive. As to the concept of method, probably Piccolomini would not have been as austere as Zabarella in discarding all but two methods as Aristotelian. However, this

[32] Franciscus Piccolomineus, *Comes Politicus,* f. 13ᵛ.
[33] For example, on a doctrine of Augustine used by Scotus in commenting on the *Sentences* of Peter the Lombard: "Ordo est congruens dispositio plurium, vel disciplinarum vel partium eiusdem disciplinae, cum inter se, tum ad unum primum, ex rerum natura a dirigente deprompta, ut disciplinae pro facultate naturam rerum aemulentur, distincteque legentium animis eam offerant." See *Universa philosophia de moribus,* p. 18.

is only a conjecture, for Piccolomini's main concern was with the concept of order and with the idea that knowledge corresponds in some sequential fashion with its subject matter.

METHODOLOGY AT THE UNIVERSITY OF PISA: MAZZONIUS

The influence of Greek and Arab commentators upon Aristotelian doctrines of method may again be seen in a 'Comparison of Plato and Aristotle' [34] written by Jacobus Mazzonius, or Jacopo Mazzoni, of Cesena (1548-98), a teacher of philosophy (both Aristotelian and Platonic) at Pisa. Mazzonius distinguishes from general logic a particular kind of logic that results when general logic is applied to a particular science. Averroes had called this, following the introductory section of the *Parts of Animals*, a kind of *paedeia*, by means of which we can know, independently of substantive acquaintance with a science, whether someone who is expounding that science is proceeding correctly or not.[35]

This directive or applied logic contains nothing more than the criterion and method of that science. In a previous passage Mazzonius had given the name "criterion" to that faculty of the soul by which method and order are discriminated in the sciences: it is this faculty by which the more known and the less known in any discipline are determined.[36] "Method" can be taken in two senses, one more broad and the other more strict. When taken broadly it contains in itself both demonstration and order, or, as Averroes would say, *ordo doctrinae* and *via doctrinae*.[37]

In this broad sense, method might seem to be adequately defined by Galen in the *De Hippocratis et Platonis dogmatis*, but in fact Galen's description does not sufficiently distinguish order

[34] Jacobus Mazzonius, *In universam Platonis et Aristotelis philosophiam praeludia, sive de comparatione Platonis et Aristotelis* (Venice, 1597).

[35] "Dicimus quod omnis universali Logica paratus, dum ad scientias accedit Logicam illam universalem, ad quendam particularem modum contrahet, atque faciet Logica particularem, quam ut 'paediam' simpliciter cognoscit Averroes multis in locis. . . ." *Ibid.*, p. 165.

[36] "Est autem scientiae Criterium facultas illa animi, per quam in scientiis iudicatur methodus et ordo, et secundum hanc facultatem ante omnia constituendum est notius et ignotius." *Ibid.*, p. 162.

[37] *Ibid.*, p. 165.

from method.[38] Hence Mazzonius prefers the definition of method given by Alexander of Aphrodisias, as a "progress toward that which can be known by a certain correctly ordained way," since in the words "toward that which can be known" is contained a reference to the characteristic that distinguishes method, which has a relation to demonstration, from order, which has not.[39] More strictly taken, *methodus* signifies only what Averroes called the *via doctrinae*, that is, the genus of demonstrating. It is distinguished from order by the fact that it disposes the things which can be known in a science, and disposes them according to their priority in that science.[40] Unlike order, which simply designates that one thing should follow another, method dictates that one follows from another (logically), and hence this specific method signifies nothing other than demonstration. For if division, which does not belong to order, sometimes seems to play a part in the sciences, it does so only for the sake of demonstration, and so can be subsumed under that heading.[41]

Mazzonius' discussion has been introduced in order to show that the Italian methodology was commonly accepted by scholars who worked with the same sources: Aristotle, the Greek and Arab commentators, and Galen. We need not assume any absorbing preoccupation with empirical research, or any anticipation of such a preoccupation—although, to be sure, this theoretical discussion may have later become absorbed into the language of

---

[38] *Ibid.*

[39] "Melius itaque Alexander utramque methodi facultatem amplexus videtur, quando (referente Simplicio in primo textu *Physicorum*) definivit methodum ut sit progressus ad id quod cognosci potest cum quadam via recte ordinata. In prioribus verbis, nempe in illis, 'Methodus est progressus ad id quod cognosci potest,' habet relationem ad demonstrationem, in sequentibus vero ordinem respicit." *Ibid.*

[40] "Si vero methodus strictius sumatur significat solum id quod appellavit Averroes *viam doctrinae*, id est, genus ipsum demonstrandi, et distinguitur ab ordine, quia ordo consideratur inter varia quae declaranda occurrunt, ita ut dicat solum situm, et collocationem quandam scibilium. Atque sic illa prius collocantur, quae notiora sunt secundum criterium eius scientiae...." *Ibid.*

[41] "Methodus autem consistit in unius rei per alteram explicatione. Et quemadmodum ordo dicit hoc post illud, ita methodus dicit hoc ex illo, et proinde methodus haec specifica nihil aliud significat, nisi demonstrationem. Nam etiam si interdum reperiatur divisio, quae ad ordinem non pertinet, quia tamen in gratiam demonstrationum fit ideo maxima cum ratione ad eas reducitur et sub earum nomine intelligitur." *Ibid.*, pp. 165-66.

description. It has been shown that the whole discussion can be regarded as one of exegesis, chiefly of the Aristotelian texts. Its elements were drawn in clearly recognizable fashion from centuries of commentaries, and there is no need to assume an anticipation of seventeenth-century science on the part of these scholars to make the discussion intelligible to the modern reader.

SUMMARY

From our examination of the views on method of some of the more traditional teachers of philosophy in northern Italy, it should be clear that Renan's estimate concerning the part played by the doctrines of Averroes in shaping the intellectual climate of Italy during the sixteenth century was not far off, so far as this one philosophical problem goes. If we add to the doctrines of Averroes those of the newly translated and fashionable Greek commentators, and the methodological views of Galen, we have the materials out of which Italian Aristotelians shaped their methodology. Contrary to the usual interpretation, we have seen no reason to ascribe to these Averroistic Aristotelians a strongly empirical orientation. Had they been interested in developing an empirical methodology, they could have found some suggestions in Galen—but these suggestions were not what they discussed. Instead great attention was paid to the elaboration of Aristotle's doctrine of the scientific syllogism, in a manner that had been part and parcel of the Scholastic tradition for centuries. As we have seen in Part One, the relation of this syllogistic procedure to demonstration in mathematics had been hotly debated at Padua and elsewhere even during the early part of the sixteenth century. This controversy, with the doubts it raised as to the connection between Aristotle's analysis of science and mathematics, helped to estrange the incipient mathematical analyses of nature from the Aristotelian tradition.

The most original and the freshest treatment of method was that of Zabarella. It is significant that Keckermann, a fairly astute critic in logical matters, singled out Zabarella as the *only*

Italian who was not a slavish follower of Averroes and Aristotle, but a man who dared to approach his subject with a fresh view. For the majority of academic figures, Renan's judgment as to the sterility of academic and Averroistic philosophizing would seem to hold.[42] Not all Italians, however, followed so slavishly in the footsteps of the commentator, and to some of the more original Aristotelians we shall turn in our next chapter.

[42] At least with regard to this particular discussion of method. In other fields— that of philosophical psychology, for instance—the thinking of the Italian Averroists may well have been more productive.

Chapter 8. SOME OTHER ITALIAN ARISTOTELIANS

Not all Italian Aristotelians clung so tenaciously to the path set by Averroes and the Scholastics as did those considered in our previous chapter. Some Italian writers on method broke away from these conservative and time-honored ways of thinking and wrote separate treatises on the subject which are written in a more "modern" style, and which represent stages in that transition from Scholastic argumentation to the modern philosophical treatise to be completed in Descartes' *Discours de la Méthode*.

This non-Scholastic trend is illustrated by Giacomo Aconzio, a Protestant émigré who devoted an essay to the subject of method, and by Girolamo Borro, professor of philosophy at Pisa, who was teaching there when Galileo was a student. In neither of these works do we find that heavy treatment usually accorded the subject by Averroist students of Aristotle. Whereas method had been marginal for the Averroists (since Averroes did not have a clear doctrine on the subject), these writers devote whole treatises to the topic.

Differing from these two in style and yet equally independent of the Italian school traditions was Giulio Pace's methodical *Institutiones logicae*, published toward the end of the century. As a result of his intimate knowledge of the Greek Aristotle (gained while translating the *Organon* and other works) or perhaps because of his receptiveness to all sorts of ideas, Pace compiled a list of no less than twelve methods, "drawn from the writings of Aristotle," as he assures the reader on the title page of his work. Pace felt that his account of method would make up for the absence of such an account from the *Organon*.

Finally we offer as evidence for the continued interest of Italian
Aristotelians a discussion of method from the next century by
Scipione Chiaramonti, also a professor of philosophy at Pisa, who
relayed the doctrines of his predecessors and added yet another.

ACONZIO'S "MODERN" TREATISE ON METHOD

In 1588, after the initial furor over Ramus' method but prior to
the Zabarella-Piccolomini controversy, there appeared a modest
treatise, 'On Method, that is, the Correct Manner of Investigating and Transmitting the Arts and Sciences,'[1] the work of an
Italian exile named Giacomo Aconzio. Peter Ramus, who apparently read the work shortly after its publication, wrote to the
author some years later that it was not altogether at odds with
his own doctrine yet did not clearly agree.[2] Leibniz characterized
it as a treatise on "general methodology,"[3] and the description is
perhaps apt. The absence of quotations and authorities gives this
book a modern appearance that has misled recent scholars into
assuming that its author was farther ahead of his time than he
in fact was. The work also illustrates the remark made by Jacob
Burckhardt, that the modern prose treatise evolved from the

---

[1] The full title is *Jacobi Acontii Tridentini De Methodo, hoc est recta investigan-
darum tradendarumque [artium ac] scientiarum ratione* (Basel, 1558). In contrast
to most Renaissance works on philosophy, which have seldom been reprinted, this
work has received two modern editions, one by Giorgio Radetti and the other by
Herman J. de Vleeschauwer. I shall cite the former.

[2] The remark occurs in a letter Ramus wrote to Aconzio asking whether the latter
had written anything on geometry and mechanics—subjects in which Ramus was
currently interested: "Libellum autem de methodo multo jam antea legeram, non
abhorrentem quidem ab institutis nostris, sed neque plane convenientum." *Petri
Rami Collectaneae, praefationes, epistolae, orationes . . .* (Marburg, 1599), p. 173.

[3] Leibniz mentions it in his *Nova methodus discendae docendaeque juris pruden-
tiae . . .*, originally published in Frankfurt in 1667. It is reprinted in the *Philo-
sophische Schriften, hrsg. von der preussischen Akademie der Wissenschaften*, I, 280:
"Methodologia seu ars disponendi versatur circa methodum. Methodus autem est vel
naturalis, cuius haec est regula, quicquid sine altero cognosci potest, non vero alterum
sine ipso, illud alteri praeponi debet; vel occasionalis, cuius nulla generalis regula
tradi potest, sed variat infinitis modis: qua de re plura disserunt Jacobus Acontius
in libello de methodo, et Epistola Stratagematis Sathanae addita; et Joh. Neldelius,
et Abrahamius Calovius." The other references are to two works by German scholars
of the next century—the latter work being one that Peter Petersen calls the "most
significant work on methodology from the Protestant side" (*Geschichte der Aristotelischen Philosophie im protestantischen Deutschland* [Leipzig, 1921], p. 213):

Humanist essay after the endless classical quotations began to be
dropped.[4] The residue was the modern essay or treatise such as
we see it in Aconzio's little book—devoid of the citations from
antiquity that characterize earlier works and yet not much different in substance from other writings of the time. Still the fact
that the subject of method occupies a whole treatise, instead of
being smuggled into a commentary on a classical author, certainly reflects a new emphasis on the topic.

What then is the substance of Aconzio's book on method? He
begins by remarking that although no art or science can be correctly transmitted or known except by a diligent and certain
method, yet no one had thought to give clear and absolute
precepts to this art of method itself, which lends light to all the
others.[5] Even dialectic lacks method, to say nothing of other
arts, faculties, and sciences.[6] Aristotle has a good deal on the
subject in his writings, especially in the *Parts of Animals*, but he
did not embrace the whole art: he deals with the subject only in
order to present the rationale of his own writings. (From such
a remark we may conclude that Aconzio's treatment of method is
going to be less restricted in scope than that of the Averroistic
Aristotelians.) Galen wrote a book, now lost, on the constituting
of arts, which Martinius Akakia (=Sans-Malice, a French writer
contemporary with Aconzio) and other medical men have attempted to restore, but their own writings suffer from a lack of
method. Galen entertained the belief that an art could not be
contemplated and taught in the same manner, which is contrary

Tractatus novus de methodo docendi et disputandi, printed in the *Scripta philos.
Wittenberg,* 1673. This material has not been explored since Petersen's time.
Leibniz's writings are full of such references to the methodological discussions of
the sixteenth century. Incidentally, to my knowledge, this quotation contains the
first occurrence of the term *methodologia,* but there are probably earlier ones.

[4] Jacob Burckhardt, *The Civilization of the Renaissance in Italy* (London, 1928),
pp. 243-44. The remark is made in connection with moral treatises of the Humanists,
but the same process took place later on with Humanistically trained philosophers,
who also began to drop the classical references. Montaigne's essays, of course, still
belong to the earlier stage—they are replete with classical quotations.

[5] Jacobus Acontius, *De methodo e opuscoli religiosi e filosofici,* ed. Giorgio
Radetti (Florence, 1944), pp. 76-78.

[6] *Ibid.,* pp. 78-80.

not only to Aristotle but also to reason and experience.[7] Aconzio accordingly intends to fill this gap by producing a methodical treatise on method, brief and slanted toward use, not cognition.[8] It is to be presented in the form of precepts (something of a concession to the arts methodology).

There follows Aconzio's definition of logic,[9] with some general statement of more or less watered-down traditional Aristotelian views. Logic is (as many define it) the correct rationale of contemplating and teaching. Logic consists of two parts,[10] the consideration of questions and the consideration of themes; method, although needed in the first part, must be applied in the second. Method is a certain correct rationale by which one shall be able to prosecute an inquiry into the truth and knowledge of anything and be able to teach properly what has been found.[11]

The discussion that follows is couched in traditional terms taken for the most part from Aristotle's theory of knowledge. Perhaps its chief merit is the author's conscious intent to present his doctrine without unduly cluttering up his presentation with names and citations from authorities. Since the end of method is the knowledge of something,[12] Aconzio is led into a long-winded but oversimplified exposition of Aristotelian doctrine from the *Posterior Analytics* and the *Topics*. He defines the resolutive method in the usual way as proceeding from the notion of an end

---

[7] *Ibid.,* p. 80. Radetti suggests that the work of Akakia to which Aconzio refers might be his commentary on the *Ars medica,* but since this work of Galen's *exists,* it cannot be the one Akakia and others have attempted to *restore.* Possibly Aconzio was thinking of the lost work on demonstration by Galen.

[8] "Nam cum artium utilitas non ex earum cognitione sed usu constet, necesseque sit, si quidem arte aliqua uti velis, eius tibi praecepta esse in promptu, non secus atque literarum elementa scribere aut legere volenti: diligenter videtur in tradendis artibus verbositas omnis fugienda." *Ibid.,* p. 84.

[9] "Est vero Logica, meo quidem iudicio (utcunque eam definiant multi) recta contemplandi docendique ratio. . . ." *Ibid.,* p. 86.

[10] "Logicae duae sint partes, quarum altera pertineat ad quaestiones, altera vero ad proposita: quam nunc explicandam suscipimus. Quanquam enim veri quoque ac falsi examen recte fieri non sine methodo aliqua potest, magis tamen nomen methodi ad eam videtur pertinere rationem, qua recta ordinataque propositorum fit discussio." *Ibid.*

[11] "Sit igitur methodus recta quaedam ratio qua citra veritatis examen et rei alicuius notitiam indagare et quod assequutus fueris docere commode possis." *Ibid.* [12] *Ibid.,* p. 89.

to be achieved,[13] to it is opposed the compositive method, which must begin with the first step toward that end. He warns against confusing this legitimate meaning with other meanings often but mistakenly given to the phrase "resolutive method"—as, for example, the "order of proceeding from the more common to the less universal," or "that which proceeds from composites to simples" or from "whole to parts." These different senses of "order" must be kept distinct and each applied only in its proper place.[14] (One of the new features of Aconzio's presentation is his technique of giving traditional doctrines in the form of precepts to follow rather than in the form of interpretations of the writings of Aristotle or Galen. Another is the attempt he makes to distinguish clearly between contemplative and teaching methods.) The order in these two pursuits [15] ought to be the same, namely, from the more known to the less known—with this difference, however, that often many things must be gone through that do not pertain to the matter at hand and many "divisions" attempted that bring no usefulness; since very often things worth knowing lurk among the useless. Aconzio maintains this order against Galen and his followers, who believe that the arts cannot be transmitted by the resolutive order but regard the compositive order as far more suitable for that purpose.[16]

Of Galen's third "method" (from the *Ars medica*), Aconzio says that it corresponds to the precepts he has previously given for defining and dividing. He adds (with considerable historical insight) that this is the method that Crassus, in Cicero's *De Oratore*, advocates. Although this method may be suitable for

---

[13] "Sed illud diligenter observandum est, ut a fine seu effectu semper ad proximas quasque causas procedatur: et ad illas quidem quae per se causae sunt, non autem quae fortuito, sive, ut dicunt, per accidens. Appellantque hanc methodum resolutivam a finis notione: sicut contrariam vocant compositivam. Ille ordo cogitanti est commodissimus, hunc vero (compositivum inquam) sequi in operando oportet: finis enim omnium ultimum est, quae operantes efficimus, in excogitando autem primum." *Ibid.*, p. 140.   [14] *Ibid.*, pp. 140-42.

[15] "Ordo . . . idem esse debet in docendo atque in cogitando, ut scilicet a notioribus ad minus cognita semper procedatur, illud tamen interest, quod contemplanti multa saepe sunt percurrenda, quae ad rem non faciunt, multae tentandae divisiones, quae nullam afferent utilitatem; quia scilicet lateant persaepe inter inutilia, quae scire operae pretium sit." *Ibid.*, p. 160.

[16] *Ibid.*, p. 162.

putting into writing an art already constituted, Aconzio does not believe that it is at all suitable for constituting an art that has not yet been found. "For it does not always preserve the order from the better known to the lesser, which we have shown to be absolutely necessary to the investigator: and if it sometimes coincides with that order, it coincides with the resolution of the end, and for this reason it will be disapproved of even in teaching.[17] Galen himself openly says that this third method is only useful as a short cut and for memorizing: Aconzio regards it as useless even for these purposes.[18]

Having presented his precepts of method, Aconzio recommends constant practice to those who wish to become methodical.[19] The demand for examples of his method is legitimate, Aconzio remarks, but he unfortunately cannot furnish any. For although Galen left a work 'On the Constitution of the Medical Art,' in which he seems to have followed the resolutive order, still in many places we admire rather a certain great force of intellect than the perpetual and never-broken thread (of method) we require.[20] Aconzio's precepts of methods, being much more complex, cannot be found fully exemplified in any one work, although careful reading of Plato and Aristotle will reveal many illustrations of method.[21] When a person has been sufficiently exercised in singular instances, it will then be easy for him, following Aconzio's precepts, to join all things together as required by the subject matter and to constitute the whole method of any theme.[22] Aconzio closes with the hope that his little book has not itself been unmethodical in its treatment of method.

Aconzio's work strikes scholars who are not familiar with other writings of the period as extremely original and modern. Yet he moves within the circle of ideas common to authors of his time. His writing lacks the usual polemical tendency, to be sure, but his authorities are still basically Plato and Aristotle. His concern for teaching and the communication of the arts puts him into what we have been calling the arts group of methodologists,

[17] *Ibid.*, p. 168.   [18] *Ibid.*   [19] *Ibid.*, p. 170.
[20] *Ibid.*, p. 172.   [21] *Ibid.*, p. 174.   [22] *Ibid.*

while he still retains sufficient respect for the Aristotelian theory
of science to remain more or less traditional in that regard. Concern for the *utility* of dialectic is another Humanist characteristic
exhibited by Aconzio. His willingness to advance his views in
the form of precepts is refreshing, but not altogether novel, for
Ramus after all had also reduced method to a single precept—
that the more general must precede. Aconzio, while not guilty
of such oversimplification, still did not offer anything that in-
dicated greater insight into the problems with which he dealt so
abstractly.

While Aconzio's work was no doubt read (although probably
not as widely as his other work, the 'Stratagems of Satan,' a
piece of religious pamphleteering), it did not arouse the antagonism that the dialecticians evoked. Without the academic following and position of Melanchthon and Ramus, Aconzio did not
carry their weight and remained comparatively unnoticed in the
methodological controversies of the time.

A HUMANIST PRESENTATION OF PERIPATETIC METHODOLOGY: GIROLAMO BORRO

An Italian teacher who showed a greater familiarity with the
"artistic" trend of methodology, and less subservience to Averroes than most of his colleagues, was Girolamo Borro or Hieronymus Borrius (1512-92) of Arezzo, who taught philosophy at
Pisa.[23] In 1584 Borro published a 'Defense of the Peripatetic
Method of Teaching and Learning.'[24] This work is an attempt
to outline and defend Aristotle's method against its *contemptores*.
His own program boils down to a threefold method very familiar
by now: synthesis, analysis, and diaeresis. But the details of his
discussion are a good deal richer than many former treatments,

---

[23] For Borro's life, see Angelo Fabroni, *Historia Academiae Pisanae* ... (Pisa,
1792), II, 341-44. For the influence on Galileo of a work Borro wrote on physics,
see Ernest A. Moody, "Galileo and Avempace," JHI, XII (1951), 163-93 and
375-422.

[24] Hieronymus Borrius, *De peripatetica docendi atque addiscendi methodo* ...
(Florence, 1584).

while his style and approach are quite different from those of the Averroistic Italians, being more in the Humanist vein.

The Dedicatory Epistle, addressed to Francesco Maria, Duke of Urbino, is interesting for its references to the contemporary scene. Borro mentions the ease of acquiring textbooks owing to printing: in spite of this ease, the study of philosophy has not prospered, in his view. In contrast to the usual Humanistic tendency to complain about the length of time wasted on philosophy or dialectic, Borro cites Aristotle's example to show that students of philosophy should be prepared to spend long years of study in their subject.

To us in our time, having scarcely saluted the threshold of humane letters from afar, it seems too much to spend one year in dialectic and one or two or at most three years in physics. Few there are who finish five years, very few who achieve six. And with no reasoned plan of books or teachers, we read any books that we happen to find and hear any teachers, without discrimination. And (what is the root of the whole matter) we despise order and method, which should be highly regarded, because everything rests on them.[25]

Borro starts out by stating that he intends to set forth the method he practices as a writer, teacher, and friend, and which he understands to be the method of Aristotle. Citing Aristotle on the impossibility of inquiring into a science and into its method at the same time, he insists that before we begin to prosecute a scientific inquiry we must first determine what order and method we are to follow.[26] Borro had absorbed enough of the Humanist revolt in education to protest against the lack of order and method in teaching, and yet he was enough of a traditionalist to maintain that the order and method needed was that practiced and preached by Aristotle himself.[27]

Borro conceives of method as instrumental in finding, disposing, setting out in words, or teaching any good thing, and understanding what has been found by others and disposed or handed down to posterity and communicated to others.[28] He

---

[25] *Ibid.*, Dedicatory epistle.   [26] *Ibid.*, pp. 4-5.   [27] *Ibid.*, pp. 6-7.
[28] *Ibid.*, pp. 8-9.

distinguishes between order and method, maintaining that order is a necessary condition for method but not a sufficient one. Aristotle required order of things so as to avoid an infinite which the mind cannot grasp; hence we need a relation of prior and posterior, and a first member of the series in order to establish order among things. "But this finite order of knowing things is not method but is conjoined with it so that no violence however great can separate it from method: for unless something were first, to which the posterior things can be referred by that chain of order which cannot be dissolved, the whole rationale of method would be completely overthrown."[29]

Borro then gives the questions about method that he will attempt to answer in order. It is interesting to note the general resemblance of this list to those methodical lists proposed by the dialecticians, e.g., Melanchthon. Borro proposes seven questions: (1) what does the word "method" signify? (2) what is method? (3) how many intermediate genera (or species) of method are there? (4) what is each species of method? (5) what is the use or function of each of these species? (6) does Aristotle use this method and its species always and everywhere in his writings? (7) how are Aristotle's arguments rendered by this method each to its own place, figure, and form? [i.e., how does Aristotle arrange his arguments syllogistically?][30] This sort of treatment is clearly reminiscent of the division of dialectical method, with the weighing of the relative merits of each according to its function, as made by neo-Platonists or commentators.

Following this scheme Borro gives the etymology of μέθοδος that we have already noted on p. 65, one which stresses the brevity and ease of method. Although Borro here enumerates the "customary" Latin translations of μέθοδος and announces that he is going to follow the best usage with *via*, he in fact speaks of *methodus* throughout (as one might guess from the very title of his book). He then defines method provisionally as "that short way by whose guidance we ascend as quickly as possible to some

---

[29] *Ibid.*, p. 11.   [30] *Ibid.*, p. 12.

knowledge or skill"[31]—stressing the time element to a degree unusual for a Peripatetic.

Relying very heavily upon the metaphor of the short cut, Borro maintains that method must exhibit the characteristics which Aristotle set for measure in the *De caelo*[32]: it must be short, straight, certain, terminated, easy, and single. This results in a fuller definition incorporating these requirements.[33] The method that answers this description is that *paideia* described by Aristotle at the beginning of the *Parts of Animals*, which enables skilled students to know whether the method followed in disputing is adequate, regardless of the truth or falsity of what is presented.[34] "He who grasps this method firmly will philosophize with great facility, great brevity, and great progress. Other than this one, there is no way of philosophizing; he who holds to this, although he proceed by degrees or even very slowly, will be led finally to the chosen end—and the more hurriedly he runs, the quicker. Beside this straight way all others are crooked and he who enters upon them rather goes away from the end the quicker he runs." Borro remarks that his definition excludes many things that might otherwise be considered methods. For example, in adding that it is a way that leads "to doctrine and skill" (*ad doctrinam ac peritiam*), he has excluded ways that do not lead to such doctrine and skill: e.g., reasoning, demonstration, induction, example, definition, and enthymeme. These are not methods but the *termini* to which Borro's method leads.[36] (Thus Borro has identified "method" not with "way of doctrine" in the usual Averroist manner but with a "way leading to doctrine and skill.")

To those who might argue that Aristotle includes two of the above ways, demonstration and definition, among his methods, Borro spells out the following reply:

[31] "Methodus ergo est via compendiaria perdiscendi, qua duce, ad doctrinam atque peritiam quam celerrime ascendimus." *Ibid.*, pp. 14-15.
[32] *Ibid.*, p. 15.
[33] "Methodus ergo est via brevis, recta, certa, terminata, facilis, et una, qua duce, ad doctrinam atque peritiam comparandam ascendimus...." *Ibid.*, p. 16.
[34] *Ibid.*, p. 17.   [35] *Ibid.*, p. 18.   [36] *Ibid.*, pp. 16-17.

Readers should take note. . . that Aristotle not infrequently was inclined to use "way and method" not just for the way but also for the terminus conjoined with the way and method. . . . The way and its terminus are one and the same in subject and differ only conceptually (*ratione*). . . . Hence [in this sense] demonstration and definition are way and method, since each is the terminus of a way, yet neither of them is properly the way. But both are merely termini, and are ways only in so far as they finish and terminate the ways of which they are the extreme parts.[37]

None of the Greek commentators captured the peculiar force and nature of method. "Nor is there any other method above and beyond that which we have tried to teach; many who do not realize this depart from the truth when they multiply ways and methods beyond necessity."[38] There is only one method, but it is threefold. Its kinds are (1) analysis, which is a progression from the end to all parts, both great and small, down to the very smallest; (2) synthesis, a returning from the smallest parts to the greater, and thence to others until the end is reached; and (3) diaeresis, which is "when the supreme genus is divided by all differentiae into its species and distributed into its forms, and again the species of species are divided by new differentiae as far as they can be divided."[39] "Analysis" and "synthesis" are originally geometrical terms that Aristotle has appropriated in the *Nicomachean Ethics*: they are actually the same, differing only in direction.[40] Borro then examines the function of each of these species: in general, analysis is useful for finding, synthesis for writing, and diaeresis for defining—although ease of teaching may require a shift in order.[41] Diaeresis is really only a subsidiary species of method, a feeble kind of proof.[42]

The finding method has a fourfold function, drawn from the *Posterior Analytics*: (1) to demonstrate properties of the subject matter, (2) to find its principles, (3) to investigate its parts, and (4) to conclude by demonstration the proper affections found for the subject matter, principles, or parts.[43] Borro then gives some examples of method—one (his own) of the nature of man, another taken from the whole of Aristotle's natural philosophy. In

---

[37] *Ibid.*, p. 19.   [38] *Ibid.*, pp. 20-21.   [39] *Ibid.*, p. 26.   [40] *Ibid.*, p. 32.
[41] *Ibid.*, p. 47.   [42] *Ibid.*, p. 45.   [43] *Ibid.*, p. 50.

Chapter 35 he gives an example of syllogistic or methodical treatment that is hardly new, dating as it does back to Greek commentaries on the same passage (the proemium to the *Physics*). Although Borro quotes Averroes on the *Physics* (p. 79), he does not specifically discuss Averroes' distinction of *ordo doctrinae* and *via doctrinae*. In Chapter 34 Borro discusses, with examples, the way in which Aristotle's arguments can be cast into syllogistic form. This procedure (which even its expounder finds tedious) is necessary practice for those who wish to acquire a firm grasp of method. In spite of Borro's insistence on the utility of his method in finding and writing, it is obvious that its primary value for him lies in its application to our reading of Aristotle.[44] In all fairness, however, it must be conceded that this scholarly reading of Aristotle was beginning to recover the sense of open-minded inquiry so conspicuously displayed by the original.

There follows a somewhat halfhearted attempt to give precepts for the finding of suitable middle terms for demonstration and for presenting chains of syllogisms exhibiting the nature of the subject under discussion. He concludes with a characteristically Humanist protest against the mass of huge and unwieldy commentaries, whose size and denseness is due, in his opinion, to ignorance of method.[45]

JUDGMENT OF BORRO

Borro represents the unusual combination of a Humanist approach and a quite traditional Aristotelian or "Peripatetic" (as he himself calls it in his title) methodology. This Pisan teacher of philosophy combines some of the Humanist protest against medi-

[44] Cf. the following passages: "Haec Methodus, intus et incute cognita et parata, non tantum plurimum confert ad ipsam apud Aristotelem agnoscendam et agnitam ex Aristotele eruendam, sed etiam ad intelligendas virtutes Aristotelis illiusque dictionis et ad discernandas varias apud Aristotelem argumentationes, easdemque suis propriis formis ac figuris reddendas..." (*ibid.*, p. 65). "Apud Aristotelem hanc maxime necessariam Methodum agnoscere hanc agnitam eruere, non est facile: immo illam, vel etiam longe, in Aristotele videre, et illam ex Aristotele foras ducere, non nisi assuetis admodum longo usu, longaque ac diligenti lectione Aristotelis, et nostras hasce praeceptiones ad manus habentibus, datum est..." (*ibid.*, p. 66).
[45] *Ibid.*, pp. 104-5.

eval logic with a thoroughgoing defense of Aristotle's method as he saw it, relying upon all the *testimonia* from Aristotle that were in favor with the Italians. Yet even while leaning upon these traditional passages for support, Borro manages to avoid the interpretations of Averroes with respect to the *via doctrinae*. The most original feature of his presentation is his rather clever adaptation of Aristotle's definition of measure in the *De caelo* as a criterion in his general definition of method. Also original is his penchant for striking images and figures of speech, among which we may note especially his characterization of the man without method as a wanderer lost in the dark of night.[46] We are reminded of Descartes' lost traveler stumbling slowly along in the dusk.

THE EXTREME OF METHODOLOGICAL PLURALISM: PACE

The most determined pluralist among all the writers on the subject of method was Giulio Pace or Pacius (1550-1635), whose varied career as a teacher of law and logic in many countries and as both a Catholic and a Protestant must have exposed him to a multiplicity of influences.[47] His listing of no less than twelve methods has made him notorious in histories that take cognizance of the subject at all. Pace develops his methodological views in his little textbook of logic.[48] Method and order of doctrine are

[46] "Ut haec Methodus ex Aristotelis libris in quibus abdita latitat eruatur: cuilibet huius rei periculum facere cupienti, primum hoc, et praecipuum esse debet: ut Methodum quam eruere tentat, omnino cognitam habeat: quod si secus contigerit, per densissimas, obscurissimasque intempestae noctis tenebras, incertus quid quaerat, aut quo tendat, vagabitur: nec eruendam Methodum, eruet: at qui quid sit Methodus, quot, et quae sint Methodorum genera et quae illarum sint vires, et naturae atque proprietates et usus explorare teneat, ab eruenda Methodo non admodum aberit." *Ibid.*, pp. 64-65.

[47] For Pace's life, see Fedele Lampertico, "Materiali per servire alla vita di Giulio Pace, giureconsulto e filosofo," *Atti del Reale Istituto Veneto di Scienze, Lettere, ed Arti,* Ser. VI, Tomo 6¹ (1885-86), pp. 735-68. Another article is chiefly on his jurisprudence: Antonio Franceschini, "Giulio Pace da Beriga e la giurisprudenza dei suoi tempi," *Memorie del Reale Istituto Veneto di Scienze, Lettere, ed Arti,* XXVII (1903), 1-103.

[48] The title of the textbook gives prominence both to the section on method and to the methodical nature of the presentation: Julius Pacius, *Institutiones logicae, quibus non solum universa Organi Aristotelici sententia breviter, methodice, ac*

practically synonymous for Pace, although the latter can be used in a broader sense. In a science three things must be taken into account: the *subiectum*, or that which is inquired into; the *quaesitum*, or that which is asked; and the *medium*, that by whose means one arrives at the cognition of what is sought. With respect to each of these, particular methods must be adhered to: seven methods pertain to the subject, one to the question, and four to the means.

For each of these methods Pace has a special name. The seven dealing with the subject are as follows: (1) the "distributive" method (from genus to species); (2) the "inductive" method (from particulars to universals); (3) the "partitive" method (from whole to member); (4) the "coagmentative" method (from members to whole); (5) the "resolutive" method (by which the whole is resolved into its parts); (6) the "compositive" method (from the essential parts to the whole); and (7) the "adjunctive" method (by which part is adjoined to part).[49] For each method Pace is able to cite a passage in which Aristotle makes use of it: e.g., in the *Physics*, Aristotle makes use of the resolutive method when he resolves a natural body into its principles, matter and form.

With respect to the *quaesitum* the "inquisitive" method tells us in what sequence we ought to ask questions: (1) what does the name signify? (2) does the thing signified exist or not? (3) what is it? (4) of what sort is it? (5) why is it such? (6) how manyfold is it?[50] By a comparison of *medium* with *quaesitum* we arrive at three demonstrative methods—to which, in order to be perfectly safe, Pace adds the fourth method, the "cumulative," which is just a name for the piling up of arguments of the other three sorts, as Pace himself admits.[51] (One cannot help regretting that the comments of students on this list have not been preserved.)

Although Pace certainly must be given credit for an impressive

---

perspicue continetur, sed etiam syllogismi hypothetici, et methodi, quorum expositio in Organo desideratur, et in vulgatis Logicis aut omittitur aut imperfecte traditur, plene ac dilucide explicantur (Sedan, 1595).
[49] *Ibid.*, ff. 48r-49r.   [50] *Ibid.*, f. 49r.   [51] *Ibid.*, ff. 49r-49v.

display of nomenclatorial versatility, it cannot be said that his doctrine had any originality or intrinsic merit other than clarity of presentation. It must have been increasingly clear to Peripatetics by this time that they were in the position of having "more methods than results," in the phrase used by Henri Poincaré to describe the sociologists of his time. To be sure, each of Pace's methods is faithfully illustrated by an alleged example of Aristotle's use of that method, but such "results" were hardly new. Pace has not strayed far from the path of the commentators.

ITALIAN METHODOLOGY IN THE NEXT CENTURY: CHIARAMONTI

The methodological tradition of the commentaries continued to occupy some Italian scholars into the seventeenth century, among them another professor of philosophy at Pisa, Scipione Chiaramonti or Claramontius (1565-1652), one of Galileo's favorite targets in the *Two Chief World Systems*. Chiaramonti wrote a work in 'Four Books, concerning Doctrine, in which all the controversies agitated among serious philosophers about order and methods are discussed one by one.'[52] The author makes no pretense of originality so far as the theoretical discussion of his topic goes, but he does claim to offer something new—a section on application or *praxis*, which he feels has been seriously neglected:

We all recognize the utility of Method in the sciences and faculties, [but] we do not all understand its nature and species and terminology in the same way. Or at least we do not agree in our understanding, but what relates mostly to matters of theory (if we may call it that) we read as matters of dispute, [while] matters of use, wherein lies the whole utility [of Method] lie neglected and lost. These lie in Aristotle as gold in a vein rich but deep, whence they may not be dug out without much difficulty. I have applied myself to bringing out the applications (*praxes*) that contribute to this end: how useful these will be, use itself will show. Those who read accurately will realize that I have decked out completely new applications in an old argument. However, unless vanity deceives me, these will be like a

[52] Scipio Claramontius, *De methodo ad doctrinam spectante, libri quattuor, in quibus controversiae omnes de ordine et methodis inter graves philosophos agitatae singillatim discutiuntur* ... (Cesena, 1639).

golden thread for those who use them, leading them through the labyrinths of the sciences and out again, secure of exit. I shall divide this treatise into two main parts: in the first . . . will be contained the matters in dispute about the nature and species of Method: in the second . . . the proposed applications will be advanced, and whatever pertains to them. In the former I shall defend the ancient and old opinions against the new. In the latter, in the course of explicating Aristotle and digging out his deepest meaning, much that is new will be brought out.[53]

In the exposition that follows, Chiaramonti analyses the views of many of the men we have been discussing. Piccolomini and Zabarella receive a considerable amount of attention, as does Borro, while even Ramus is mentioned by name, although the author seems to have been familiar with his ideas mostly by way of Carpentarius' refutation of them. Chiaramonti explicitly regrets not having seen Cardinal d'Ossat's work on method. The Greek commentators are discussed, together with Averroes and Avicenna, with the sources cited in convenient fashion. Some other Italians are mentioned, for example, Federigo Pendasio,[54] who taught at Bologna and Padua. Before giving his own views, Chiaramonti faithfully expounds the opinions of all these writers *singillatim*, as he has promised.

Chiaramonti then presents his own views. Method is a "way leading the human mind to cognition without error."[55] He follows Pendasio and Zabarella in regarding order as a species of method, since it helps to lead the mind to cognition.[56] He defines order as the "disposition of the things to be considered

---

[53] *Ibid.*, p. 1.

[54] I have not been able to locate a copy of the *Progymnasmata* in which, according to Chiaramonti, Pendasio's views on method are presented. There exists no monograph on Pendasio (Federicus Pendasius), although he is mentioned briefly by Ernest Renan, *Averroès et l'Averroïsme* (Paris, 1866), pp. 403-4. See also Bruno Nardi, *Saggi sull' Aristotelismo Padovano dal Secolo XIV al XVI* (Florence, 1958), p. 413.

[55] "Dicamus tamen ipsam methodum esse viam ad cognitionem absque errore promoventem humanam mentem. . . ." *De methodo ad doctrinam spectante*, p. 8.

[56] "Pendasius contra ordinem sub methodo collocat. . . . Eandem sententiam tuetur et sequitur Zabarella, qui eam in schola tum peripatetica tum medicorum obtinuisse affirmat lib. I. *De Methodis,* cap. i. Ego quoque ipsam amplector, et probo ordinem esse methodi speciem. Quoniam est ipse quoque progressio cum a priori ad posterius procedat, et ad cognitionem promoveat: iuvat enim ordo ad rerum cognitionem assequendam, sicut confusio impedit ac perturbat." *Ibid.*, p. 10.

in a doctrine whereby first one thing then another is dealt with, with the same relation of prior and posterior prevailing throughout, but not including the subordination of one thing as providing the cognition of another."[57] Furthermore, there are two orders, compositive and resolutive, corresponding to two ways of knowing—"confused" (from that which is more known to us) and "distinct" (from that which is simply or absolutely more known).[58] The special sense of method is defined by Chiaramonti as a "progress from the cognition of one thing to the cognition of another, when the cognition of the antecedent contributes to the cognition of the consequent either by inference or by helping in another way."[59] As to the number ("species") of methods, he maintains that there are two main ones: demonstrative (which has illative force) and definitive (which does not). The latter is described as "progress from the distinct cognition of the parts of a definition to the distinct cognition of the whole definition, and thus of the thing defined." Four subsidiary methods, all to be found in Aristotle, play minor roles: the inventive method, the resolutive, the divisive, and the compositive.[60]

Like most scholars of the late Renaissance, Chiaramonti was aware of the exceedingly great diversity of meanings of *resolutio*, and he gives detailed attention to the mathematical sense of *analysis* found in Euclid. The second section of the book, that devoted to *praxis*, contains the usual rules for syllogizing, quite similar to those presented by Borro or many other writers.

Hence we see that Renaissance methodology continued to run its course while the modern era had well begun. This traditional Aristotelian felt no obligation to point out the use of Peripatetic theories of method by Galileo: his discussion deals only with the text of the Master.

[57] *Ibid.*, p. 19.

[58] *Ibid.*, p. 22. The distinction between confused and distinct knowledge suggests Scotist influence: see Etienne Gilson, *Jean Duns Scot: introduction à ses positions fondamentales* (Paris, 1952), pp. 73-74.

[59] "Est scilicet methodus progressus a cognitione unius ad cognitionem alterius cum praecedentis cognitio ad subsequentis cognitionem deserviat vel inferendo vel aliter iuvando." *Ibid.*, p. 47.

[60] *Ibid.*, p. 49.

Chapter 9. ECHOES OF THE METHODOLOG-
ICAL CONTROVERSY IN ENGLAND

In England the first stirrings of independent philosophical activity during the sixteenth century concerned methodology, displaying at first strong affinities with the continental
discussions. Torn by religious dissensions that separated society
into three factions, Anglican, Puritan, and Catholic, British scholars were almost wholly absorbed in the consideration of theological issues, especially during the first part of the century.
Neither Oxford nor Cambridge enjoyed the prosperity of earlier
times, owing to the dislocations attendant upon religious strife,
but of the two schools Cambridge was the more flourishing. It
has been customary to represent Cambridge as more receptive to
the new Humanistic studies and Oxford as conservative and
scholastic. As a matter of fact this picture is erroneous: both
schools felt the influence of Humanism, yet neither school entirely abandoned the study of the medieval authors.[1] In short the
range and content of studies at both places was characteristic of
the Renaissance.

PRE-RAMIST LOGIC AT CAMBRIDGE: SETON, WILSON, AND LEVER

In order to gain some idea of the philosophical atmosphere
that prevailed in Cambridge before the doctrines of Ramus

[1] See Mark H. Curtis, "Library Catalogues and Tudor Oxford and Cambridge,"
Studies in the Renaissance, V (1958), 111-20, which corrects the widely received
view derived from James Bass Mullinger, *The University of Cambridge*... (Cambridge, 1884). Curtis has found new evidence in the form of inventories of students'
books at Oxford, one of which he gives in full. From this list it is clear that Oxford
felt the breath of Humanism as well as Cambridge: the names of Ramus, Erasmus,
Sturm, Melanchthon, Vives, and Agricola appear frequently. Hemmingius is represented by several volumes, including his work on methods. By far the greatest

reached there, we must examine a little manual of dialectic that circulated in manuscript form for some time before it was finally printed in 1545.[2] The author of this work, which soon became "the textbook of the university,"[3] was John Seton (c. 1498-1567) a Roman Catholic who taught philosophy in St. John's College before entering the priesthood and serving as chaplain to several important prelates. He was finally forced to flee from England because of his adherence to his religious faith. Although Seton's *Dialectic* contains simplified expositions of such Terminist concepts as *suppositio* and *aequipollentia*, it nonetheless shows the influence of the recent dialecticians, especially of Rudolph Agricola, whom the author follows in the "finding part of dialectic."[4] Seton's work seems to cover in brief all the content of dialectic as it was taught during the early part of the century.[5] In spite of the fact that Seton was familiar with Melanchthon's dialectical textbook, his own book has no section on *methodus* and makes no mention of the topic. Seton's conception of the nature of dialectic is definitely "modern" (if we may use such a term to denote the recent revival of an ancient conception). Hence if this textbook reflects the actual teaching of dialectic at Cambridge, we may assume that the subject of method had not yet begun to occupy the attention of British students in the fourth decade of the century.

number of logical authors listed are Renaissance dialecticians: in fact, of the writers known to me only Paul of Venice could be called "scholastic and conservative" in Mullinger's sense. Of course one would not expect to find Scotist works in either student inventories or library catalogues: they had been pretty well weeded out after the Henrician Injunctions of 1535.

[2] John Seton, *Dialectica . . .* (London, 1545). On English logic, the recent work of Wilbur Samuel Howell, *Logic and Rhetoric in England, 1500-1700* (Princeton, New Jersey, 1956), should be consulted: it offers a wealth of information concerning the influence of Ramus on both logic and rhetoric, with very thorough bibliographic references. For Seton's *Dialectica* in particular, see pp. 49-56.

[3] According to Mullinger, *The University of Cambridge*, p. 41.

[4] Seton announces his intent in the following words: "Dialectica est artificium, docens de quavis materia probabiliter disserere: hanc in duas secant partes, nimirum, inveniendi et iudicandi. De priori diligenter et satis copiose scripsit Rodulphus [Agricola]. De altero vero nos (volente Deo) dicere aggrediamur." John Seton, *Dialectica,* Liber II. In his dedicatory epistle, Seton remarks that Melanchthon's textbook seems more suitable for teachers than for learners.

[5] "Dialectica est scientia, probabiliter de quovis themati disserendi. Huius munus est recte dividere, definire, et ratiocinare." *Ibid.,* Liber I.

By the middle of the century, the dialectical concept of method, as found in Melanchthon's writings, had taken hold at Cambridge sufficiently to permit Thomas Wilson (c.1525-1581) to introduce the subject into his *Rule of Reason*, one of the first philosophical works in English. Wilson's section on method is entitled "The manner of handlyng of a single question, and the readie waie how to teache and set forthe any thyng plainly and in order as it should be, in Latin Methodus." He goes on to give eight ways of examining any single question:

In handlyng of any single question, the preceptes and rules given before in the common woordes, in the most generall woordes, in the definition and division dooe verie good service, and helpe towardes the orderyng of every sutche matter. The whole nature of suche questions are throughly seen by usyng of this order. Every single question is eight waies examined, first to aske whether the thing be or no. . . . The second question is to aske what a thing is. And this commeth from the definition whiche is of twoo sortes, either of the substaunce of any thing, or els of the name. . . . The third question is to aske what are the causes, and especially what is the efficient cause, and what is the finall cause, or the ende of any thyng. . . . The fift question is, when the effects, the office, or proper woorkyng is examined. . . . The sixte question is, when thinges be asked that happen after, or the whiche have great affinities or likelihood together. . . . The seventh is, to aske what are disagreeyng. . . . The eight question is to bryng in witnesse, and to shew by whose authorities. . . . And this lesson ought diligently to bee learned of all, that evermore thei begin from the generall, and come to every severall part. As in declaryng what vertue is, first to tell the Nature of it generally, and after to handle every vertue by itself. And this order both Tullie hath followed in his books *De Officiis,* and also Aristotle in his *Ethikes* hath doen the like, to the greate admiration of all they that be learned.[6]

Such doctrine was apparently acceptable, or at least not objectionable, to English Aristotelians, although another Cambridge scholar, Ralph Lever (died 1585), raised an indignant voice in protest against the "rhetoricizing" of good Aristotelian logic. His charming and quaint book, *The Arte of Reason, Rightly Termed Witcraft,* is devoted to establishing the possibility of

---

[6] Thomas Wilson, *The Rule of Reason, Conteinyng the Art of Logike . . .* (London, 1580), ff. 16ᵛ-17ʳ. The first edition appeared in 1551.

teaching logic in plain ordinary English. Lever follows Aristotle, except in a few sections in which he claims a certain originality; but he stubbornly refuses to countenance any rhetoricizing in his logic. "As for Ciceronians and suger-tongued fellowes, which labour more for fineness of speach, then for knowledge of good matter, they oft speake much to small purpose, and shaking foorth a number of choise words and picked sentences, they hinder good learning, wyth their fond chatte."[7] Needless to say, no section on method appears in this work.

THE SINGLE METHOD OF RAMUS VERSUS THE DOUBLE METHOD OF DIGBY

The methodology of Ramus, on the other hand, met with sharp and instant opposition. Ramist logic began to be taught at Cambridge University sometime after the middle of the sixteenth century by Laurence Chaderton (1536?-1640), a fellow of Christ's College, and later master of newly founded Emmanuel College. Christ's College subsequently became the center of Ramist activity in England.[8] Opposition to Ramist logic developed in another college, St. John's, in the person of Everard Digby (c.1550-1592), a teacher of logic until his expulsion from that college in 1587. Digby's *magnum opus* on "analytic theory," published in 1579, purports to "show the way to the mastery of the sciences," in a vein quite foreign to continental methodology.[9] On the continent, method was the preoccupation of the more sober philosophers: very little fantastic speculation is to be found in the pages dealing

[7] Ralph Lever, *The Arte of Reason, Rightly Termed Witcraft, Teaching a Perfect Way to Argue and Dispute* (London, 1573), "Forespeache."
[8] For the Ramist movement in England, see Howell, *Logic and Rhetoric in England, 1500-1700*. On Chaderton in particular, see p. 179. Chaderton clearly deserves priority over Gabriel Harvey as far as the teaching of Ramist *logic* goes. The first works on Ramist logic published in England, however, were those of Roland MacIlmaine, a Scot.
[9] Even the title of Digby's work gives on idea of its unusual character: *Theoria analytica, viam ad monarchium scientiarum demonstrans, totius philosophiae et reliquarum scientiarum, necnon primorum postremorumque philosophorum mysteria arcanaque dogmata enucleans* (London, 1579). His use of the term "arcana" gives Digby away as belonging to what might uncharitably be called the lunatic fringe of Renaissance thought: it was a favorite term with occultists.

with the subject. Digby, however, while basically a Scholastic, interlards his traditional Thomist and Scotist material with views drawn from neo-Platonic, Cabbalistic, and Hermetic sources.

Far from being simply an "analytic theory of knowledge"— whatever that might be—Digby's work is a full-fledged essay in metaphysics, complete with Angels, Spirits, and Ideas. To his astonishing acquaintance with ancient philosophy and literature (if we may judge safely from citations of dozens of authors) and to his use of the traditions of *Lichtmetaphysik* and the Cabbala, we may add a number of names familiar to us from Digby's own century, e.g., those of Jacob Schegk, Jacobus Carpentarius, and Nicolaus Grouchius. Carpentarius' discussion of Albinus was evidently known to Digby, for he cites it in connection with the various meanings of "analysis," which for Digby is the supra-rational, almost mystical way that leads to the sciences:

The same Method, Analysis, is the only proper one for both the discovery and transmitting of the sciences. It claims for itself the simple perfection of the first principle, from which it lights its first flame, and displays the first certitude to the gaze of the inquirer. . . . For since the good is one, the certain is one, the first is one, so will that first primitive reason be one, fashioned by nature in such a way that it admits no duplication in itself either of nature or of judgment. Although there is no reach of human wit great enough, no power of contemplation or quickness of thought strong enough either to apprehend the so divine form of this [method] and . . . its venerable holiness, or to gaze upon or imitate it by reaching out according to the almost infinite discourse of human wit—yet it strives with the greatest effort, a certain image having been adumbrated by nature in describing different paths by which it may represent to human eyes the heavenly path itself, led by the cardinal points of East and West and the vertices of the Poles. Thus it [i.e., the human mind] creates out of the simplicity of nature the multiplicity of method, by which it has come about that what in its own nature is simple and whole has been distorted through the duplicity of human judgment into various methods greatly at variance with one another. In addition to these evils it also befalls us that among so many and so great teachers of method not one [or just one] has really revealed the method of science as it is in its perfection and for itself.[10]

Since this bombastic declaration was accompanied by more direct insults offered to the name of Ramus, it could not fail to

[10] *Ibid.*, pp. "49" (89)-90.

give offense to loyal Ramists. Only a short time later, one of Digby's own students took up the challenge implicit in his master's doctrine. William Temple (1555-1627), who was later to become provost of Trinity College in Dublin, had espoused Ramist logic after "spending three years in Aristotelian logic" at Cambridge.[11] Under the pseudonym "Franciscus Mildapettus," Temple addressed a reproach to Digby for impugning the single method of Ramus.[12] Digby immediately replied with a "Response,"[13] printed in the same year, in which he added more fuel to the flames by speaking of the Ramist method as a "poisonous doctrine" spreading over Europe. In the same-year, prodded by Temple's challenge, Digby set forth in detail his reasons for rejecting the single method of Ramus, in a little dialogue on the "double" method.[14] The speakers in this dialogue are an Aristotelian and a Ramist. The latter complains that he is disturbed by the conflicting views philosophers hold as to the method by which we may pursue the sciences. The Aristotelian replies that in this, as in other philosophical matters, it is safest to follow the majority or the most wise. When the Ramist objects, "Who is so wise as to be able to teach the true method to the sciences?" the Aristotelian answers that upon this question turns the whole

---

[11] Since Temple was attending Cambridge at the same time as Francis Bacon (although in a different college), scholars have taken an interest in his polemic with Digby for the light it throws on the intellectual climate in which Bacon gained his education and against which in part he revolted. See especially Jacob Freudenthal, "Beiträge zur Geschichte der englischen Philosophie," AGP, IV (1890-91), 450-77 and 578-603; V (1892), 1-41.

[12] *Francisci Mildapetti Navarreni ad Everardum Digbeium Anglum, de unica P. Rami methodo reiectis caeteris retinenda* (London, 1580).

[13] Quaestio (quae nulli dubium esse potest philosopho) inter Aristotelicos et Verbalistes [i.e., the Ramists] est, utrum scientiis docendis, unica sit methodus secundum Aristotelem. Haec non multo pridem e cerebro Petri Rami enata, postquam semel naturali nido evolasset, publice agitata est Lutetiae. Ubi opinio P. Rami de unica methodo secundum Aristotelem, tanquam venenata pestis, et corruptela studiorum ac iuventutis totius Europae, ab excellentissimis pene illius aetatis Philosophia, et per Regis literas patentes explosa est, error recentissimus indicata, ac perinde eodem nomine condemnata; ut vere et aperte refert Iacobus Carpentarius Claramontanus . . . digressione sua super Alcinoo." *Everardi Digbei Cantabrigiensis, admonitioni F. Mildapetti Navareni de unica P. Rami methodo retinenda, responsio* (London, 1580), incipit.

[14] Everardus Digbeus, *De duplici methodo, libri duo, unicam P. Rami methodum refutantes, in quibus via plana, expedita, et exacta, secundum optimos autores, ad scientiarum cognitionem elucidatur . . .* (London, 1580).

controversy which today is raging over method: "I came upon the answer to it a little strengthened by the fact that I found it in Plato, Aristotle, Galen and other men of highest authority. Having kept silent about it for so long, I sought a companion with whom to share the fruit of such pleasant labor, so that together we might carry on friendly discussions of the double method, neither one yielding to the other or opposing him, but both of us yielding only to reason." The Ramist then exclaims, "What a miserable state for students to be in, when they are advised to imitate fighting philosophers! Our master now teaches only one, you teach a double method."

In order to inform his pupil of the true double method, the Aristotelian launches into an exposition of it, with support drawn from Plato, Aristotle, and Galen. With bold if not always precise scholarship, Digby equates correlative terms from each of these authors with his "two methods," one proceeding from that which is prior to us (equivalent to Plato's *genesis*, Galen's *synthesis*, or Aristotle's *inductio*), the other proceeding from that which is posterior (equivalent to Plato's *diaeresis*, Galen's *analysis*, or Aristotle's *resolutio* or *demonstratio*).[15]

Obviously anyone who can unblinkingly equate terms in such wholesale fashion is going to run roughshod over the nicer points of interpretation—and this Digby does with a vengeance. The meaning of "analysis" seems to shift with the context, and it is difficult to pin him down to a single meaning.

In one sense, the same analysis is used both in finding and in transmitting the sciences; and yet, as we already have suggested, it is not absolutely the same . . . since the name "analysis" is used for the descent either from the end to the means, or from the general to the particular. By "analysis" in the former sense men were at first stimulated to the invention of the arts; they used the latter in explaining them. Whence we conclude, along with the most learned Peripatetics, that the method of finding the sciences is contrary to the method of teaching them. Nevertheless if we understand a more perfect method of teaching, each of these is analytic and has division in common. . . . Ramus, impatient of every distinction, wishes there to be just one method—and that the most powerful and demonstrative, which

15 *Ibid.*, Caput 19: "Methodus una nobis, alia natura notior."

is more suitable for the exact finding and teaching of the sciences than for instructing us.[16]

Digby insists that the most perfect method, that of analysis, is not suitable for beginners in learning an art: it is to be ranked among the most difficult matters and reserved to those more advanced in knowledge, as the "most learned Carpentarius" taught Ramus.[17] According to Galen, method ought to be so ordered from the nature of the subject matter that its procedure will be plain and direct to us. A harmony must be established between the degree of difficulty of the material presented and the ignorance of the student.[18]

Digby cites the Platonic dialogues as well as Aristotle for his methodology:

The function of both methods is to guide the inquirer from the beginning of his road to the chosen end. This involves the procedure of the art itself as well as the accommodation of the student, as we learn from Plato. For in the *Philebus* and *Phaedrus* he asserts that the most necessary art for the constitution of the arts is that of dividing and composing, and he instructs us to become proficient in these in two ways: first, to ascend by composition from the most particular to the first genus; second, to descend from the first nature, which is most general, to the things which permit no further cutting, through the middle differentia such as make up definitions, as he taught in the *Statesman* and *Sophist*.[19]

Digby is aware of the use made by Galen of these sources. Definition and division, as expounded by Plato, are not themselves methods but rather most powerful instruments for correctly producing method: both Plato and Galen call them "most beautiful ways."[20]

---

[16] *Ibid.*, Cap. 21: "Non eandem esse methodum scientiis inveniendis et docendis."

[17] *Ibid.*, Cap. 31: "Analysis docenti quam discenti accommodatior."

[18] "Methodus (secundum Galenum) a materiae subiectae natura eo usque ordiri debet, quousque nobis ea ratio plana erit et directa. Itaque sive in sublimioribus, sive inferioribus versetur doctrina, sic tamen erit disponenda, et ad eam humilitatem graduum, facilitatemque, ut sit proportio quaedam et harmonia inter ignorantiam discentis et artem docentis, ut neque abiecta nimis sit prima artis constitutio, modo eam discipulus negligat, nec nimis alta et elata, ut eam desperet: sed similis naturae omnino cum animo discentis, ut facile eam apprehendat simile gaudens suo simili." *Ibid.*, Cap. 33: "Methodo nobis facillima artes sunt discendae."

[19] *Ibid.*, Cap. 40: "Compositionis et resolutionis usus."

[20] "Definitio et divisio non sunt illa quidem methodi ... etsi Plato et Galenus

Obviously Digby had absorbed a good deal of the arts methodology, and hence it is not surprising to find him defending the
method of the dialecticians, the method for explicating "simple
themes." Digby's remarks on the subject [21] offer a good sixteenth-
century example of how the Aristotelian tradition could adopt
some Humanist innovations in doctrine of method and yet reject
the Ramist methodology. The basic method given by Digby for
explaining a simple theme is the scheme of four questions set
forth by Aristotle in the *Posterior Analytics*: for a fuller explanation, others have added other questions to these four (Digby
cites Melanchthon's list of ten questions as an example).[22]

In discussing the question as to what methods are suitable for
the exposition of an art, Digby quotes a passage from Carpentarius that we have already examined.[23] In brief elucidations
and in the explanation of a simple theme, artificers (constructors
of arts) begin from definitions.[24] When Galen gives a full and
copious treatment of medicine, of course, he begins with its first
elements, but in the *Ars Parva* he begins by defining medicine.
In full treatments of the arts, the ancients (namely, Euclid,
Ptolemy, Boethius, Proclus, Plato, and Aristotle) never began
with definitions nor yet with *summa* of the subject (this would
have been tedious to the learner) but with its first elements.[25]

Digby concludes the theoretical section of the dialogue on
method as follows:

We today are not such outstanding masters of arts as the venerable Philosophers of old because we do not proceed by the same simplicity of Method
but by a mixed and confused one, so that just as what we have learned
already is partly known to us and partly obscure, so also our Method is
mixed, partly clear and partly obscure to nature and to us. Moreover there
are lacking men like Pythagoras, Euclid, Plato, and Aristotle, by whose
living voice we might be guided to knowledge, step by step, as by a magic

duas pulcherrimas vias, eadem appellarunt. Sed duo sunt potissima instrumenta recte
producendi methodum, ut patet apud Galenum in hunc modum: 'Rationalis artium
constitutio sine exercitatione compositionis et divisionis, fieri nullo modo potest.' "
Ibid.
    [21] *Ibid.*, Cap. 48: "Methodus qua utimur in simplici themate seu singulis gradibus
explicandis."   [22] *Ibid.*   [23] On p. 151 above.
    [24] *De duplici methodo,* Cap. 53: "Quando a definitione ordiri debet methodus
et quando non."   [25] *Ibid.*

wand [one of Digby's favorite expressions]. A plain and distinct Method, therefore, is lacking, as are studious, erudite, and high-minded professors who neither cherish a sordid love of money, nor yet are destitute of wealth and honor.[26]

The second part of the work is given over to considerations of practical applications.

Digby was by no means immune to the Humanists' methodology of the arts. One can see this from a list of current definitions of "exact method" he gives in the eighteenth chapter.[27] As luck would have it, he does not give the source of any of his citations: had he done so, we would have a solid basis for knowing what methodological sources were available and used by English students. Familiar as all these ideas are, we cannot ascribe any of them with certainty to a particular source, for the language was so much in the air as to defy localization. The last definition is the only one specific enough to warrant our ascribing it, with fair probability, to a particular source—in this case, Galen. Digby discusses Galen's philosophy quite frequently; the omission of his name from among Digby's chief sources is the major point in which Freudenthal's otherwise acceptable interpretation needs correction. Digby's main authorities in method were Plato, Aristotle, and Galen; but to these standard names he adds some less common ones (e.g., Plotinus) and a host of "recent" writers (e.g., Reuchlin). Dialectic is the *methodi magistra,* but he takes "dialectic" in a wide sense in which it covers all sorts of speculation, and thus opens the door to authorities not commonly cited in methodological works.

WILLIAM TEMPLE'S DEFENSE OF HIS MASTER

Temple replied to Digby's apology for his double method with a defense of Mildapettus—this time writing under his own

---

[26] *Ibid.,* Cap. 55.

[27] "Exacta autem methodus (ut quidam definiunt) est [1] ordo et constitutio rerum aptis et accommodatis locis collocandarum.

"[2] Alii: Methodus est via, qua ingressi, propositum eius ductu assequamur.

"[3] Alii: Methodus est certa et regularia ratio docendi, discendique ex definiendi dividendique praeceptionibus constituta.

name.[28] The first sixty-three pages of the work present Temple's analysis of Digby's heated personal attacks (he lists five pages of "calumnies" directed against him by Digby), to which Temple replies in like vein. His worst accusation is that, to judge from Digby's *Theoria analytica* and his dialogue on the double method, one would take him for a follower of Aquinas—a dangerous charge at the time in England.[29] Temple accuses Digby of wishing to revive the sophistries of Scotist logicians, and delights in taunting him with the names of Dorbellus (Nicolaus de Orbellis, fl. 1445-55, a French Franciscan and Scotist) and Javellus (Chrysostomus Javellus, c.1471-c.1538, an Italian Dominican whose philosophical affiliations remain to be identified), whom Digby had indeed quoted.

Having disposed of the attacks upon his person, Temple launches into his counteroffensive against Digby's observations on the single method of the Ramists. These had included fifty-two quotations (Temple was careful to count them) from Aristotle on method: sixteen from the *Posterior Analytics,* eleven from the *Metaphysics,* the remainder from other works.[30] Temple objects to Digby's tendency to merge these statements with those of Aristotle's commentators, instead of relying upon Aristotle alone for defense of his "twofold method."[31] Had Digby offered the testimony of Aristotle upon method, Temple would not have refused it: however, he proposes to examine Digby's quotations

---

"[4] Alii: Methodus est compendiosa via veritatis inveniendae et docendae, in quacunque facultate.
"[5] Alii: Methodus est praecedentium et consequentium artificiosa dispositio.
"[6] Alii: Methodus est in multis ad eandem finem pertinentibus Eutaxia." From *ibid.,* Cap. 18: "Methodus alia popularis, alia exacta."
[28] William Temple, *Pro Mildapetti de unica methodo defensione contra Diplodophilum* [Digby], *commentatio Gulielmi Tempelli, e regio Collegio Cantabrigiensi* (Frankfurt, 1583). The first edition appeared in England in 1581, but is scarce.
[29] "Dum Analyticam theoriam et illum de duplici methodo dialogum intueor, facile adducor, te ut sectorem Aquinatis esse putem." *Ibid.,* p. 25.
[30] *Ibid.,* pp. 62-63.
[31] "Nam si id tibi propositum fuerat, ut adversus Petrum Ramum confirmationem bipartitae methodi Aristotelis testimonio disceptare, cur artificialis argumenti vim tam saepe attulisti? Cur aliorum hominum authoritates tam solicite aggregasti? Cur nomen Trismegisti, Platonis, Galeni, Plotini, Lovaniensis Academiae, Thomae, Alberti tam frequenter inculcasti? Cur Petri Rami errorem citantis ex Aristotele testimonia meliore interpretatione non refellisti?" *Ibid.,* p. 63.

and show him that they by no means support the double method
he favors.[32]   Temple then refutes one by one the fifty-two
testimonia from Aristotle. To most of them he devotes only a
brief rebuttal, asserting that they do not support Digby's double
method. To one Temple gives a fuller treatment— the Scholastic
favorite from the *Ethics*, "That which is last in resolution is first
in generation." After eight pages of argument, Temple concludes:

Wherefore that disputation of yours about "analysis" and "genesis" is
inconsistent with the precept of dialectical method [and] is the fabrication
of a sluggish and torpid theory. For it is not the business of method to
demonstrate a conclusion from general principles or to revise a completed
demonstration, or to separate a whole into parts, or to resolve an end into
means. These are done not by the precept of method but by the help of
some other rule.[33]

It may readily be seen that, as with most Ramist-Aristotelian
controversies, this one turns on the meaning to be assigned to
methodus.

Only after about a hundred pages does Temple finally begin
the exposition of his own methodology. He explains the Ramist
formula with almost overbearing condescension, which probably
accounts for the caustic and malignant tone in which Digby
answered Temple's attacks. In the course of his exposition,
which is pretty conventional, Temple takes care to state what
method is not; needless to say, it is none of the things Digby
wanted it to be.

Method is not the way of finding an argument or an art, nor the procedure
for drawing up a proposition, nor the law of concluding and demonstrating
a question, nor (I repeat) the precept of defining anything or dividing it
into its members or resolving it into its means or of analyzing (*retexendae*)
it into its terms—but it is a rule for disposing in a certain order matters
(*res universas*) that have already been conceived and found by some precepts
and defined and distributed by other precepts; [a rule] that must be
learned and explored not only with the judgment of the proposition but
also, if necessary, with that of the syllogism, and which must be arranged
in an order guided by the methodical theorem.[34]

[32] *Ibid.*, p. 67.   [33] *Ibid.*, p. 95.   [34] *Ibid.*, pp. 118-19.

Obviously not much agreement could be hoped for from two scholars who drew their defense so much from the writings of Aristotle, and yet could take exactly the same classical texts and draw from them diametrically opposite conclusions. Both sides, in this as in most other Ramist-Aristotelian disputes, argued from their own premises, which were hopelessly different, and hence there was no clear joining of issues. In such an impasse the only constructive possibility was to scrap the whole controversy over method—at least, in its original terms—and to strike out anew without relying upon the testimony of the ancients, which could yield such rival interpretations.

LOGIC AT OXFORD: JOHN CASE

Meanwhile at Oxford we also hear of students who felt the attractions of Ramist doctrine. They are mentioned briefly and adversely by an Oxford writer on logic, John Case (died 1600), who was forced to teach privately because of his leaning toward Roman Catholicism. Case wrote a 'Summa of the Ancient Commentators upon the Universal Dialectic of Aristotle, Showing How Truly or Falsely Ramus Assails Aristotle.'[35] Case himself seems to follow closely the teaching of Aquinas and Franciscus Toletus (1532-96), author of a Jesuit textbook of logic. Case inveighs against the preoccupation of the Scotists, Thomists, Nominalists, Realists, and their like with metaphysical problems arising out of the *De interpretatione*, but he is not above consulting the "ancient interpreters of Aristotle"—as of course his title would lead us to expect.

For I have brought together the streams of many ancients into one rivulet, as it were; I have condensed their volumes into a brief epitome, the volumes, that is, of those whom I, after having followed [them] in my lectures for

---

[35] John Case, *Summa veterum interpretum in universam dialecticam Aristotelis, quam vere falsove Ramus in Aristotelem invehatur ostendens* (London, 1584). This work went through several editions in England and Germany. Case wrote similar compendia for the *Ethics* and *Physics* of Aristotle and for the pseudo-Aristotelian *Economics*. Howell, *Logic and Rhetoric in England, 1500-1700*, pp. 190-92, suggests that Case was not entirely hostile to Ramus.

seventeen years, have considered most worthy to be summoned from their present resting places into our schools. If you ask for names, I give you Thomas and Boethius, Lambert and the Venetian school, Nifo and golden Catena—to whom, if I should not offend the ears of this fastidious age, I should wish to add two: Scotus and Burleigh.[36]

Obviously these authorities would be out of favor at Oxford; we are reminded of the well-known statute of the University excluding "all sterile and inane questions departing from the ancient and true philosophy" of Aristotle.[37]

Case is fully sensitive to the noisy claims of the Ramist method, but he does not develop a rival method as Digby had done. He contents himself with stating the time-worn distinction between "order of nature" and "order of doctrine." In the seventh chapter of his compendium, which bears the title, "In teaching the precepts of dialectic, ought one to begin with definition and the question 'what is it?'" he remarks:

In learning an art thoroughly, they hardly proceed correctly who, learning many things without order, are forced to unlearn not a few without profit: for as the center in the circle, the thread in the labyrinth, so is order in the study of the sciences. Just as sailors in a dark night often shipwreck both themselves and everything else, so those who attempt something without order dash themselves against the rocks of blindness; nor do they act otherwise than those who undertake a long journey and do not start upon the right path. Wherefore, as in all things, so or especially so in the arts must it be striven for that we should be directed by order as by a gnomon. Indeed since order is twofold—that of nature, which is from the confused to the certain, from the simple to the composite, and that of doctrine, which is the converse—I think that the latter, which is of doctrine, ought alone to be imitated in teaching the first precepts.[38]

Case defends Aristotle's theory of demonstration against those who regard it as useless and those who think that we can know nothing:

Dialectic should be the art of sharply defining, dividing, demonstrating: which it clearly would not be if demonstration were completely excluded from the ends of Dialectic. . . . If Dialectic teaches us to know by means

---

[36] *Ibid.*, p. "293".

[37] This statute is given in Strickland Gibson's edition of the *Statuta antiqua universitatis Oxoniensis* (Oxford, 1931), p. 437.

[38] *Summa veterum interpretum in universam dialecticam Aristotelis*, p. 12.

of causes, if it explains the way and method of finding causes, if it correctly discriminates what has been found in other sciences, if it excels in all these through demonstration, then I do not see why demonstration should not be called the hand, as it were, of Dialectic. For as a thing is grasped by the hand, so the knowledge of a thing is acquired by demonstration.[39]

Case's definition of dialectic resembles the medieval one up to a point: "Dialectic is the art of arts and science of sciences"; but then it diverges, "indeed it serves as a hand, as they say, to the rest of the sciences, for it provides the manner of proving in all." [40] Just as Case leaves out the usual clause, "having the way to the principles of all methods," so he leaves unspecified his doctrine of method. This is more or less typical of those who retreated to the *verbum magistri*, in whom no explicit doctrine of method could be found.

SUMMARY

We have seen that a number of English philosophers had already engaged in controversy over method before Bacon entered the arena with his crushing indictment of previous learning. We have also seen that this British debate was carried on in terms borrowed from continental methodology. Students at Oxford and Cambridge followed with interest the Ramist methodology as they had that of the dialecticians before Ramus. The influence of the more traditional scientific methodology that culminated in Zabarella is not so immediately apparent in pre-Baconian philosophy. Yet such an influence might well be expected in view of the well-known fact that many British medical and scientific men were trained in the Italian universities in the sixteenth century. It is worth suggesting that Hobbes' views on method, for example, may owe something to the thinking of Italian Aristotelians. In my opinion, the British concern with method can be regarded as completely derivative from the previous discussions on the mainland. We have found evidence to indicate that Englishmen were

[39] *Ibid.*, p. 174.   [40] *Ibid.*, p. 3.

also beginning to feel that the lack of a clear method was what handicapped them in their pursuit of knowledge, and that until they could recapture the power of ancient thinking through its methods they would not be in a position to duplicate its results.

Chapter 10. THE CLASH OF ARISTOTELIAN AND RAMIST METHODOLOGY IN GERMANY

The philosophical climate of the German universities during the sixteenth century was dominated by two factors: the revival of Aristotelian studies due to the encouragement of Melanchthon, and the diffusion of Ramist doctrines, first brought to northern Europe by Ramus himself on his trip up the Rhine in 1568 and subsequently disseminated by German adherents to his reforms. Melanchthon's own rather dilettantish eclecticism could not satisfy the more philosophical minds: careful study of Aristotelian metaphysics came into vogue only after his death, toward the end of the century.[1] Aristotelian logic, on the other hand, shared in the earlier revival of the direct study of Aristotelian texts. The *Organon*, which at first had suffered replacement by the dialectical compendia, especially those of Melanchthon, began to receive greater attention, possibly owing in part to the threat of Ramist methodology. Challenged by Ramists to produce a method from the doctrine of Aristotle, German Aristotelians naturally turned to the commentaries of Jacopo Zabarella, whose logical writings were widely read in Germany as well as in England.[2] Zabarella presented a clear and positive doctrine of method, one that could satisfy the most orthodox Aristotelian. The merger and clash of "Philippism," Ramism, and Aristotelianism in Germany produced that welter of school labels—"semi-Ramist," "Philippo-Ramist," and so on[3]—which has helped to

---

[1] See Max Wundt, *Die deutsche Schulmetaphysik des 17. Jahrhunderts* (Tübingen, 1939).

[2] Peter Petersen, *Geschichte der Aristotelischen Philosophie im protestantischen Deutschland* (Leipzig, 1921), pp. 196-99. Also Wundt, *Die deutsche Schulmetaphysik*, pp. 38-39.

[3] For this curious party-splitting, see Friedrich Ueberweg, *Die Philosophie der*

discourage scholars from inquiring into a certain number of really interesting Renaissance thinkers.

To be sure, few of the many works on logic produced in Germany as a result of this clash reached a foreign audience: their scarcity in libraries outside Germany today is testimony to this fact. It might seem, therefore, that the profusion of logical literature turned out during this period could be of interest to the historian of German philosophy alone—except that there are certain ideas and tendencies in these works that were destined to play a significant role later. I am thinking in particular of the famous systematizing tendency of German thought, clearly discernible—in philosophical theory, at least—even at this time.

Perhaps one reason for the neglect of this earlier German material is the fact that Germany did not immediately produce a methodologist of the caliber of Bacon or Descartes. It finally did produce Leibniz, but his thought was so cosmopolitan that it would seem somewhat parochial to investigate only German antecedents for his methodology. At any rate, we must leave the investigation of this material to those who have readier access to it.

BARTHOLOMEW KECKERMANN OF DANTZIG

There was one German writer, however, whose works did circulate abroad (even to America) and who enjoyed a very favorable reputation for his philosophical acumen. This was Bartholomew Keckermann (c.1572-1609), whose odd name was cited frequently in English and continental logic of the period. From his logical writings, which gather together all the currents of the period, we can see that method occupied a central place in the German controversies between Aristotelians and Ramists, as it had in the English debates between those schools. But where Digby, for example, had relied on Plato, Aristotle, and Galen for his doctrines of method, German Aristotelians also had at

---

Neuzeit (Berlin, 1924), pp. 109-10, and Petersen's *Geschichte der Aristotelischen Philosophie*, pp. 127-43.

their command the influential treatise of Zabarella on method; hence the German disputes centered on Galen and Zabarella on the one hand, and Ramus on the other.[4] Melanchthon's dialectical version of method, being reconcilable with neither of these poles of opinion, seems to have dropped out of sight.

A native of Dantzig, Keckermann studied at several German universities, including Wittenberg, and taught philosophy in the Gymnasium of his native town.[5] He was in general a conscientious and "progressive" Aristotelian; thoroughly aware of the criticisms that had been leveled against Aristotle in recent years and cognizant of their force, he was ready to reconstruct the Master's thought to answer these criticisms. He was also familiar with the "artistic" stream of methodological thought. He was certainly the most constructive and sophisticated expositor of an interesting concept that had been developing in that tradition— the idea of a system. Keckermann was the first to devote a theoretical discussion to this concept, now so familiar: following the lead of the Stoics, he used the term *systema* for the set of precepts that make up an art. For example, logic is a *systema praeceptorum logicorum*, where of course the "precepts" are not the grasping sense impressions of Stoic epistemology but the rules of the medieval writers. Keckermann went on, as we shall see, to set up certain criteria for determining whether a body of doctrine can be called a system. He himself wrote "systems" of logic, rhetoric, and politics.[6]

[4] Petersen, *Geschichte der Aristotelischen Philosophie*, pp. 212-13.

[5] Keckermann deserves a better monographic study than that given in W. H. van Zuylen's slim dissertation, *Bartholomäus Keckermann: Sein Leben und Wirken*, diss. Tübingen (Borna-Leipzig, 1934).

[6] The systems of geography, astronomy, physics, and of the Hebrew language that were published in Keckermann's name after his death would not have conformed to his usage, since he would not have regarded these subjects as arts. See Otto Ritschl, *System und systematische Methode in der Geschichte des wissenschaftlichen Sprachgebrauchs und der philosophischen Methodologie* (Bonn, 1906), p. 30.

Another German teacher, Clemens Timpler, followed Keckermann in this usage, maintaining in his *Metaphysicae systema methodicum* (Hanover, 1606) that metaphysics is an art, if art, in the sense of Lucian, be taken "pro systemate vel pro notitia certorum praeceptorum methodice dispositorum ad finem aliquem utilem in vita humana, non autem quatenus sumitur pro habitu cum recta ratione efficiendi," the latter being the strict Aristotelian definition, or perhaps the alternate Stoic definition of Cleanthes. Quoted by Ritschl, *System*, p. 31.

"TEXTUAL" VERSUS "SYSTEMATIC" PHILOSOPHIZING

A clear indication of Keckermann's general position in the intellectual currents of his time may be obtained from his treatise on the *praecognita* of logic, a sort of propaideutic to logical study.[7] In this work he develops a distinction, reminiscent of Patrizzi's, between the textual explication of a philosophical author and original or "systematic" philosophizing. In his preface to the reader Keckermann described the current tendencies in logic as Aristotelian, Ramist, and Lullian: the last he dismissed with the remark that it had engaged the attention of many learned men. As for the other two schools, Keckermann, while he was familiar with the views of Ramus and had considered them carefully, remained convinced of the solidity of Aristotelian logic, especially as expounded by Zabarella.[8] He quotes with obvious pleasure from the work of a moderate Ramist, Rudolph Snell, who had expressed dissatisfaction with the oversimplified definitions and dichotomies of Ramist logic. Keckermann had earlier written that the objections of Ramus and his followers applied not so much to the precepts of Aristotle himself as to the lengthy discussions of the commentaries. This sentiment he found echoed by Snell, who added that neglect of the distinction between Aristotle and his commentators had given rise to the erroneous notion, held by many Aristotelians, that there was not a single method in Aristotle, but many.[9] The Ramists, by Snell's own confession, are "too curious and overconcerned with Method": in trying to be brief they become obscure. They do not read the writings of Aris-

---

[7] Bartholomaeus Keckermannus, *Praecognitorum logicorum tractatus III,* 2d ed. (Hanover, 1606). This work contains a complete bibliographic history of logic from the time of Adam to that of the writer, in which Keckermann tells us not only what works he read and in what edition he read them but also what works in logic he had not been able to read. A complete picture of the range and extent of a typical Renaissance student's reading in logic may thus be gained from a perusal of this list. Petersen (*Geschichte der Aristotelischen Philosophie,* p. 138) calls this work (which he cites in an edition of Hanau, 1612) the "most detailed critique of Ramist method from the Aristotelian camp."

[8] Keckermann, *Praecognitorum logicorum,* pp. 11-12.

[9] *Ibid.,* pp. 12-13. The passages Keckermann quotes are from Snell's *Tomus primus syntagmatis philosophici* (Frankfurt, 1596).

totle but scorn them for their own pitiful compendia and arts.[10]

Keckermann gives a list of the principal points at issue between the Aristotelians and the Ramists; seventh in the list we find the following: "Whether, although there is only one method from the more known and more general to the less known and general, there are nevertheless diverse applications of this one method to the theoretical and to the operative or practical disciplines."[11] He admits that the *Organon* is not a complete treatment of logic: in particular, as Zabarella had pointed out, there is nothing whatever on the subject of the method or order of disciplines.[12]

In his general introduction to the study of philosophy,[13] Keckermann maintains that philosophy is properly taught by giving first the general *praecognita* (in this case, giving the nature of philosophy and then the correct way to begin its study), and then afterwards the special method or system of the singular parts of philosophy.[14] Keckermann describes method as the soul and form of disciplines, without which things themselves cannot cohere nor the thoughts of men concerning these things.[15] His interest in methodizing the study of philosophy is clearly inspired in part at least by his knowledge of a similar trend in other fields, e.g., theology, jurisprudence, and medicine.[16]

In line with the distinction he has previously made, Keckermann divides Peripatetics into two groups: "textual" philosophers and "methodical" ones. The former are those Aristotelians who follow the text laboriously, without omitting a word and without introducing any ideas of their own.

Such for the most part were those ancient Peripatetics who are called interpreters par excellence: Alexander of Aphrodisias, Simplicius, Themistius, Philoponus, Ammonius, and also Averroes—as well as those recent philosophers who follow them, Italians and Spaniards especially, who spend all

---

[10] Keckermann, *Praecognitorum logicorum*, p. 16.
[11] *Ibid.*, pp. 27-28.   [12] *Ibid.*, p. 196.
[13] Bartholomaeus Keckermannus, *Praecognitorum philosophicorum libri duo; naturam philosophiae explicantes et rationem eius tum docendae tum discendae monstrantes . . .* (Hanover, 1612).
[14] *Ibid.*, pp. 1-2.
[15] "Methodus est anima et forma disciplinarum, since qua nec cohaerent res ipsae, nec cogitationes hominum de rebus." *Ibid.*, p. 1.
[16] *Ibid.*, p. 129.

of their time and that of their students turning the text of Aristotle over and over, apparently little concerned to develop absolute Methods and Systems of disciplines from Aristotle's font.

Keckermann goes on to observe that two disadvantages result: (1) students never grasp a whole and methodical discipline, and (2) they are detained in the *cursus philosophicus* much longer than they need be. The "methodical" Aristotelians, on the other hand, are those who develop a discipline by the rules of system or method first, and then accommodate the text of Aristotle to that method and to "the use of our century," clearly and succinctly.[17] In his chronology of logic, Keckermann frequently complains that a writer was not systematic or did not write methodically. For example, Plato, although he included a good many logical precepts in his dialogues, failed to present a complete system or method of any discipline.[18]

Against the single method of Ramus, Keckermann upholds the traditional twofold distinction of compositive and resolutive —by this time universally denominated "synthetic" and "analytic," in which form they were to remain current in philosophical discourse for centuries:

I admit that Method is only one in genus, but this genus is divided into two forms or species: from the nature (*ex ratione*) of the subject treated and from the order of thinking or teaching. I have remarked before that the precepts of logic are to be measured by the subject matter and by our intellect, not the converse. But subjects dealt with in the Disciplines are twofold, either purely theoretical or practical: hence our way of thinking of subjects is also twofold. For sometimes our mind comes upon correct knowledge in the very act of thinking, beginning from the most simple and general; sometimes it desires to know and to think of things of such a sort that it is not satisfied by thought alone but goes on until man may from there gain some further end in functioning and acting. . . . And the Peripatetics call this form of natural Method the "Analytic," as they call the former the "Synthetic." This doctrine is most simple, and congenial both to our own nature and to that of the things to be ordered. Nor surely do those who desire the perspicuous truth—such as the most celebrated Zabarella, supreme artificer of methods, has taught it in Books One and Two of the *De methodis*—desire anything other than the light of noon itself.[19]

[17] *Ibid.*, pp. 160-61.   [18] *Ibid.*, p. 78.   [19] *Ibid.*, pp. 142-44.

Keckermann remarks that the Galenists had fabricated many methods, which may have led Ramus to champion the elimination of all but one for the sake of simplicity.[20]

In his work on logic, Keckermann gives two sets of criteria for deciding whether a given treatment of logic constitutes a formal system, criteria based in part on the Stoic idea of an art and in part on Aristotle's observations on the part-whole relationship. The *Organon*, says Keckermann, is inadequate to serve as a model for a formal system of logic because we do not have all of it and what we have does not satisfy the criteria given. The formal aspect of a logical system consists of two things: (1) the determinate distribution of the parts and (2) the coordination of these parts to the end or purpose of the whole system and to each other.[21]

After giving nine requirements that a system must satisfy in order for the parts to be properly distributed within the whole, Keckermann examines some prevailing divisions of logic by these criteria and finds them wanting—among others the Stoic and dialectician's division of logic into *inventio* and *iudicium*. He then gives five further requirements for the proper relation of the parts to the End of the whole system, in this case the use to which logic is to be put.

The details of Keckermann's theory are interesting and deserve further study than we can give to them here. In Keckermann's view, no extant writings, Ramist or Aristotelian, fulfill the stringent requirements he sets forth. Among the "more notable defects of the Peripatetics with regard to the structure of a logical system" is the fact that they tend to neglect the role of logic in teaching: "Philip Melanchthon wished the end of logic to be not merely cognition but also the faculty of teaching someone else capably that which you have already learned."[22] The textual interpreters overlook the fact that there is much in Aristotle that is added for the sake of illustration and argument and does not bear on the "direct and expeditious method of the art."[23]

---

[20] *Ibid.*, p. 144. [21] *Praecognitorum logicorum*, p. 198.
[22] *Ibid.*, p. 225. [23] *Ibid.*, pp. 236-37.

SUMMARY

In almost all of the doctrinal controversies of the day, Keckermann pursues a moderate course, answering objections and for-
mulating his own views without the rancor and party-spirit so
visible in his predecessors. Keckermann was a conciliator and
reconciler of the two main traditions of methodology we have
been speaking of; yet a careful reading of his works will reveal
how original and fresh such a merger could be. Although he
regarded Aristotle's works as the embodiment of method and as
a sound norm for the methodical treatment of disciplines,[24] his
qualifications and answers to objections on that score make it
clear that Keckermann was no blind adulator. The idea of apply-
ing external and explicitly formulated criteria to the works of
Aristotle and to the distinctions of recent writers lifts Keckermann above the melee of controversy of the times and establishes
him as one of the most original and constructive of the writers
on method. But although he echoed Zabarella's wish for philosophers who would look to things themselves rather than to the
text of Aristotle,[25] Keckermann was not much less bound by
tradition than his mentor.

[24] "Textus enim Aristotelici mensura prima est Methodus integra Disciplinae,
ad quam omnia sunt inter resolvendum atque explicandum regulanda." *Ibid.*, p. 150.
    "Aristotelica scripta continent expeditam Methodum, id est, formam disciplinarum
Philosophicarum, quae aliorum Philosophorum libris et scriptis deest." *Ibid.*, p. 151.
[25] *Ibid.*, p. 154.

CONCLUSION

Although there were many writers on method from the sixteenth century whom we have not even mentioned, enough have been sampled to give a fairly complete picture of the methodology of the late Renaissance. However divergent the various trends of this discussion may appear, the ancient Greek basis of it can always be traced. When we survey the results of this century of debate, we must admit that originality was not one of its chief merits. Yet lack of originality was not exclusive with the "methodologists": preoccupation with the printed word was a salient feature of the philosophizing of the times. Sixteenth-century philosophy in general presents a curious contrast between the exceedingly standardized and conventional Aristotelianism of the schools and the wild flights of speculation of the mystics, Rosicrucians, nature philosophers, and Light-Metaphysicians— traditions so thoroughly discredited by the next century that even William Gilbert's mild (and correct) fancy that the earth was a large magnet met only with scorn from the most advanced thinkers, because of its hint of the fantastic.

Renaissance philosophical discussions, with certain exceptions, were not so much objective controversies as rival interpretations of philosophical texts. In the subject with which we have been dealing, the interpretations varied not so much because of differences in philological technique as because of differences in motivation. The "controversy" over method arose not from general genuine disagreement over issues but rather from a conflict of purposes. The one category of writers—the methodologists of the arts—was concerned with the efficiency of teaching and with the application of the useful arts to life. The other group—the methodologists of science—was concerned with methods of strict demonstration and proof. The two purposes clashed in logic because logic could be regarded as an art or as a science, and because its inventor, Aristotle, had found it useful both in speaking and in scientific analysis. Yet why should the two purposes have inevitably led to a clash? Why could not a truce have been arranged in which the *Topics* was marked off for the art-ists and the *Posterior Analytics* for the scientists? Why should the entire learned world have been split into two rival camps by a bitter feud between the partisans of scientific method and the Humanistic educational reformers?

The answer seems to be that sixteenth-century teachers of medicine and philosophy viewed the Humanist reforms as a threat to their own cherished ideal of strict science. When Humanists such as Vives and Ramus criticized traditional methods of teaching and offered their own alternatives, the "subject-matter teachers" of the day closed ranks and fought back with their own methodology, that of a strictly interpreted and mathematical Aristotle, supplemented by Galen, Proclus, and the Greek commentators. Through Humanist usage, the term *methodus* had come to have an almost rhetorical meaning: a writer who presented an art or science in brief, clear fashion, according to cut-and-dried rules, was said to have "reduced the subject to method." The traditionalists avoided this sense of the term: they repudiated the criterion of communicability or ease of teaching and emphasized instead the scientific, or science-producing, character of their method, which was not intended to make it easy for the pupil, or to improve the rhetorical effectiveness of a teacher's presentation: it was aimed exclusively at producing "science" or knowledge, as opposed to rhetorical persuasion and probable opinion. Theirs, in a phrase which was only beginning to gain currency during the late Renaissance, was the *methodus scientificus*.

Hence, viewed in historical perspective, the sixteenth-century debates on method represent simply another episode in the age-old rivalry between philosophy and rhetoric. This conflict could have been easily reconciled, or at least so it would seem, by a theory of education which accounted for the desirability of introducing students to their subjects gradually and easily and yet retained a sense of the necessity for strict procedure and precision in advanced education and research. But then—even granting the difficult feat of accounting for all scientific demonstration wholly in terms of the Aristotelian syllogism—this rapprochement would not have been satisfactory to the following century, for neither camp of methodological thought really dealt with the problems involved in the "finding of the arts," or the discovery of new scientific truths, as we would phrase it—nor did either recognize the necessity for having a way of categorically eliminating the false and invalid from the body of knowledge.

The fact is that the sixteenth-century philosopher was not yet really impressed by the necessity for winnowing out the wheat from the chaff in the received doctrine. The astronomical theories of Copernicus did not gain immediate general acceptance, while the anatomical discoveries of Vesalius, although quickly accepted, were considered only minor revisions of the body of medical lore and were often published with the collected works of Galen as an appendix or supplement. Galileo's theories, on the other hand, really shook the complacence of scholars, and his brusque and uncompromising defense of his own theories and those of Copernicus dramatized the need for a complete reevaluation of the received doctrine. As a result, the seventeenth-century methodologies, in particular that of Descartes, were more imperative in their critical demands.

With regard to experimentation as a confirming stage in the application of scientific method, we have found no evidence of an explicit formulation of such a doctrine in our period. In view of the fact that the sources which played such a predominant part in setting the stage for philosophical debate are silent on the subject of experimentation, this is hardly strange. When the notion of experimentation begins to be formulated expressly, by Francis Bacon, it is framed not in the terms of the scientific methodology but in those of the artistic methodology. Although the "finding" of the arts and the finding of arguments in dialectic were favorite topics during the preceding century, they had been treated in rather doctrinaire and dispirited fashion. Bacon transformed the debating procedure of the *Topics* into a transaction in which Nature replaced the respondent and the challenger became the scientist.

As to the place of mathematics in the methods advocated, it must be painfully clear that the sixteenth century, when it considered the subject at all, was on a somewhat different track from that taken by the mathematizing physicists of the new era. Virtually all Peripatetics retained the belief that the syllogism, in its Aristotelian form, was the instrument of mathematical reasoning, and framed their discussions accordingly. Yet, actual mathematical discovery and the application of mathematics to physics were taking an entirely different tack. Descartes could model his philosophical method upon that of mathematics without mentioning the syllogism, while Galileo expressly set apart the syllogism from those chains of mathematical reasoning which are the "true instrument" of the physicist.

Not much remains that is distinctively modern, then, in the conception of method which the Renaissance developed, aside from a very general idea of an infallible and reasoned procedure to be followed in the pursuit of knowledge.

The underlying obstacle to the development of a theory of empirical research, which was what the times really called for, was the fact that "philosophy" as then understood included disciplines which we would regard as empirical sciences: that is, fields in which the investigator needs to gain special firsthand experimental evidence, such as biology and physics. The classical treatment given these fields (aside from the biological) by Aristotle was still, one might say, "dialectical"—that is, concerned with the analysis of concepts by logic or methodical discussion. Hence methods of philosophizing and methods of science were one and the same, and were both dialectical. The methods of the Platonists—division, resolution, demonstration, and definition— were not methods of doing anything either, but methods of discussing and analyzing concepts. For the enterprise in which

Socrates enlisted them—the gaining of moral insight—they were indeed useful, and still are so today. But they can hardly be considered methods of research. So long as there was no clear-cut distinction made between empirical and logical, then, the methods of logical discussion could be confused with methods of research, to the disadvantage of both.

This accounts for the fact, otherwise rather foreign to our way of thinking, that the comparison of Aristotle's actual practices with the methods he advocated could be considered, in the Renaissance, a satisfactory empirical test of those methods. We might wonder why methodology in any domain whatsoever could not be empirical—that is, based upon the empirical examination of inquiry in that domain which has produced valid results— were it not for the wise reminders of Whitehead and Dewey that theory and method sometimes go hand in hand, and that development of method must often proceed simultaneously with the development of theory. Philosophical theory was stagnant in the period we have been investigating, except for the nature philosophies that seem to have developed chiefly in reaction to the rigid and oversober philosophical tradition of the schools.

The most fruitful of the diffuse discussions we have been examining were those in which the methodologist himself could employ the method he claimed to have developed: for instance, when the legal writer could actually try to "reduce law to an art," or the grammarian could personally teach his method of learning the languages. When a logician, on the other hand, spoke of "analyzing effects into causes," he did not speak from firsthand experience, but could only offer the usual traditional examples from the text of Aristotle. There is evidence throughout the period of a growing dissatisfaction with those hackneyed examples from Aristotle's *Posterior Analytics*, the nontwinkling star and the nonbreathing wall. This dissatisfaction became more acute when the Greek cosmology found in Aristotle began to be discarded. In a sense, it is only part of the general rejection of bookish learning that made men turn to the Book of Nature in the next century. The Renaissance had fully explored the books

that contained the thought of antiquity and had drained them of
all that could be useful. The interest in the methods by which
Aristotle arrived at his results was surely progress. In studying
Plato it was impossible to avoid observing his methods, so that it
is no wonder that Platonically oriented Humanists developed an
interest in the subject of method. When thinkers of the next
century came to devise new sets of rules, they could not help
incorporating, consciously or unconsciously, much that had been
carried along as inert ideas in the philosophical tradition of centuries. But Bacon, with his immense practical vision, and
Descartes, with his philosophical penetration, gave to these inert
ideas new life.

La difference qu'il y a entre eux et nous, est qu'on se picquoit bien plus
d'érudition dans le siècle passé, que dans celuy-ci. . . . C'estoit le genie
de ce tems-là, où rien n'a esté plus en vogue, que la grande capacité, et une
profonde litterature: on étudioit à fond les Langues: on s'appliquoit à
reformer le texte des ancien Auteurs par des interpretations recherchées,
à pointiller sur une équivoque, à fonder une conjecture pour bien établir
une correction: enfin on s'attachoit au sens litteral d'un Auteur, parce qu'on
n'avoit pas le force de s'élever jusqu'à l'esprit, pour le bien connoître:
comme on fait à present, qu'on est plus raisonnable, et moins sçavant: et
qu'on fait bien plus d'estat du bons sens tout simple, que d'une capacité
de travers.[1]

These proud words of a French savant express perfectly the
attitude of the seventeenth century toward its immediate past.
Before the turn of the century, mere erudition reigned supreme—
nothing was heard but the turning over of pages and the rustling
of pens making marginal notes. Yet was Père Rapin's boast
entirely justified? In his "Comparison of Plato and Aristotle," he
himself wrote a section entitled "La methode de Platon et d'Aristote" which would not have impressed the erudite scholar of the
sixteenth century as essentially new.

If we cast aside our impressions gained from the reading of
histories of philosophy—and also those gained from reading
seventeenth-century writers, who are not quite objective—*nemo*

---

[1] Père Rapin, preface (written about 1681) to his "Comparaison de Thucydide et
de Tite Live," *Les oeuvres* (Amsterdam, 1709), I, 175-76.

iudex in casu suo—we can see many ways in which the famous methodologists of the new era are indebted to their humble predecessors. Francis Bacon (1561-1626), for all his originality, is clearly much indebted to the Humanistic arts methodology. A man who was a lawyer and a student of the classics interested in rhetoric and history could hardly have escaped noticing the discussion of method in his chosen fields. Moreover, Cambridge University while Bacon attended it was a seething hotbed of Ramist doctrine: Bacon was well aware of "the controversy which Method hath moved in our time," and he devoted not a little space to rejecting the single method of Ramus.

In Bacon's rich prose one can find embedded countless references to the methods of the previous century, whose Greek names betray their Humanist provenance. His criticisms of both the Scholastic and the Humanist methods were informed and convincing. But in discarding the *Posterior Analytics* and adapting the method of the *Topics* to his own purposes, he was following in the Humanist trend of methodology.

Also very much influenced by the Humanist movement, although just as firm in renouncing its methodology, was Pierre Gassendi (1592-1655), whose youthful outburst against the Aristotelian logicians[2] owed much to its Humanist predecessors. In this work, Gassendi pokes fun at the Humanists who had set up method as the "scales of truth, the measure, judge, and rule of the Arts." Away with this talk, says Gassendi, the proper criterion of truth is experiment, not your dialectic.[3] Yet the idea of dia-

---

[2] Petrus Gassendus, *Exercitationes paradoxicae adversus Aristoteleos ...* (The Hague, 1656).

[3] "Praesentio quid sis responsurus: dices nempe Dialecticam non discernere quidem speciatim hoc verum aut falsum tanquam ex officio, sed tradere tantum quandam generalem methodum, qua scientiae omnes deinceps utantur, quo valeant ipsa discernere. Haec nempe est causa cur Dialectica vocetur libra, trutina, et examen Veritatis: cur mensura, judex, et regula Artium; cur vestibulum, janua, et clavis Scientiarum; cur Sol, fax, et oculus Mentis. Quanta farrago, Deum immortalem! at quaeso te bona fide, quaenam tandem haec est methodus? vel ut unum seligam ex tam multis epithetis, quaenam est haec trutina, qua veritas alicuius rei ponderanda sit, ut sitne ignis calidus, an non; Sol lucidus an tenebrosus? non procul sane abnuerem; hoc est enim *Iudicatorium*, seu ut Graeci dicunt κριτήριον quod ex tam multis propositis videtur esse eligendum; at experimentum est sensus, vel facultatis naturalis, non autem Dialecticae, tuque aliud nobis proponas." *Ibid.*, p. 9.

lectic which he was rejecting in this passage—as giving only a certain general method, of which all the sciences may make use in order to distinguish the true from the false—was the very notion that René Descartes (1596-1650) proclaimed.

The youthful Descartes, in the fourth of the rules which he set up for the direction of the mind, felt that a method was necessary for investigating the truth of all things, and by "method" he understood "fixed and easy rules such that whoever observes them strictly will never take anything false for true and, without uselessly expending any mental effort, but gradually always increasing [his] knowledge, will arrive at the true understanding of all things of which he is capable." Taken by itself, this definition sounds quite like those of the previous century. But when we recall that Descartes has first required the slate of knowledge to be cleaned, we touch upon the crucial difference. There was never a suggestion in the previous century that a man who would reach true understanding must start from scratch, nor that he could reach such a final terminus in his quest.

Careful reading of the *Regulae*, so much richer in details than the *Discours*, will disclose the extent to which Descartes uses language and ideas current in the methodology of the previous century—but with such a freshness and consummate skill that we are tempted to believe that they were indeed the result of an angel's visit. One need not delve too far back into the medieval period to find doctrines of method reminiscent of those proposed with such exactitude by Descartes—but one must go back as far as the Greeks to find a spirit of inquiry so penetrating and so philosophical.

It should be observed that one tenet shared by all these writers was clearly a heritage from the Humanists: the relegation of the syllogism to a comparatively minor role in the discovery, or even the demonstration, of the sciences. The doubts entertained by Peripatetics of the sixteenth century concerning the applicability of Aristotle's syllogistic analysis to mathematics, and hence to the exact sciences in general, now rebounded when mathematics replaced logic as the "instrument" of natural philosophizing.

"Very well," we seem to hear the seventeenth century say. "If Aristotle's theory of science does not permit us to call mathematics a perfect science, then so much the worse for his theory of science." Many of Aristotle's general doctrines as to the place of principles in science, and their character, were retained. But the syllogism, which had been the stumbling block for doubtful Peripatetics, now became a touchstone separating those who were willing to start afresh with mathematics—algebra and geometry —as research tools for the natural philosopher, and those who clung to the Scholastic or Aristotelian tradition.

For the traditional views continued to be held: the new methodology did not carry the day immediately. For instance, Cartesian doctrine reached Germany rather slowly, and before it did, Peripatetics of every persuasion had fought tooth and nail over the traditional doctrines of order and method. Indeed some later writers, viewing the seventeenth century's efforts at methodological analysis, considered that Descartes had added nothing whatsoever to Peripatetic discussions of method.[4] The German savant Daniel Georg Morhof (1639-91) attributed the sterility of these treatments of method to the fact that they were written by men with no firsthand experience in mathematical art and physics, "the more solid foundation of demonstration."[5]

Now there is undoubtedly a good deal of truth in Morhof's remark, but little justice. For, we must ask, were the seventeenth-century philosophical "methodologies," for all their professed empiricism, any closer to the actual practice of scientific investigation? Can the methods of science be safely excogitated from a

---

[4] For a jaundiced view of the whole discussion of method, see Johann Heinrich Zedler's *Grosses vollständiges Universal-Lexicon* ... (Halle and Leipzig, 1739), Vol. XX, article "Methodus." Zedler remarks that the subject of method had been "completely confused by the Peripatetics," but was being cleared up by recent logicians.

[5] "Nam caeteri Autores Peripatetici, qui de methodo tractarunt, parci admodum sunt in exemplis distincte proponendis. Quoniam enim plerique ex illis mathematicae artis et solidioris physicae, et praecipue ἐμπειρίας naturalis rudes fuere, quae firmiorem ἀποδείξεων fundum huic doctrinae substernunt, mirum videri non debet, si mutilam illam et in multis erroneam dederint. Ceterum nihil pene novi ab illis, qui tamen nova se dixisse putant dictum est, quod non commoda deductione e principiis Aristotelicis arcessi possit." *Polyhistor* ... (Lübeck, 1714), I, 389.

philosopher's chair? Or, for that matter, can they be sketched out by a scientist before he has reflected a good deal upon successful procedures in his field? Is not a theory of experimentation—which is what the modern student inevitably looks for in a "methodology"—rather by its nature something that will be developed *ex post facto*?

Actually, the development of an explicit doctrine of experimentation did not come, in my opinion, until after the experimentation of Galileo had provided a solid base for theorizing. There is, of course, an almost irresistible temptation to assume that because Galileo was such a brilliant and ingenious experimentalist he must have operated upon a carefully formulated theory of experimentation. Those who succumb to this temptation can find passages in his dialogues which seem to sustain their view. One passage often quoted is from the *Dialogue concerning the Two Chief World Systems*. The spokesman for Galileo's theories, Salviati, has just argued that Aristotle would have changed his mind concerning the immutability of the heavens if he had lived until the present century and could have witnessed some of the new observations which were changing the cosmological picture. "Had Aristotle been living in our time," Salviati remarks, "he would have changed his mind on this point, because he always put *sensata esperienza* before natural discourse."[6]

Some of those who have interpreted this passage[7] have translated *sensata esperienza* by the impressive phrase "well-chosen experiments," which makes Galileo sound very modern. Unfortunately there are some difficulties with this translation. For one thing, there is the uncomfortable fact that it makes Aristotle, who conducted, as is well known, only one ill-chosen experiment, a champion of "well-chosen experimentation." Furthermore, this interpretation runs into other and more serious difficulties. If we replace the Italian phrase with its suggested equivalent in other places in Galileo's writings, we emerge with some rather strange

[6] Galileo, *Le Opere,* national edition (Florence, 1890-1909), VII, 75.
[7] Among them Edward Strong, *Procedures and Metaphysics* (Berkeley, 1936), p. 146.

readings.[8] The intrusion of modern concepts into Galileo's language can play havoc with the interpertation of his thought. Obviously *sensata esperienza* is the Italian equivalent of the very traditional "sense experience"—which is a far cry from an experimental basis of physical science.

It should be clear that much of the earlier discussion did not even touch upon the method of gaining valid and useful knowledge, but concerned only the method of transmitting an "already-established art," or of pursuing a successful course of study. Putting these methods aside, there remains, to be sure, a faint residue of philosophizing that seems to concern the method of science, and many descriptions of method that sound surprisingly modern. But they are only descriptions, not prescriptions. A modern historian of science would probably accept Everard Digby's judgment that the men of his time were lacking a trustworthy method such as had enabled Pythagoras and Euclid to make their discoveries and conclusions. But he would hardly be convinced that Digby had provided the type of method he himself called for.

We may take this, then as our general conclusion concerning this whole movement of thought. So far as practical effect upon methods of scientific investigation goes, the result of these long and wordy controversies was minimal, although in a few fields of thought the arts methodology laid the grounds for the revamping of techniques of exposition, for instance, in law or history. So far as theoretical effect goes, there is no question but that in reviving the subject of method and in studying the philosophical works of the ancients, these Renaissance scholars were setting up a demand for a method which was to be answered, in the form of philosophical programs, in the next century, and were also furnishing some hints from classical thought which do not altogether disappear from view even though the seventeenth century did not care either to mention or to read what their predecessors had written on the subject.

[8] As, for instance, in the following passage (*Le Opere*, V, 378): "*Well-chosen experiments* show us that the flow to and fro of marine waters is not a swelling and compression of the parts of that element ... etc." For my part, I find it hard to see how even Galileo could manage a "well-chosen experiment" with the tides.

Appendix: METHODUS IN TITLES OF BOOKS IN THE LATE RENAISSANCE

The intent of this list is merely to suggest the ways in which the word *methodus* began to be used during the sixteenth century, especially in titles of pedagogical works. It is arranged chronologically.

Desiderius Erasmus. Ratio seu methodus compendio perveniendi ad veram theologiam. Basel, 1520.

Aelius Donatus. Methodus Grammatices. Strasbourg, 1522 (this is the *Ars Minor*, reprinted under similar titles at Cologne, 1525; Lyons, 1536; Nuremberg, 1536; and Magdeburg, 1547).

Christophorus Hegendorphinus (Hegendorf). Methodus conscribendi epistolas, antehac non edita. Dragmata locorum tum rhetoricorum quam dialecticorum una cum exemplis ex optimis quibusquam autoribus depromptis.... Antwerp, 1527.

Hermogenes.Περὶ μεθόδου δεινότητος. De methodo gravitatis sive virtutis commode dicendi. Paris, 1531. On this work, see Walter J. Ong, *Ramus, Method, and the Decay of Dialogue* (Cambridge, Mass., 1958), p. 231.

Joannes Visorius. Ingeniosa nec minus elegans ad dialectices candidatos methodus. Paris, 1534. Visorius relies on Cicero, Quintilian, and Rudolph Agricola for his discussion of invention.

Joannes Lonicerus. Graecae grammaticae methodus. Basel, 1536.

—— Artis dicendi methodi ex optimis utriusque linguae autoribus deprompta. Basel, 1536.

Conradus Celtis (Conrad Pickel). Methodus conficiendarum epistolarum. Printed along with Joannes Ludovicus Vivus (Juan Luis Vives), *De conscribendis epistolis.... libellus* and Erasmus, *Compendium,* in Cologne, 1537.

Reinerus Gemma. Arithmeticae practicae methodus facilis.... Antwerp, 1540.

Emanuel Moschopoulos. Grammaticae artis graeci methodus. Basel, 1540.

Matthaeus Gribaldus. De methodo ac ratione studendi libri tres. Lyons, 1541.

Conradus Lagus (Conrad Hase). Juris utriusque methodica traditio. Frankfurt am Main, 1543. Roderich von Stintzing, *Geschichte der deut-*

schen Rechtswissenschaft (Munich and Leipzig, 1880-1910), p. 300, calls this the "oldest complete compendium of law."

Ambroise Paré. Méthode de traicter les plays faictes par hacquebutes. Paris, 1545.

Joannes Drosaeus (Jean de Drosai). Juris universi Justinianea methodus.... Paris, 1545. Mentioned by Stintzing, *Geschichte der deutschen Rechtswissenschaft,* p. 143.

Erasmus Sarcerius (Sarzer). Locorum communium ex consensu divinae scripturae et sanctorum patrum ad certam methodum clarissima simul et copiosissima confirmatio. Basel, 1547.

Michael Neander. Methodorum in omni genere artium brevis et succincta ὑφήγησις. Basel, 1556.

Petrus Ramus (Pierre de la Ramée). Quod sit unica doctrinae instituendae methodus: locus e nono Animadversionum.... Paris, 1557. Part of Ramus' 'Remarks on Aristotle,' reprinted separately: see Walter J. Ong, *Ramus and Talon Inventory* (Cambridge, Mass., 1958). p. 303.

Florian Trefler. Methodus exhibens per varios indices, et classes subinde quorumlibet librorum, cuiuslibet bibliothecae, brevem, facilem, imitabilem ordinationem. Augsburg, 1560. According to Archer Taylor, *Renaissance Guides to Books* (Berkeley and Los Angeles, 1945), p. 113, this is a librarian's manual.

Nicolaus Vigelius (Vigel). Juris civilis totius absolutissima methodus; in qua ... non solum omnes totius iuris civilis titulos, sed et singulas singulorum titulorum leges ... habes.... Basel, 1561.

Joannes Camillus. De ordine ac methodo in scientia servandis liber unus. Venice, 1561.

Nicolaus Hemmingius (Niels Hemmingsen). De lege naturae apodictica methodus concinnata. Wittenberg, 1562.

Leopoldus Dickius. De optima studiorum ratione in omni facultatum genere methodus. [Basel], 1564.

Arnaldus Ossatus (Arnaud d'Ossat). Expositio Arnaldi Ossati in Disputationem Iacobi Carpentarii de methodo. Paris, 1564. See Ong, *Ramus and Talon Inventory,* p. 500.

Joannes Bodinus (Jean Bodin). Methodus ad facilem historiarum cognitionem. Paris, 1566.

Nicolaus Hemmingius (Niels Hemmingsen). De methodis libri duo, quorum prior quidem omnium methodorum universalium et particularium, quarum usus est in philosophia, brevem ac dilucidam declarationem, posterior vero ecclesiasten sive methodum theologicam interpretandi concionandique continet. Leipzig, 1570.

Nicolaus Taurellus. Philosophiae triumphus, hoc est, metaphysica philosophandi methodus, qua divinitus inditis menti notitiis humanae rationes eo deducuntur, ut firmissimis inde constructis demonstrationibus aperte rei elucescat et quae diu philosophorum sepulta fuit autoritate philosophia victrix erumpat . . . Basel, 1573.

Thomas Blundeville. The True Order and Methode of Wryting and Reading Hystories, According to the Precepts of Francisco Patricio and Accontio of Tridentio. . . . London, 1574.

Simon Simonius (Simoni). Artificiosa curandae pestis methodus libellis duobus comprehensa. . . . Leipzig, 1576.

Valentinus Nabod. Astronomicarum institutionum libri tres, quibus doctrinae sphaericae elementa methodo nova traduntur. Venice, 1580.

Nicolaus Taurellus. Medicae praedictionis methodus . . . hoc est, recta brevisque ratio coram aegris praeterita, praesentia, futuraque praedicendi . . . . Frankfurt, 1581.

Reinerus Reineccius (Reinhard Reineck). Methodus legendi cognoscendique historiam tam sacram quam profanam. . . . Helmstadt, 1583.

Celsus Martinengus. De praevidendis morborum eventibus libri tres . . . . Ejusdem de methodis commentarius, deque artium structura libellus. Venice, 1584. This must be the work mentioned by Francesco Piccolomini in his *Comes politicus* (Venice, 1594), f. 20^r.

Joannes Beurer. Synopsis historiarum et methodus nova. Hanau, 1594.

Joannes Althusius (Johann Althaus). Politica methodice digesta atque exemplis sacris et profanis illustrata. Groningen, 1610.

Nicolaus Vigelius (Vigel). Methodus universi iuris pontificii absolutissima, in quinque libros distincta: nunc demum additionibus methodi iuris controversi aucta. Basel, 1616.

Nicodemus Frischlinus (Frischlin). Methodus grammatica. Leipzig, 1626.

Joannes Alstedius (Johann Heinrich Alsted). Compendium philosophicum, exhibens Methodum, Definitiones, Canones, et Questiones, per universum philosophiam. Herborn, 1626.

Joannes Amos Comenius (Jan Amos Komensky). Porta linguarum trilinguis reserata et aperta, sive seminarium linguarum et scientiarum omnium, hoc est, compendiaria Latinam, Anglicam, Gallicam (et quamvis aliam) linguam una cum artium et scientiarum fundamentis sesquianni spatio ad summum docendi et perdiscendi methodus, sub titulis centum, periodis mille comprehensa. London, 1631.

SELECTIVE BIBLIOGRAPHY

Articles or books that were found especially relevant are cited here, in addition to a few works not explicitly discussed or referred to in the text which provided useful background reading. The usual histories of philosophy—Zeller, Ueberweg, Gilson, etc.—were used, as were the biographical dictionaries of Michaud, Jöcher, DNB, Allgemeine Deutsche Biographie, etc.

A. ABBREVIATIONS USED

AGP   Archiv für Geschichte der Philosophie
BAW   Bayerische Akademie der Wissenschaft
BGP   Beiträge zur Geschichte der Philosophie des Mittelalters
CAG   Commentaria in Aristotelem Graeca
CR   Corpus Reformatorum
JHI   Journal of the History of Ideas
PAW   Preussische Akademie der Wissenschaften
SVF   Stoicorum Veterum Fragmenta

B. PRIMARY SOURCES FROM THE SIXTEENTH CENTURY

(Location of copies in American libraries is given by the standard symbols used in the Union List of Serials.)

Acontius, Jacobus (Giacomo Aconzio). De methodo e opuscoli religiosi e filosofici. Ed. Giorgio Radetti. Florence, 1944.

Agricola, Rudolph (Roelof Huusman). De inventione dialectica libri tres, cum scholiis Joannis Matthaei Phrissemii. Paris, 1529. NNC.

Ascham, Roger. The Scholemaster, or Plain and Perfite Way of Teachyng Children to Understand, Write, and Speake, the Latin Tong.... London, 1570. NNC.

Bacon, Francis. The Works of Francis Bacon. Ed. J. Spedding and R. L. Ellis. London, 1887.

Barocius, Franciscus (Francesco Barozzi). Opusculum, in quo una oratio, et duae quaestiones, altera de certitudine et altera de medietate mathematicarum continentur. Padua, 1560. NNC.

Bodinus, Joannes (Jean Bodin). Methodus ad facilem historiarum cognitionem. Oeuvres Philosophiques de Jean Bodin. Ed. Pierre Mesnard. Paris, 1951.

Borrius, Hieronymus (Girolamo Borro). De peripatetica docendi atque addiscendi methodo. Florence, 1584. CtY.

Buccaferrea, Ludovicus (Ludovico Boccadiferro). Explanatio libri I. Physicorum Aristotelis. Venice, 1558. NNC.

Budaeus, Gulielmus (Guillaume Budé). Annotationes... in quatuor et viginti Pandectarum libros.... Paris, 1535. NNC.

Caesarius, Joannes. Dialectica Ioannis Caesarii viri undecunque doctissimi, nunc recens Hermanni Raiiani Vuelsdalii fructuosis scholiis illustrata.... Venice, 1559. NNC.

Canus, Melchior (Melchior Cano). Opera.... Bassano, 1776. NNC.

Cardanus, Hieronymus (Girolamo Cardano). Opera omnia.... 10 vols. Lyons, 1663. NNN.

Carpentarius, Jacobus (Jacques Charpentier). Animadversiones in libros tres dialecticarum institutionem Petri Rami. Paris, 1555. NNC-film.

―― Platonis cum Aristotle in universa philosophia comparatio, quae hoc commentario in Alcinoi institutionem ad ejusdem Platonis doctrinam explicatur. Paris, 1573. MH.

Case, John. Summa veterum interpretum in universam dialecticam. Aristotelis, quam vere falsove Ramus in Aristotelem invehatur, ostendens. London, 1584. NNC-film.

Claramontius, Scipio (Scipione Chiaramonti). De methodo ad doctrinam spectante, libri quattor, in quibus tum controversiae omnes de ordine et methodis inter graves philosophos agitatae singillatim discutiuntur .... Cesena, 1639. NNC.

Dasypodius, Conradus (Rauchfuss), ed. Euclideae demonstrationes in syllogismos resolutae.... Strasbourg, 1564.

Digbeus, Everardus (Everard Digby). Admonitioni F. Mildapetti Navareni de unica P. Rami methodo retinenda, responsio. London, 1580. See Ong, Ramus and Talon Inventory, p. 507.

―― De duplici methodo, libri duo, unicam P. Rami methodum refutantes, in quibus via plana, expedita, et exacta, secundum optimos autores ad scientiarum cognitionem elucidatur.... London, 1580. University Microfilm.

―― Theoria analytica, viam ad monarchium scientiarum demonstrans, totius philosophiae et reliquarum scientiarum, necnon primorum postremorumque philosophorum mysteria arcanaque dogmata enucleans. London, 1579. NN-UTS.

Dounamus, Georgius (George Downham). Commentarii in P. Rami regii professoris dialecticam, quibus ex classicis quibusque auctoribus praeceptorum Rameorum perfectio demonstratur, sensus explicatur, usus exponitur.... Frankfurt, 1605. NNC.

Erasmus, Desiderius. Ausgewählte Werke. Ed. Hajo Holborn. Munich, 1933. NNC.

Flacius, Matthias (Flack). Clavis scripturae sacrae, seu de sermone sacrarum literarum in duas partes.... Jena, 1674. NN-UTS.

Gassendus, Petrus (Pierre Gassendi). Exercitationes paradoxicae adversus Aristoteleos, in quibus praecipua totius Peripatetica doctrinae fundamenta excutiuntur.... The Hague, 1656. NNC.

Goveanus, Antonius (Antonio de Gouveia). Opera iuridica, philologica, philosophica.... Rotterdam, 1766. NNC.

Hegendorphinus, Christophorus (Christopher Hegendorf). Dialecticae legalis libri quinque, recogniti.... Antwerp, 1534. DLC

Keckermannus, Bartholomaeus (Bartholomew Keckermann). Praecognitorum logicorum tractatus III.... Hanover, 1606. NNC-film.

—— Praecognitorum philosophicorum libri duo; naturam philosophiae explicantes at rationem eius tum docendae tum discendae monstrantes .... Hanover, 1612.

Leonicenus, Nicolaus (Niccolò Leoniceno). In libros Galeni greca in latinam linguam a se translatos prefatio communis. [Venice, 1508.] NNN.

Lever, Ralph. The Arte of Reason, Rightly Termed Witcraft, Teaching a Perfect Way to Argue and Dispute. London, 1573. NNC-photostat. On this work, see Howell, Logic and Rhetoric in England, pp. 57-63.

Manardus, Joannes (Giovanni Manardi). In artem Galeni medicinalem luculenta expositio.... [Basel, 1529.] NNN.

Mazzonius, Jacobus (Jacopo Mazzoni). In universam Platonis et Aristotelis philosophiam praeludia, sive de comparatione Platonis et Aristotelis, liber primus. Venice, 1597. NNC-film.

Melanchthon, Philippus (Philip Schwarzerd). De dialectica libri quatuor recogniti an. xxxvi. Wittenberg, 1536. CtY.

—— "Erotemata dialectices...," in CR, Halle, 1846. Vol. XIII. NNC.

Morhofius, Danielus Georgius (Daniel Georg Morhof). Polyhistor, sive de notitia auctorum et rerum commentarii.... Lübeck, 1688-92. NNC.

Nizolius, Marius (Mario Nizzoli). De veris principiis et vera ratione philosophandi contra pseudophilosophos libri IV. Ed. Quirinus Breen. 2 vols. Rome, 1956. First published in Parma, 1553.

Pacius, Julius (Giulio Pace). Institutiones logicae, quibus non solum universa Organi Aristotelici sententia.... continetur, sed etiam syllogismi hypothetici, et methodi, quorum expositio in Organo desideratur.... explicantur. Sedan, 1595. NNC-film.

Patritius, Franciscus (Francesco Patrizzi). Discussionum peripateticarum tomi IV, quibus Aristotelicae philosophiae universa historia atque dog-

mata cum veterum placitis collata eleganter et erudite declarantur . . . .
Basel, 1581. CtY.

Pererius, Benedictus. De communibus omnium rerum naturalium principiis et affectionibus, libri quindecim . . . . Cologne, 1595. NNC.
DLC.

Perionius, Joachimus (Joachim de Périon). De dialectica libri tres. Lyons,
1551. NNC.

—— Topicorum theologicorum libri duo, quorum in posteriore de iis
omnibus agitur, quae hodie ab haereticis defenduntur . . . . Paris, 1549.
NN-UTS.

Petrus Hispanus (Peter of Spain). Summulae logicales, cum Versorii
Parisiensis clarissima expositione . . . . Ed. Martianus Rota. Venice,
1580. NNC-Teachers College.

Piccolomineus, Alexander (Alessandro Piccolomini). In mechanicas quaestiones Aristotelis paraphrasis paulo quidem plenior; Eiusdem Commentarium de certitudine mathematicarum disciplinarum, in quo de
resolutione, diffinitione, et demonstratione necnon de materia, et in
fine logicae facultatis, quamplura continentur ad rem ipsam tum mathematicam, tum logicam maxime pertinentia. Venice, 1565. DLC.

Piccolomineus, Franciscus (Francesco Piccolomini). Comes politicus, pro
recta ordinis ratione propugnator . . . . Venice, 1594. NNC-film.

—— Discursus ad universam logicam attinens. Marburg, 1606. NNC-
film.

—— Universa philosophia de moribus . . . . Venice, 1583. NNC.

Picus de Mirandula, Joannes (Giovanni Pico della Mirandola). Disputationes adversus astrologiam divinatricem. Ed. Eugenio Garin. 2 vols.
Florence, 1946. NNC.

Ramus, Petrus (Pierre de la Ramée). Aristotelicae animadversiones. Paris,
1543. IU. NNC-film.

—— Aristotelicarum animadversionum liber nonus et decimus in Posteriora Analytica. Paris, 1553. NNC-Teachers College.

—— Collectaneae, Praefationes, Epistolae, Orationes . . . Marburg, 1599.
NNC-Teachers College.

—— Defensio pro Aristotele adversus Jac. Schecium. Lausanne, 1571.

—— Dialecticae institutiones . . . . Paris, 1543. NNC-film.

Recorde, Robert. The Pathwaie to Knowledge, Containyng the First
Principles of Geometrie . . . . London, 1574. NNC.

Ringelbergius, Joachimus Fortius (Ringelsbergh). Dialectica Paris, 1540.
NNC.

Sarcerius, Erasmus (Sarzer). Dialectica multis ac variis exempli illustrata,
una cum facillima syllogismorum, expositioriorum [sic], enthymematum, exemplorum, inductionum, et soritum dispositione. Marburg,
1537. NNC.

Setonius, Joannes (John Seton). Dialectica. London, 1545. University microfilm.

Snellius, Rudolphus (Snel van Roijen). De ratione discendi et exercendi logicam per analysin et genesin facili et perspicua, libri duo .... Herborn, 1599. ICU.

Sturmius, Joannes (Johann Sturm). Institutionis literatae .... Thorn, 1586. NNC.

—— Partitionum dialecticarum libri duo. Strasbourg, 1539. IU.

—— Prolegomena, hoc est, praefationes in optimos quosque utriusque linguae tum bonarum artium, tum philosophiae, scriptores .... Zurich, n.d. NNC-Teachers College.

Tempellus, Gulielmus (William Temple). Francisci Mildapetti Navarreni ad Everardum Digbeium Anglum admonitio, de unica P. Rami methodo reiectis caeteris retinenda .... London, 1580. "Franciscus Mildapettus" was a pseudonym used by Temple in this first of his attacks on Digby in defense of Ramus.

—— P. Rami Dialecticae libri duo scholiis G. Tempelli Cantab. illustrati .... Cambridge, 1584. NNC.

—— Pro Mildapetti de unica defensione contra Diplodophilum .... Frankfurt, 1583. NNC.

Titelmannus, Franciscus (Francis Titelmans). Dialecticae considerationis libri sex, summam Organi Aristotelici complectentes. Paris, 1539.

Trapezuntius, Georgius (George of Trebizond). Dialectica brevis. Basel, 1552. NNC.

Triverius, Jeremias (Drivere). In Texnhn Galeni clarissimi commentarii. Lyons, 1547. NNC.

Vicomercatus, Franciscus (Francesco Vimercato). Commentarii in tertium librum Aristotelis De Anima .... Venice, 1574. NNC.

Viottus, Bartholomaeus (Bartolomeo Viotti). De balneorum naturalium viribus libri quatuor .... Lyons, 1552. NNN.

—— De demonstratione libri quinque .... Paris, 1560. NNC.

Visorius, Joannes. Ingeniosa nec minus elegans ad dialectices candidatos methodus. Paris, 1534. CtY.

Vivus, Joannes Ludovicus (Juan Luis Vives). Opera .... 8 vols. Valencia, 1782-90. NNC.

Willichius, Jodocus (Wilcke). De formando studio in quolibet artium, et sacrorum et prophanarum genere consilium. N.p., 1564. NN-UTS.

Wilson, Thomas. The Rule of Reason, Conteinyng the Art of Logike .... London, 1580. NNC.

Wolfius, Joannes (Wolf), ed. Artis historicae penus .... Basel, 1579. NNC-film.

Zabarella, Jacobus (Jacopo Zabarella). In libros Aristotelis Physicorum

commentarii, nunc primum in lucem editi. Venice. 1601. NNC-film.
—— Opera logica. Treviso, 1604. NNC-film.
Zanchius, Hieronymus (Girolamo Zanchi). Opera theologica ... Geneva, 1619. NN-UTS.

C. SECONDARY SOURCES

Brown, John L. The Methodus ad Facilem Historiarum Cognitionem of Jean Bodin: A Critical Study. Washington, 1939.
Brucker, Jakob. Historia critica philosophiae .... 6 vols. Leipzig, 1742-47.
Buisson, Ferdinand E., ed. Répertoire des ouvrages pédagogiques du XVIᵉ siècle. Paris, 1886.
Burckhardt, Jacob. The Civilization of the Renaissance in Italy. London, 1928.
Burtt, Edwin Arthur. The Metaphysical Foundations of Modern Physical Science. London, 1925.
Busson, Henri. Le rationalisme dans la littérature française de la Renaissance. 2d ed. Paris, 1957.
Butterfield, H. The Origins of Modern Science, 1300-1800. London, 1951.
Cassirer, Ernst. Das Erkenntnisproblem in der Philosophie und Wissenschaft der neueren Zeit. 2 vols. Berlin, 1906.
Cassirer, Ernst, Paul O. Kristeller, and John H. Randall, Jr., eds. The Renaissance Philosophy of Man. Chicago, 1948.
Crombie, A. C. Robert Grosseteste and the Origins of Experimental Science, 1100-1700. Oxford, 1953.
Dainville, François de. La naissance de l'humanisme moderne. 2 vols. Paris, 1940.
Dilthey, Wilhelm. Weltanschauung und Analyse des Menschen seit Renaissance und Reformation. Gesammelte Schriften, Vol. II. Leipzig and Berlin, 1921.
Duhem, Pierre. Le système du monde; histoire des doctrines cosmologiques de Platon à Copernic .... 8 vols. Paris, 1913-54.
Durkheim, Emile. L'évolution pédagogique en France. 2 vols. Paris, 1938. These are lectures given by Durkheim in his capacity as lecturer on the history of education at Paris. Suggestive.
Eucken, Rudolph. Geschichte der philosophischen Terminologie. Leipzig, 1879.
—— Die Methode der Aristotelischen Forschung in ihrem Zusammenhang mit den philosophischen Grundprincipien des Aristoteles dargestellt. Berlin, 1872.
Freudenthal, Jacob. "Beiträge zur Geschichte der englischen Philosophie," AGP, IV (1890-91), 450-77, and V (1892), 1-41.

Garin, Eugenio. "Aristotelismo e platonismo del rinascimento," *La Rinascita*, II⁸, (1939), 641-71.

—— La filosofia. 2 vols. Milan, 1947.

Gilmore, Myron. The World of Humanism, 1453-1517. New York, 1952.

Grabmann, Martin. Die Geschichte der Scholastische Methode. 2 vols. Freiburg im Breisgau, 1909.

—— Mittalterliches Geistesleben: Abhandlungen zur Geschichte der Scholastik und Mystik. 3 vols. Munich, 1926-56.

Haskins, Charles Homer. Studies in the History of Mediaeval Science. Cambridge, Mass., 1924.

Heath, Sir Thomas. Mathematics in Aristotle. Oxford, 1949.

Howell, Wilbur Samuel. Logic and Rhetoric in England, 1500-1700. Princeton, New Jersey, 1956.

Humbert, L'Abbé Auguste. Les origines de la théologie moderne. I. La Renaissance de l'antiquité chrétienne (1450-1521). Paris, 1911.

Johnson, Francis R. Astronomical Thought in Renaissance England: A Study of the English Scientific Writings from 1500 to 1645. Baltimore, 1937.

Kristeller, Paul O. The Classics and Renaissance Thought. Martin Classical Lectures, Vol. 15. Cambridge, Mass., 1955.

—— Studies in Renaissance Thought and Letters. Rome, 1956.

Krumbacher, Karl. Geschichte der byzantinischen Litteratur. Munich, 1897. The section entitled "Fortleben des Aristoteles" is informative.

Le Blond, J. M. Logique et méthode chez Aristote: Étude sur la recherche des principes dans la physique Aristotélicienne. Paris, 1937.

Lockwood, Dean Putnam. Ugo Benzi: Medieval Philosopher and Physician, 1376-1439. Chicago, 1951.

MacClintock, Stuart. "Heresy and Epithet: An Approach to the Problem of Latin Averroism," Review of Metaphysics, VIII (1954-55), 176-99, 342-56, and 526-45.

McKeon, Richard. "Rhetoric in the Middle Ages", *Speculum,* XVII (1942), 1-32.

Miller, Perry. The New England Mind: The Seventeenth Century. New York, 1939.

Moody, Ernest A. The Logic of William of Ockham. New York, 1935.

Müller, Iwan. "Ueber Galens Werk vom wissenschaftlichen Beweis," Abhandlungen, philosophisch-philologische Classe, BAW, XX (1897), 405-78.

Nardi, Bruno. Saggi sull' Aristotelismo Padovano dal secolo XIV al XVI. Florence, 1958.

Ong, Walter J., S.J. Ramus and Talon Inventory: A Short-Title Inventory of the Published Works of Peter Ramus (1515-1572) and of Omer

Talon (ca. 1510-1562) in Their Original and in Their Variously Altered Forms. With Related Material: 1. The Ramist Controversies: A Descriptive Catalogue. 2. Agricola Check List: A Short-Title Inventory of Some Printed Editions and Printed Compendia of Rudolph Agricola's Dialectical Invention (De Inventione Dialectica). Cambridge, Mass., 1958.

—— Ramus, Method, and the Decay of Dialogue. Cambridge, Mass., 1958.

Petersen, Peter. Geschichte der Aristotelischen Philosophie im Protestantischen Deutschland. Leipzig, 1921.

Prantl, Carl von. Geschichte der Logik im Abendlande. 4 vols. Leipzig, 1855-70.

—— "Ueber Petrus Ramus." Sitzungsberichte, BAW, II (1878), 157-69.

Randall, John Herman, Jr., "The Development of Scientific Method in the School of Padua," JHI, I (1940), 177-206.

Rashdall, Hastings. The Universities of Europe in the Middle Ages. 2 vols. Oxford, 1895.

Renan, Ernest. Averroès et l'Averroïsme. Paris, 1866.

Rice, Eugene, Jr. The Renaissance Idea of Wisdom. Cambridge, Mass., 1958.

Ritschl, Otto. Dogmengeschichte des Protestantismus. 2 vols. Leipzig, 1908.

—— System und systematische Methode in der Geschichte des wissenschaftlichen Sprachgebrauchs und der philosophischen Methodologie. Programm zur Feier des Gedächtnisses des Stifters der Universität König Friedrich Wilhelms III. Bonn, 1906.

Robinson, Richard. Plato's Earlier Dialectic. 2d ed. Oxford, 1949.

Sandys, John Edwin. A History of Classical Scholarship. 3 vols. Cambridge, 1908.

Solmsen, Friedrich. Die Entwicklung der Aristotelischen Logik und Rhetorik. Neue Philologische Untersuchungen, Viertes Heft. Berlin, 1929.

Stintzing, Roderich von. Geschichte der deutschen Rechtswissenschaft. 3 vols. in 4. Munich and Leipzig, 1880-1910.

Taylor, Henry Osborn. Thought and Expression in the Sixteenth Century. 2 vols. New York, 1920.

Thorndike, Lynn. A History of Magic and Experimental Science. 8 vols. New York, 1923-58.

Underwood, Edgar Ashworth, ed. Science, Medicine, and History: Essays on the Evolution of Scientific Thought and Medical Practice Written in Honour of Charles Singer. 2 vols. London, New York, 1953.

Van Steenberghen, Ferdinand. Aristotle in the West: The Origins of Latin Aristotelianism. Louvain, 1955.

Waddington, Charles. Ramus: Sa vie, ses écrits et ses opinions. Paris, 1855.

Walzer, Richard. "Arabic Transmission of Greek Thought to Medieval Europe," *Bulletin of the John Rylands Library, Manchester,* XXIX (1945), 160-83.

Woodward, William H. Vittorino da Feltre and Other Humanist Educators: Essays and Versions. An Introduction to the History of Classical Education. Cambridge, 1921.

Wundt, Max. Die Deutsche Schulmetaphysik des 16. Jahrhunderts. Tübingen, 1939.

INDEX

99 ff.; and analysis, 151; and Piccolomini, 174; and Digby, 205
*Arte of Reason, Rightly Termed Wit-
craft, The* (Lever), 199
Artes historicae, 79
Artifex methodi, 125-27
Art of Rhetoric (Aristotle), 76*n*
Arts, methodology of, xxi-xxii, xxiv-xxv,
65-66; Socrates on, 3-4; defined, 11*n*,
12*n*, 43*n*, 48*n*, 70*n*, 77-78; Stoic doctrine of, 11-13, 69-71, 111; Galen on,
18-19; history of term, 43-44; and
dialectic, 57; law as an art, 96; and
Humanists, versus "scientific" commentators, 120, 222-23; and Ramist
method of, 130-44; and Borro, 186-91
Ascham, Roger, 113
Astronomy, 81
Authority, Renaissance attitudes toward,
35-38, 67, 164
Averroes, on *Physics,* 26, 105; and Aristotle, 28, 51-54, 154; and Renaissance
methodology, 30, 164-76; and medical
method, 98, 101; and Italian Aristotelians, 178-79, 180-81, 186-95; and
Keckermann, 217
"Averroism," 52*n*-53*n*; *see also* Averroes
Avicenna, 195

Bacon, Francis, 114, 202*n*, 211, 223,
226-27
Bacon, Roger, 67, 86
Baduel, Claude, quoted, 72
Barker, Sir Ernest, 42
Barozzi, Francesco, 87, 91
Barrow, Sir Isaac, quoted, 91, 92
Bebel, Heinrich, 94
Boccadiferro, Ludovico, *see* Buccaferrea,
Ludovicus
Bodin, Jean, 79-80
Boethius, 25, 50, 77, 81; and dialectic,
125; and Digby, 205; and Case, 210
Bologna, University of, 54, 100
Bonitz, Hermann, 41-42
Borrius, Hieronymus, *see* Borro, Girol-
amo
Borro, Girolamo, and *methodus,* 64-65,
71; non-Scholastic, 180; and "artistic"
trend, 186-92; and Chiaramonti, 195
Bruni, Leonardo, 61-63
Bruno, Giordano, xxiii, 35
Buccaferrea, Ludovicus, 166-67
Budé, Guillaume, 64, 94, 97
Burckhardt, Jacob, 181-82

Burleigh, Walter, 210

Cabbala, 201
Caccialupis, Johannes Baptista de, 94
Calvin, John, 109
Cambridge University, 78, 197-200, 211,
227
Canis, Johannes Jacobus, 94
Cano, Melchior, 109
Carpentarius, Jacobus, and Aristotle, 36;
versus Ramus, 145-51; merits of, 151-
52; and Galen, 157; and Chiaramonti,
195; and Digby, 201, 204-5
Case, John, 91, 209-11
Cassirer, Ernst, xiii, 172-73
Catena, Petrus, 90*n*, 210
Catholics in England, 197
Celtis, Conrad, 84
Chaderton, Laurence, 200
Charpentier, Jacques, *see* Carpentarius,
Jacobus
Cheke, Sir John, 113
Chiaramonti, Scipione, 181, 194-96
Christ's College (Cambridge), 200
Cicero, translated, 12; and *methodus,* 49,
75-76; 125; and art, 70, 95-96; and
Nizzoli, 72; and Sturm, 78; and
Ramus, 131, 146; and Carpentarius,
151; and Schegk, 160; and Aconzio,
184; *De Officiis,* 199
Ciceronians, 200
Claramontius, Scipio, *see* Chiaramonti,
Scipione
Clavius, Christopher, 90
Cleanthes, 43*n*
Clement of Alexandria, 32-33
Codex, of Justinian, 96
Collège Royal, 61
Commandino, Federigo, 34, 82, 89
Commentaries: Greek, on method, 24-
27, 34, 46-48, 136-37, 164 ff., 222;
medieval Latin, 27-31; geometric me-
thod in, 31-35; Arab, 52-164 ff.; scien-
tific, versus "artistic" Humanists, 120;
Latin, 164 ff.; *see also individual
commentators*
"Commonplaces" in theological method,
108-9
'Comparison of Plato and Aristotle'
(Mazzonius), 176
'Comparison of Plato with Aristotle'
(Carpentarius), 147
Compendia, 56-60, 112-15
Compositive method, xiii, 184

science, 222; *see also Methodos; Methodus*

'Method for the Easy Cognition of Histories' (Bodin), 79; quoted, 80

Method of Healing (Galen), 19

Methodos, 5, 12; history of, 39-48

Methodus, in Renaissance, xxv; history of, 39, 48-55; and Boethius, 50; and Aquinas, 54-55, 60; as Latin philosophical term, 56-66; Humanist distaste for, 60-63; Renaissance etymologies of, 64-66; in education, 69; as "short form of art," 69; Averroes on, 177; and Seton, 198; Humanist usage of, 222

Methodus (Erasmus), 107

Methodus ad facilem historiarum cognitionem (Bodin), *see* 'Method for the Easy Cognition of Histories'

Methodus medendi (Galen), 20, 21

"Mildapettus, Franciscus," *see* Temple, William

Mill, John Stuart, 11

Morhof, Daniel Georg, 229

Mos Gallicus, 94

Mos geometricus, 15n

Mos Italicus, 95

Music, 81

Nashe, Thomas, 113

Neo-Platonism, 28-29

Neo-Scholastics, 30

Nicomachean Ethics (Aristotle) 9, 47, 115, 190

Nifo, Agostino, 59, 210

Nizolius, Marius, *see* Mario Nizzoli

Nizzoli, Mario, 13, 64, 72

Ognibene da Lonigo, 102

Olympiodorus, 70

On Demonstration (Galen), 20

'On Demonstration' (Viotti), 153

'On Method, that is, the Correct Manner of Investigating and Transmitting the Arts and Sciences' (Aconzio), 181

'On the Constitution of the Medical Art' (Galen), 185

On the Doctrines of Hippocrates and Plato (Galen), 45

'On the Establishing of the Medical Art, to Patrophilus' (Galen), 16

'On the Method of Healing' (Galen), 152

'On the Opinions of Hippocrates and Plato' (Galen), 138

On the Parasitic Art (Lucian), 111

Orbellis, Nicolaus de (Dorbellus), 207

Order, 187-88

"Order of doctrine," 54, 167-69

Ordo, 69

Organon (Aristotle), 26, 76n, 115; and logic, 77; geometric application of, 84; and Ramus, 132, 135-36, 141-42, 163; and *methodos,* 133; and Schegk, 158, 161; and Zabarella, 168-69, 171; and Pace, 180; in Germany, 213, 217, 219

Ossat, Cardinal d', 195

Oxford University, 197, 209-11

Pace, Giulio, 180, 192-94

Pacius, Julius, *see* Pace, Giulio

Pandects (Justinian), 64, 96

Pappus of Alexandria, xvi, 34, 82, 99

Paracelsus, xxiii

Paris, University of, 109, 130, 145

Parmenides, 40

Partitiones (Hermogenes), 78

Parts of Animals (Aristotle), 6, 146, 165, 176, 182, 189

Patrizzi, Francesco, xxv, 114-15, 216

Patrophilus, 16-17

Pendasio, Federigo, 195

Perceptio, 12

Pererius, Benedictus, 91

Périon, Joachim de, *see* Perionius, Joachim

Perionius, Joachim, 109

"Peripatetic Method of Teaching and Learning" (Borro), 65

Peripatetics, and Platonic dialogues, 4; as logicians, 90-91; four doctrines of, 104-5; and Ramus, 145; and Borro, 186-92; and Galileo, 196; and pluralism, 194; and Digby, 203; and Keckermann, 217-29; and syllogism, 224, 228-29

Peter Lombard, 109-25

Peter of Auvergne, 55

Peter of Spain, 57, 74, 77

Petrarch, 71

Phaedrus (Plato), 3 ff., 45, 59; *methodos* in, 40; and Galen, 139; and Ramus, 150; and Piccolomini, 175; and Digby, 204

Philebus (Plato), 7, 131, 139, 175, 204

"Philippo-Ramists," 127, 213

Philoponus, and Aristotle, 28, 30, 47-48, 88, 154, 165, 168; on Greek defini-